EDUCATING MINDS AND HEARTS

SOCIAL EMOTIONAL LEARNING AND THE PASSAGE INTO ADOLESCENCE

Series on Social Emotional Learning

Teachers College Press
in partnership with The Project for Social Emotional Learning, Teachers College,
and The Collaborative for the Advancement of Social Emotional Learning (CASEL)

Jonathan Cohen, *Series Editor*

CONSULTING EDITORS:
Maurice Elias, Norris Haynes, Roger Weissberg, and Joseph Zins

EDITORIAL ADVISORY BOARD:
L. Lawrence Aber, Diana Allensworth, Michael Ben-Avie, Robert Coles,
James Comer, Pearl R. Kane, Catherine Lewis, Ann Lieberman,
Karen Marschke-Tobier, Nel Noddings, John O'Neil,
Seymour B. Sarason, Thomas Sobol

Social emotional learning is now recognized as an essential aspect of children's education and a necessary feature of all successful school reform efforts. The books in this series will present perspectives and exemplary programs that foster social and emotional learning for children and adolescents in our schools, including interdisciplinary, developmental, curricular, and instructional contributions. The three levels of service that constitute social emotional learning programs will be critically presented: (1) curriculum-based programs directed to all children to enhance social and emotional competencies, (2) programs and perspectives intended for special needs children, and (3) programs and perspectives that seek to promote the social and emotional awareness and skills of educators and other school personnel.

EDUCATING MINDS AND HEARTS

SOCIAL EMOTIONAL LEARNING AND THE PASSAGE INTO ADOLESCENCE

Edited by Jonathan Cohen

Foreword by Howard Gardner

Association for Supervision and Curriculum Development
Alexandria, Virginia

For my Mother and the memory of my Father,
whose love and good counsel provided the foundation

Association for Supervision and Curriculum Development
1703 N. Beauregard Street • Alexandria, VA 22311-1714 USA
Telephone: 1-800-933-2723 or 703-578-9600 • Fax: 703-575-5400
Web site: http://www.ascd.org • E-mail: member@ascd.org

Printed in the United States of America.

ISBN 0-87120-348-0
ASCD Stock No. 199001   s3/99
ASCD member price: $18.95   nonmember price: $21.95

Library of Congress Cataloging-in-Publication Data
    Educating minds and hearts : social emotional learning and the passage
    into adolescence / edited by Jonathan Cohen.
        p. cm. — (Series on social emotional learning)
    Includes bibliographical references and index.
        ISBN 0-8077-3839-5   (cloth : alk. paper). — ISBN 0-8077-3838-7
    (pbk. : alk. paper)
        1. Affective education. 2. Social learning. 3. Emotions in
    adolescence. 4. Middle school education. I. Cohen, Jonathan,
    1952–   . II. Series.
    LB1072.E38   1999
    370.15'3—dc   98-50749

06 05 04 03 02 01 00 99   8 7 6 5 4 3 2 1

Contents

PART III: Implementation and Future Directions 171

Note from the Series Editor

School life colors and shapes how students and educators experience themselves and others in a way that extends far beyond school hours and activities. Just think about your favorite teacher. For most of us, our favorite teacher was someone we felt really cared about and/or challenged us: someone who recognized us and reached out to us. And for many of us, those favorite teachers continue to exert a strong influence throughout our lives, because that relationship fundamentally altered our sense of ourselves.

We all know that how we feel about ourselves and others can profoundly affect our ability to concentrate, to remember, to think, and to express ourselves. Many educators appreciate that we simply cannot separate "academics" from the social and emotional lives of the classroom and the student. Some educators spend lifetimes working to create safe, secure classrooms and/or schools so that students will not only learn but soar! Most educators wish that they had more time to think about and work toward these goals.

To grow up in healthy and responsible ways we all need the capacity to learn from our own emotional and social experiences. Awareness of ourselves and others provides the foundation for social and emotional competencies: a sense of self-worth; the abilities to solve problems and make responsible and helpful decisions, to communicate and collaborate with others, to become self-motivating. Being aware of ourselves and others also provides the foundation for academic learning, in addition to fostering respect for democratic values. Optimally, social and emotional learning (SEL) needs to be an integral part of children's education, in conjunction with linguistic, mathematical, aesthetic, kinesthetic, and ethical learning. How do we further these modes of learning in schools? How can we promote these processes more effectively?

This volume is the first in a new series—the Series on Social Emotional Learning, from Teachers College Press—that we hope will begin to address these questions. Cosponsored by the Project for Social and Emotional Learning (PSEL) at Teachers College and the Collaborative for Social and Emotional Learning (CASEL), its primary goal is to provide resources for educators who are struggling to promote SEL. Many of the volumes that emerge from this series will present and discuss perspectives, practical strategies, and curricula that may help teachers, administrators, and support personnel—in cooperation with parents and community members—to enhance social and emotional development within their own school communities. Interdisciplinary perspectives that broaden our understanding about a given facet of social and/or psychological functioning and development will be an integral part of the series.

This series will present innovative work within two major, overlapping approaches to furthering the SEL of children and adolescents: (1) primary prevention efforts that promote SEL for all; and (2) more traditional programs and interventions intended for children with psychosocial problems (and their families and teachers) and developed with the help of child mental health professionals. In addition, the series will present programs and perspectives that seek to promote SEL for educators themselves.

In this volume, we focus on the middle school child. The transition from childhood into adolescence is one of the most dramatic transformations in the life cycle and presents educators with special challenges and opportunities. The chapters here contribute to our knowledge of the ways in which middle schools can nurture the social and emotional growth of their students, focusing on the issues particular to early adolescence.

Jonathan Cohen
Teachers College, Columbia University

Foreword

In one sense the subject of this book is as old as education—indeed as ancient as childrearing. Adults in every society have shown concern about children's social and emotional development: this concern has been particularly manifest at crucial points in the child's development or at times when the ambient society is undergoing marked change. In another sense, then, the subject of this book is rooted in our own time—a time when all children are confronted with new challenges and new opportunities, a time when disadvantaged children find themselves at special risk in various kinds of learning.

Troubled times call for new terminology and for articulate spokespersons. In recent years, researchers and educators have begun to call explicitly for social learning, emotional learning, training in conflict resolution and intergroup relations. These messages have come to be associated with certain educators, such as Roger Weissberg, James Comer, Maurice Elias, Linda Lantieri—and especially with the gifted psychologist and writer Daniel Goleman. Without his influential book *Emotional Intelligence*, the work described here would have been unlikely to come to public attention with the speed that it has.

Like other terms that enter the consciousness of the American public, "emotional intelligence" risks becoming a buzzword—one that is overly used, misused, and eventually cast on the junkheap of fads. A principal purpose of this book is to provide a firm theoretical and practical base for the important ideas involved in "social and emotional learning." Indeed, singularly and collectively, the authors ask us to proceed beyond the catch-phrase and to appreciate the complex and fascinating space that envelops children's social and emotional life during the years of middle and late childhood.

This volume reflects the most sophisticated thinking about social and emotional development. At the same time, however, it never deviates from the experiences of young students—those experiences that are universal to youth everywhere, such as physical and psychic growing pains, and those that are exacerbated in our time, such as the power of the media and the temptations of drugs. The poignant cases of Maura and Raffi bring these fictions into sharp relief. A special contribution of the volume is to present in some detail the major ideas and practices of several well-regarded programs designed for students in America today in order to prepare them for the world of tomorrow. Anyone concerned about the development of youth today will be instructed by these pages; indeed, as the parent of three grown children and one still sprouting thirteen-year-old, I both recognized the terrain and learned new things about it.

Having set a context for this book, let me indicate how I as an educator perceive the recent interest and progress in the realm of youngsters' social and emotional learning. In its ideal realization, formal education can be thought of as a series of masteries: first, the basic literacies; then the rough building-blocks of different ways of thinking; then a systematic introduction to the major disciplines prized by the culture, among them science, mathematics, history, literature, and the arts; finally, an effort to apply these ideas to real world concerns, and, when appropriate, to synthesize the perspectives of the different disciplines.

I believe that this curricular focus should—indeed, must—be at the core of formal education. No other set of goals can justify the financial and human resources that we and other societies devote to education.

We might think of education as a lengthy highway along which all students should pass during a decade or more of study. Highways ease our journey from one place to another but they do not work without proper entrances and exits. I see social and emotional learning as providing, on the one hand, the necessary prerequisites for a formal education; and on the other, the best sense of the uses to which such an education should be put.

Let me flesh out this analogy at both ends. Unless students feel part of a community, unless they feel motivated to work, struggle, master, they will never be able to benefit from formal education. A few students may, for whatever reason, simply accept the agenda of school and sail along the highway. But for most children, it is essential that they be able to participate in the school, interact appropriately with teachers and peers, and locate themselves within the often perplexing agenda of formal schooling. In some cases, this social and emotional undergirding may be provided primarily by family, religious training, or the overall community; in most cases all over the world, however, it has become the burden of the school to provide the support, so that the student can begin to travel smoothly along the highway of literacies and disciplinary mastery.

For a journey of any length, it is necessary that one have the opportunity for frequent rest stops and refueling. Throughout any formal education, it will be important for students and teachers to have the chance to confirm the reasons for their journey. This becomes especially important at moments of crisis, which could occur either for external reasons (such as a major change in administration or educational mandate) or for internal reasons (such as personal or familial crisis). The particular interventions recommended here prove especially crucial at such times.

While education may continue throughout one's lifetime, nearly all students will eventually leave school and proceed with their lives as workers, citizens, and members of a family. To be able to effect these transitions and roles with some skill, it is imperative that students have a good understanding of other individuals (I term this "interpersonal intelligence") and a comparable understanding of themselves (the complementary "intrapersonal intelligence"). Schools can serve as prominent socializing agents in this respect. Even more important, we want citizens who proceed in responsible, ethical, and informed ways—ones who take seriously their membership in their local community and in the global society as well. Alas, even the highest IQ or the most rigorous education in the disciplines will not bring about these virtues—they reflect the character of a person.

Few would doubt that the ten or fifteen years spent in formal schooling can play a crucial role in determining such character; it matters whether the school ignores social and emotional issues, exacerbates problems in these spheres, or considers as important the psychology and social life of its students. To continue the analogy, how one acts after one has left the highway depends significantly on the social and emotional learning that has taken place along the way.

For understandable historical reasons, psychology at mid-century focused on human problems—particularly those of mental illness or mental retardation. We are entering an era where psychology has taken on a more positive role—seeking to build individuals who are strong intellectually, emotionally, and in terms of character: in short, to be preventive rather than reactive. While perhaps stimulated by the genuine problems encountered by young adolescents, the work in this book should have its greatest impact in facilitating the smooth growth of future students. Optimally, those students who are raised in a healthy home and school environment can acquire social and emotional lessons in a natural and nondidactic way. We might say that, like the accomplished commuter, such students will be able to travel competently through life; and, ultimately, they will be able to pass on their own wisdom in a natural way to those who come after them.

Howard Gardner
Harvard University

Acknowledgments

I am very grateful to George Igel, who in 1996 suggested that I organize a conference for educators and school specialists about the range of ways that we may further social and emotional learning (SEL) in our schools. Having worked as a teacher, consulting psychologist, program developer, psychoeducational diagnostician, and child psychotherapist/psychoanalyst, I was excited—and daunted—by the prospect of reviewing the many ways that educators and school specialists seek to promote SEL in schools today. Our first annual conference (held at Teachers College in October 1997) generated so much interest and excitement from educators around the country that we created the Project for Social and Emotional Learning at Teachers College. This project is now involved with a range of educative, scholarly, and consultative activities to further SEL in our schools (http://www.tc.columbia.edu/~academic/csel).

In the spring of 1997, the Collaborative for the Advancement of Social and Emotional Learning (CASEL) (http://www.cfapress.org/casel/casel.html) organized a meeting about SEL at the Fetzer Institute. This was an extraordinary, truly collaborative meeting of about 40 educators, social science researchers, mental health professionals, and others who are committed to promoting effective SEL programs in our schools. These few days set in motion the formation of new and enriching partnerships and projects. The seeds for this book series began to grow during these few days at the Fetzer Institute. From the beginning, this volume and this series have been a wonderfully collaborative process.

The creation of this volume, and of the series, grows out of a partnership between the Project for Social and Emotional Learning at Teachers College and the Collaborative for the Advancement of Social and Emotional Learning. Maurice Elias, Norris Haynes, Roger Weissberg, and Joe Zins have been integrally involved with the design of this series from its inception. The shape and spirit of this book series reflect this partnership.

Maurice Elias has been particularly involved with helping me to think about this volume on the middle school child, and I am very grateful for his support and wise counsel. Roger Weissberg has also provided many helpful ideas and support that have shaped this volume. George Igel cofounded the Project for Social and Emotional Learning, and he has been a steady and invaluable supporter of and contributor to the work. Faye Zucker, Carole P. Saltz, and particularly, Carol Chambers Collins at Teachers College Press have also been extremely helpful in guiding the development of the series. Peter Cookson, Katie Embree, Margaret Jo Shepherd, and Barry Farber have provided essential support at Teachers College that has allowed us to grow. Finally, I would like to thank Stacey, Gabriel, and Zoe for their loving presence and support.

All royalties for this volume will be donated to the Social Emotional Learning Foundation (New York City) and the Collaborative for the Advancement of Social and Emotional Learning (Chicago).

Jonathan Cohen
Teachers College, Columbia University

PART

I

Social and Emotional Learning: An Overview

Part I of this volume provides an overview to social and emotional learning (SEL) (Chapter 1) and the development of the middle school child (Chapter 2). *Social and emotional learning* is a relatively new label for an educational tradition that has existed—in one form or another—since the inception of formal education 3000 years ago. The introductory chapter presents ways of thinking about the nature of social and emotional competencies as well as the range of SEL programs and perspectives that exist today.

The second chapter in this section focuses on the developmental experiences of middle school children: the passage into adolescence. Virtually all educators and parents know that we need to be attuned to the developmental experiences of our children; this understanding provides the foundation for our empathic efforts. But "thinking developmentally" is not always so easy in practice, particularly during the bumpy years of early adolescence. Our children change so much! Bill Solodow's portraits of two middle school children help provide a common touchstone throughout the book, to ground our thinking about programs and perspectives in the developmental process that is the foundation for experience.

1

Social and Emotional Learning Past and Present

A Psychoeducational Dialogue

Jonathan Cohen

Since the beginning of formal education, there has been a dialogue about the purpose of schooling: What really matters? What is most important to teach and why and how? In recent years, teachers and researchers have rediscovered what good teachers and parents have known for many years: that knowledge of ourselves and others as well as the capacity to use this knowledge to solve problems creatively provides an essential foundation for both academic learning and the capacity to become an active, constructive citizen (Gardner, 1983; Goleman, 1995; Sternberg, 1997). Promoting social and emotional learning (SEL) helps students to learn and develop, and it helps teachers to be even more effective educators (Salovey & Sluyter, 1997).

In this chapter, I will describe how educators have conceptualized SEL over time, what is clear and what is not clear about the nature of social and emotional competencies, and the three major, overlapping ways that we can promote this kind of learning today. But, first, I want to tell you about two middle school children, Maura and Raffi. In the next chapter, Solodow will describe in some detail how these children changed over the course of their middle school years. Many of the subsequent authors in this volume will relate their particular program and/or perspective about SEL learning to Maura and Raffi.

A DEVELOPMENTALLY INFORMED PERSPECTIVE

Human development is an extraordinary process: from a single cell to the newborn; from infancy to the early childhood years; from an early middle school child to an adolescent; and from early to middle to late adulthood. We change in infinitely complex and truly astounding ways! Our experience in the moment is *always* powerfully influenced by both our past and our projections about our next developmental steps. For example, a child's conscious and unrecognized experience during the past at school and home naturally colors the expectations of what the upcoming year will bring. Similarly the child's feelings about what it means to "grow up"—and the ways in which the child is beginning to manage new challenges—shape what he or she does today.

Although we tend to focus on how much or how little we have changed, there is actually great continuity over the course of life. Human development, by its very definition, is biologically driven. Yet, there are four major forces that mold how we develop and that shape the people we become: (1) the biological strengths, weaknesses, and dispositions with which we come into the world; (2) the conscious and unconscious meanings that we attribute to experience (the intrapsychic, intrapersonal, and emotional); (3) interpersonal experiences (e.g., with family, peers, teachers, and other important figures); and (4) the larger neighborhood, cultural, and societal forces that have an impact on our lives.

As Solodow (Chapter 2) describes, Maura and Raffi change in very dramatic ways during their middle school years. The more we, as educators and school specialists, are attuned to students' developmental changes, the more empathic and supportive we can be. It is also true that many aspects of Maura's and Raffi's emerging characters and behavioral patterns are relatively consistent. When we teach children to think critically, to appreciate diversity (be it musical, literary, racial, or cultural), and to expand their own social and emotional competencies, we are affecting the course of their development.

Introducing Maura and Raffi

Here are Maura and Raffi. Maura is a petite girl, quite empathic and well liked by peers and teachers. She can usually work with others in a collaborative manner and is often a leader in class. Keep in mind that all children evidence an array of strength and weaknesses. Maura was placed in a special reading class during the third grade, due to poor performance on a standardized reading test. She had significant trouble learning to decode phonemes and words. She is a good reader now but still goes at it slowly.

Reading slowly is actually a helpful compensatory strategy as it allows her to automatically check and recheck the contents of what she is reading. Maura intellectually understands that everyone evidences some spheres of relative weakness, though she insists on seeing her decoding problems as proof that she is "dumb." This is striking and curious given that her teachers, parents, and peers perceive her as smart. She is intelligent. Maura knows that she does well in school and occasionally is confused by the discrepancy between how she feels about herself and how others see her. Paradoxically, however, she is invested in *not* paying attention to this discrepancy. She hopes that her pejorative feelings about herself will go away.

We all have relatively characteristic ways of managing problems, be they emotional, social, and/or academic. Although people differ in how they solve problems, that response is one dimension that tends to be more, rather than less, stable and consistent over time. When Maura becomes upset, she is apt to become angry and/or distraught with others. This is true even when the problem is quite minor. Although Maura has many interests and good friends, her vulnerability to anger and her striking out at others have contributed to peers and adults viewing her as somewhat testy, even oppositional. All children have problems; and this is one of Maura's. However, when good friends, teachers, and/or her parents confront her with this behavior, she is impressively able to talk about what she is feeling and what has been happening interpersonally. Maura's ability to become reflective in a relatively nondefensive manner and to take responsibility for her actions is a social and emotional strength.

Raffi is a very bright, skinny boy who often acts in a clownish and disruptive manner. He is vulnerable to having temper tantrums in and out of school. In class, Raffi is often inattentive. Some of his teachers and his parents' friends have wondered if he has attention deficit disorder, asking whether he would benefit from a trial of stimulant medication. But Raffi's inattentiveness is not chronic or pervasive; he is intermittently very anxious. Anxiety for Raffi—as for most children—complicates the ability to sustain attention. The passage into adolescence is normally tumultuous, hardly surprising given that children's bodies and minds are changing in ways more consciously dramatic than ever before. The ups and downs of the middle school years are even more exaggerated for Raffi. And, as a result, many see him as moody.

Raffi has had great trouble making friends, and he is not sure why. He feels very unhappy about himself. Sometimes these feelings are painfully conscious; often, they go unrecognized. When Raffi does feel bad about himself, he is apt to complain about physical aches and pains. Also, he is quick to find fault with others. Raffi often teases and taunts classmates in a seemingly indiscriminate manner. This represents an attempt on his part to feel the exact opposite of what he's really feeling. It seems that when he teases others, he feels in charge and in control: the aggressor instead of the victim. He desperately wants to connect with his peers as well as with his teachers. However, his teasing/taunting behavior alienates the very people he wants to reach. Whenever others make a mistake, for example, Raffi tends to laugh at them. Not surprisingly, this upsets and hurts fellow students and sometimes even his teachers. Raffi does not understand this and often feels as if *he* is the victim. Raffi's empathic capacity to "read" others is seriously impaired.

Despite this behavior, Raffi has done quite well in school. He has always wanted to "get it right" and often has been able to do just this. However, the nature of schoolwork is changing as he and his classmates move into adolescence and the middle school grades: Longer projects are assigned, and there are more demands to be reflective and to work at a higher, more disciplined level. Raffi's need to find the right answer immediately and his strikingly unreflective style are beginning to undermine his academic performance. His teachers are feeling frustrated and somewhat put off by his lack of attention, insensitivity, and disruptive behavior.

Developmental Challenges

In today's United States, middle school children like Maura and Raffi are faced with two major and often quite daunting challenges. On the one hand, as Solodow (Chapter 2) points out, children's bodies, minds, and relationships with parents, peers, and themselves are changing in confusing and frightening as well as exciting ways. The experience can be overwhelming when you consider the speed with which society—and their own lives in it— is changing. The young are facing everything from increased pressure to achieve academically to the disturbing prevalence of AIDS; from violence to premature sexual and drug-related experimentation; and, far too often, the crushing impact of prejudice and poverty (see Weissberg & Greenberg, 1997, for an excellent and recent review of these issues).

In the United States, a child is reported abused or neglected every 11 seconds; a child is arrested for a violent crime every 4 minutes; a child is killed by a gun every 98 minutes. On a typical school day, over 135,000 students bring weapons to school (Hamburg, 1997; Mott Foundation, 1994). Even in schools that are not scarred by metal bullets, "verbal" or "psychological" bullets are a normative part of school life. All teachers—and students—know that these verbal bullets, normative or not, profoundly affect children's ability to pay attention, to think, to collaborate, and to learn. From our own experience, we all know that when a child feels unsafe, that child is vulnerable to anxiety and a diminished capacity to discover, to remember, and to find joy in the process of learning.

When educators provide ongoing opportunities for children to learn "lessons of the heart" (Lantieri & Patti, 1996), this has, according to a growing body of research, an enormous impact on the children's lives as students. Effective SEL programs result in enhanced self-control. Students in such a program tend to improve their behavior and develop better skills at conflict resolution and handling interpersonal problems which, in turn, positively affects children's ability to learn (Aber, Jones, Brown, Chaudry, & Samples, 1998; Caplan, Weissberg, Grober, Sivo, Grady, & Jacoby, 1992; Elias, Gara, Schuyler, Brandon-Miller, & Sayette, 1991; Hawkins, Catalono, Morrison, O'Donnell, Abbot, & Day, 1992; Weissberg, Barton, & Shriver, 1997; Weissberg, Gullotta, Hampton, Ryan, & Adams, 1997). For example, we see a sharp decrease in the number of suspensions and expulsions. This is big and important news!

Not surprisingly, research has shown that, like any kind of learning, effective and helpful SEL programs need to be ongoing. Just as teaching reading for one semester or a year is not enough, so the same holds true for SEL (Elias et al., 1997). If we are invested in furthering SEL, it is most crucial that we consider creating a team in our school, and possibly in our community as well, that can develop a multiyear program and point of view to further that kind of learning. This is a collaborative process that, optimally, necessarily involves teachers, administrators, school support staff, parents, and students to create an effective multiyear plan (see Elias et al., 1997, for detailed suggestions about how to actually create effective, collaborative efforts).

In the last couple of decades, researchers have also discovered what many teachers and parents have known all along: for most people, academic grades and SAT scores are extraordinarily *nonpredictive* of satisfaction and productivity throughout life. Emotional well-being, on the other hand, is dramatically and positively predictive not only of academic achievement but also of satisfactory and productive experiences in the worlds of work and marriage—in fact, it even is predictive of better physical health (Goleman, 1995; Heath, 1991; Valliant, 1977, 1993).

SOCIAL AND EMOTIONAL LEARNING: FROM ANCIENT TIMES TO TODAY

Social and emotional learning is a new term that is centrally related to an educational tradition that began 3,000 years ago. Over the centuries, educators' understanding and definitions of childhood, "self," and "human relationships" have varied greatly. The specific pedagogical methods that have been employed to further particular educational goals have also evolved quite dramatically. However, I think that many good teachers have always known that we can never separate how we feel about ourselves from our mastery of any given subject. It is only in recent years, though, that more and more educators are suggesting that SEL needs to be a recognized and respected form of learning in and of itself. In other words, just as we honor language, math, and music as disciplines worth promoting for all students, social and emotional competencies are equally worth promoting. In fact, as educators, we cannot afford to ignore this essential dimension of learning.

Social learning has always been an integral facet of educating the young. The first records of formal schooling show that the purpose of education in ancient India, Egypt, and Greece was to teach students about their culture and its habits (Nash, 1968; Padel, 1992; Snell, 1982). In short, how to conceptualize and manage social relations has been a continuous educational goal from the very start. Three thousand years ago, and even today in parts of the world, terribly discriminatory lessons were taught. For example, only upper-class men were educated, and they were taught to adhere to a class and/or caste system driven by slavery (e.g., Nash, 1968).

What is sometimes called "emotional learning" was also an integral and honored goal of education from the beginning of formal education. Knowledge of self was an organizing principle of Indian and Greek education from its inception (Snell, 1982). Twenty-five hundred years ago, for example, the words *Know thyself* were carved on the wall of the Oracle Apollo at Delphi, which to the Greeks was the center of the world. Men of the educated class lived by this phrase. The Delphic precept foreshadows what Gardner, Goleman, and others now call "emotional intelligence" and "emotional learning" (Gardner, 1983; Goleman, 1995; Salovey & Mayer, 1990).

Nonetheless, the notion of childhood and who we are as social, emotional/psychological, spiritual, and intellectual beings and of how we learn to "know ourselves" has evolved quite dramatically over the centuries, particularly in the West (Nash, 1968). For example, it is well known that medieval art until the 12th century did not represent childhood at all. For most of history, children older than 7 or 8 were treated as little adults. I will not detail the fascinating evolution in our understanding of childhood and self or the educational practices that have fostered it but will only say that during the last century social and emotional competencies have come to be increasingly recognized, studied, and appreciated. Two overlapping traditions have contributed to this growing appreciation: (1) educational activities and perspectives that seek to *promote* the development of these capacities; and (2) a psychoeducationally informed perspective that has focused on which factors *interfere* with social and emotional development and therefore require particular psychoeducational interventions or even psychological or psychiatric treatment.

The emphasis on growth and activities that promote social and emotional development emerges, in turn, from several sources: the progressive educational movement; the civil rights and the women's movements; and psychoanalytic, psychological, and psychiatric "prevention" work, as well as the more recent work in education and the neurosciences that seeks to link social and emotional competencies to neurobiological developmental processes.

The notion that we can and need to understand the "whole child," including social and emotional functioning, was proposed and implemented in classrooms during the early part of the century by John Dewey, Felix Adler, and Maria Montessori. These pioneers of progressive education were soon joined by a growing number of students/teachers such as Anna Freud (who was first a teacher), Rudolf Steiner, and many others in Europe and the United States, all of whom sought to make educational curricula more relevant to the child's social and emotional experience. Progressive educators held that, optimally, we need to pay attention to *all* facets of the child; this includes an attempt to discover where each child's particular strengths and weaknesses lie, what the child's interests are, and which helpful (or unhelpful) coping strategies he or she has developed. In many ways, these ideas have become principles that most teachers and schools have accepted. To what extent teachers have actually acted on these principles varies greatly. For example, there is a tremendous range in how much training and support educators are given here. And, even when there are training and support, large class size often precludes effective, child-centered practice.

In the 1960s, the notion that emotional abilities can and should be cultivated in the classroom gained educational and popular attention as a part of the affective education movement. At the same time there were other, in some ways overlapping, social upheavals that powerfully furthered the nation's awareness of the fundamental importance of emotional and social life, among them the civil rights movement and the women's movement. In a variety of ways, these movements led, indeed galvanized, generations of students and professionals alike to learn more about psychosocial development, human diversity, and the humane (and inhumane) ways that we treat ourselves and one another. Some of this work (Belenky, Bond, & Weinstock, 1997; Gilligan, 1982) critically revealed that many of our models of human development were based on facets of male development. This work—inadvertently—slighted the importance of human relatedness and self-reflection.

Mental health professionals who work with the young have long been acutely aware of how social and emotional experience profoundly affects and even determines children's ability to learn and develop (Aichhorn, 1925/1935; Freud, 1930/1974). These professionals have differed in their approach to and/or their timing of intervention. Traditionally, early childhood mental health professionals, many of whom were originally teachers, have been primarily attuned to children who are or may be presenting with problems that "derail" development and/or effective treatments. However, Anna Freud and subsequent generations of psychoanalytically informed child therapists were primarily invested in anticipating possible problems and establishing preventive measures (Biber, 1961; Edgcumbe, 1975; Furman, 1987; Greenspan, 1993; Olden, 1953). In recent decades, various branches of psychology and psychiatry have aligned themselves with school systems, working collaboratively with teachers, parents, and administrators to promote social competencies (Consortium on the School-Based Promotion of Social Competence, 1994; Durlak, 1995; Dryfoos, 1990; Pittman, 1986). Their work remains rooted in what went before, of course, and thus overlaps, to varying degrees, with early traditions.

In the last two decades, schools have been involved in a series of programs designed to promote social competencies and to prevent social, emotional, and health problems. They are offering students character education; delinquency prevention; health, drug, and sex education; violence prevention and lessons in family life; morality and multicultural values, to name a few such programs. The intent of this effort is to intervene in a manner that will both enhance specific skills (e.g., conflict resolution, cooperative learning, peer counseling) and prevent problems in the future. Importantly, building on these efforts as well as the seminal work of Gardner (1983) about multiple forms of intelligence, the best-selling book *Emotional Intelligence* (Goleman, 1995) was a catalyzing force in furthering recognition and appreciation about the fundamental importance of SEL.

If the spotlight is increasingly on the importance of emotional competence, it is also because of the work of mental health professionals and the biopsychosocial perspective they bring to the subject. They have traditionally focused on the biological and psychological factors that complicate or interfere with social and emotional learning and development, and they employ a wide range of psychosocial and pharmacological modes of treating youngsters and their families. Their understanding of individual children (like Raffi) and/or families who are "stuck" and/or at risk contributes to our perception of the nature of development, health, and psychopathology (Cicchetti & Cohen, 1995).

SOCIAL AND EMOTIONAL COMPETENCIES

What are social and emotional competencies? I do not think that there is a consensus about how to define these competencies or what many would conceptualize as "social and emotional intelligences." It may be useful to first consider the basic building blocks or "core equipment" providing the foundation of these competencies and, then, the important ways in which people use these capacities to solve problems and generate questions.

I would suggest that *self-reflective capacities* on the one hand and the *ability to recognize what others are thinking and feeling* on the other provide the foundation for children to understand, manage, and express the social and emotional aspects of life. Just as children's ability to recognize phonemes is the basic building block of reading letters and words, I believe that being able to recognize their own experience—self-reflective ability—and the ability to recognize others' experiences are the basic building blocks of social and emotional competence. Anna Freud (a teacher and then the "grandmother" of child psychoanalysis) suggested that all children progress along a number of specific developmental lines; "self" and "social" development, she said, represent two basic dimensions, of which all teachers and parents as well as psychotherapists need to be aware (Fonagy & Target, 1997; Freud, 1965; Yorke, Kennedy, and Wiseberg, 1991).

Children's basic (neuropsychologically based) core equipment always shows variation and deviation in the various domains. Just as children evidence normal *variation* in phonetic capacity, the same holds true for self-reflective and recognition-related capacities (Baron-Cohen, 1995; Fonagy & Target, 1997). And, just as some children evince *deviation* in phonetic-related abilities (and are then labeled "dyslexic"), others evince deviation or significant problems with self-reflective and/or recognition-related abilities. The extreme example of a recognition-related deviation is autism (Baron-Cohen, 1995).

There are children in many mainstream classes who have significant trouble relating to or connecting with others. A wide range of psychological and psychobiological difficulties contributes to the problems of these children, who are often considered "geeks" by other students. To the extent that we agree that self-reflection and recognition-related abilities represent the foundation for social and emotional competencies, it behooves us to reflect on what we do in our classrooms to promote these capacities.

Social and emotional *competencies* or modes of intelligence define our capacity to solve social and emotional problems and/or to make something useful that is valued in one or more cultures. To put this another way, these competencies allow us to modulate emotions, to solve social problems creatively, to be effective leaders or collaborators, to be assertive and responsible, or to be able to ask evocative emotional and/or social questions that lead to new learning. Building on work undertaken by the Northeast Foundation for Children and described by Charney, Crawford, & Wood (Chapter 6), Elliot (1997) has identified five key dimensions that represent core attitudes and skills: cooperation, assertion, responsibility, empathy, and self-control (CARES). These dimensions overlap with what Goleman (1995) has defined as the five core facets of "emotional literacy": self-awareness, the ability to handle emotions, self-motivation, empathic capacities, and social skills. Social and emotional *learning* is the process through which we develop the skills and attitudes necessary to acquire social and emotional competencies.

Maura—often in touch with her own thinking and feelings—already has many of those abilities. She has the capacity to *use* self-awareness, further-more, in making good decisions, in empathizing with others, and in finding the ability to cooperate, collaborate, and resolve conflicts creatively. Like all of us, Maura does evidence social and emotional vulnerabilities. She is strik-ingly unreflective about her reading difficulties and the feelings they engen-der. And, as noted previously, she is prone to managing upset by becoming angry and distraught with others. At this point, these vulnerabilities do not seem to be derailing her academic or psychosocial development. They do complicate her social and emotional experiences, however, and have the potential of becoming quite problematic. Therefore, it is clear that Maura could benefit from further SEL in spite of the fact that, in many ways, she is functioning at a high level.

Raffi, on the other hand, is clearly in trouble. He is problematically unaware of himself and often of others. Even when he does recognize how classmates are feeling and thinking, he is unable to make use of this infor-mation. He is blocked, conflicted, and lacking in basic social and emotional skills. He needs help. And, for us as teachers, he raises important questions: How can we help? and What are the limits of what we can do, socially and emotionally, for the Raffis in our schools?

SOCIAL AND EMOTIONAL LEARNING: PROGRAMS AND PERSPECTIVES

There are three potentially overlapping ways that we can further SEL in schools: (1) Curriculum- and non-curriculum-based SEL programs for all children; (2) SEL programs and perspectives for at risk students; and (3) SEL for educators.

Curriculum- and Non-Curriculum-Based SEL Programs for All Children

These programs seek to promote the development of social and emotional competencies across the board. There are two major types: (1) curriculum-based SEL programs; and (2) perspectives on social and emotional devel-opment and learning that can be integrated into whatever class we are teach-ing or whatever subject is under discussion. These two methods can and often do overlap.

Curriculum-based SEL programs seek to educate children about the value of social and emotional competencies and to foster the development of specific skills in these areas. Such program seek to teach children to communicate more effectively, cooperate, resolve conflicts creatively and adaptively, reflect on self and interpersonal experience, control impulsivity, and make more thoughtful and collaborative social decisions. Today there are over 300 curriculum-based programs that purport to teach SEL. There are also many problem-prevention programs—such as conflict-resolution training or drug-prevention programs—that emphasize general social and emotional competency skills. Some of these programs have been empirically studied and shown to be helpful; many have not been studied.

Some teachers do not want or may not be able to teach SEL as a course in and of itself. Instead, they may want to think more about individual children and about their particular classrooms to discover ways of becoming further attuned to SEL and how best to incorporate it into all they do at school. There are a good many research findings available today describing how SEL can be encouraged by integrating a set of principles and practices with work that is taking place in the classroom—and on the success with which that has been done (see Chapter 6; also see Charney, 1992).

We have much more to learn about the uses and limitations of curriculum- and non-curriculum-based programs. Just as some children learn to read with little or no instruction from teachers, there are some children who need little social and/or psychologically informed instruction from educators. These children may be particularly gifted in that area and/or may come from homes where that learning is valued and—in a sense—continually practiced. Still, most children can and do benefit from instruction about the basics, whether these basics are phonics or the building blocks of social and psychological learning.

If Raffi began a curriculum- or non-curriculum-based SEL program now—in the sixth grade—I do not think that it would be helpful to him. He is too stuck. He is not interpersonally and psychologically open to this kind of learning. Raffi's negative sense of himself and others, as well as the unhelpful ways he has adopted to protect himself, have taken on a life of their own. They have become ongoing, typically unrecognized facets of his behavior. Although it will matter how educators respond to Raffi, he needs more social and emotional assistance than we, as educators, can provide in the classroom. How would Raffi be today if he had participated in a SEL class begun in kindergarten? We don't know. We do know that ongoing programs that begin earlier and continue onward tend to be most successful. I suspect that, even if Raffi's school experience had included SEL programs from the start, it would not be enough.

On the other hand, I think that Maura would certainly be able to benefit from a curriculum- or non-curriculum-based SEL program. She already shows many impressive social and emotional capacities. Social and emotional learning programs would enhance these abilities even more. On the other hand, Maura's experience of feeling "dumb" and her vulnerability to becoming angry and distraught with others are now relatively chronic and unrecognized facets of her personality. She is not aware of why she has these experiences and is defensively invested in avoiding them. Although it is unlikely that a SEL program would have a significant effect on these aspects of Maura's personality, we cannot be sure. It always is impossible to predict how the culture of a class, or of an entire school, will shape the intrapsychic and interpersonal lives of particular students and teachers.

Social and Emotional Learning Programs and Perspectives for At Risk Students

Some SEL programs and perspectives seek to address the needs of children who are psychosocially at risk of becoming stuck or are, in fact, already stuck. When we think about SEL for at risk students, it is useful to consider the following three important questions: Who are at risk students? What are the options among socially and emotionally informed programs and perspectives that could help these students? and To what extent can we work with and help at risk students? What, in other words, are our limits as educators and school specialists?

There are many models for thinking about at risk students. Coie et al. (1993, p. 1022) suggest that generic risk factors can be grouped into the following seven overlapping individual and group domains: *constitutional handicaps* (e.g., prenatal complications, biochemical imbalance, organic handicaps, and sensory disabilities); *skill development delays* (e.g., low intelligence, social incompetence, attentional deficits, reading disabilities, and poor work skills and habits); *emotional difficulties* (e.g., immaturity, conflict, poor self-esteem, and emotional dysregulation); *family circumstances* (e.g., low social class, mental illness in the family, large family size, child abuse, stressful life events, family disorganization, communication deviance, family conflict, and poor attachment patterns); *interpersonal problems* (e.g., peer rejection, alienation, and isolation); *school problems* (e.g., school demoralization and failure); and, *ecological context* (e.g., extreme poverty, neighborhood disorganization, racial injustice, and unemployment).

These categories of at risk children are overlapping; they include very different levels of functioning (e.g., biogenic, intrapsychic, interpersonal, family, societal), and they do not distinguish symptom from cause. For example, a reading or an attentional disability can be symptomatic of an under-lying constitutional, emotional, and/or family problem, but it can also induce (or be induced by) emotional, family, and/or school problems (Cohen, 1994). Then, too, the line between being at risk and being developmentally derailed (or academically, emotionally, and/or socially stuck) is often fuzzy, depend-ing on context and point of view. In this chapter, I use the terms, *stuck* and *at risk* interchangeably.

Some programs and perspectives aim to address the specific needs of at risk students. There are three general ways that this can be done: individual efforts to diagnose and treat what has (or is about to) go awry; systematic early detection and early secondary prevention; and primary prevention efforts.

INDIVIDUAL EFFORTS, EARLY SECONDARY PREVENTION AND PRIMARY PREVENTION PROGRAMS. The first and oldest method of addressing the needs of at risk students is traditional mental health work: diagnosing the nature of a student's (and/or family's) problems and mapping out an individualized plan to treat the problems. Child psy-choanalysts, school-based social workers, guidance counselors, psycholo-gists, psychiatrists, and the clergy have worked with at risk children and fam-ilies for decades. Various theories of child development and psychopathology and the choice of diagnostic, psychotherapeutic, and pharmacological meth-ods determine the understanding and the treatment of the child as does the extent to which mental health professionals collaborate with educators (see Chapter 7; also see Weist, 1997).

When faced by a seriously stuck student or a student who has not been developing (be it academically and/or psychosocially) for six or more months, mental health professionals can and often must clarify the nature of the problem and create an intervention plan. I suspect, for example, that Raffi and his family need to be evaluated and perhaps treated in this way. Although it is unclear what long-standing emotional, social, and/or neu-rocognitive problems plague Raffi, it is imperative that he and his family gain the opportunity to discover what the problems are and to address them (Cohen, 1998). Otherwise, they will increasingly derail his ability to learn and succeed in and out of school, to develop friends, and to be comfortable with himself. In fact, it is probable that Raffi's difficulties will intensify if they are not understood and addressed. Although this individually oriented, professional mental health approach can be invaluable, it is costly and ter-ribly labor intensive. It is only available to a small percentage of the students who could benefit from it. Often, the children who present with the most severe problems are from poor urban areas. This fact, plus the growing awareness that we must act sooner, rather than later, has led to the primacy of what is called "early secondary prevention" in the treatment of at risk students.

These programs emphasize early detection of potential or actual problems and advocate early intervention. And there are a growing number of them. An important example is the Primary Mental Health Project (PMHP), which has an impressive track record of identifying students' problems and potential problems early on and intervening rapidly in ways that seem to decrease psychopathology (Cowen et al., 1996). The PMHP includes school-based mental health screenings and short-term counseling by nonprofessionals who are supervised by school-based mental health professionals. Peer counseling programs, where older students work with younger ones in small groups and occasionally in a one-on-one situation (supervised by educators and/or school specialists), represent another effort that assures early detection of problems.

Although we know that the general (curriculum- and non-curriculum-based) SEL programs may be helpful to at risk as well as mainstream students (Elias & Tobias, 1996), others are aimed specifically at the at risk group. These programs use a variety of ways to reach out to these students and address their problems. For example, we know that children who tend to assume that others will be hostile experience a great deal of aggressive fantasy and are at risk of acting in aggressive/violent and antisocial ways. Conflict-resolution programs (see Chapter 8) have been shown to ameliorate the development of these responses. As such, their importance to the prevention of violence cannot be exaggerated (Aber et al., 1998; Deutsch, 1993). Other programs have been specifically developed to address particular conditions (such as deafness) that we know enhance the likelihood of at risk functioning (e.g., Greenberg & Kusche, 1993).

A growing number of practitioners who work with at risk students are involved with primary prevention efforts. School-based mental health professionals and educators who are interested in primary prevention can do so in two overlapping ways: by implementing curriculum- and non-curriculum-based programs that promote social and emotional skills and competencies; and by introducing prosocial vocabulary and behaviors to affect the climate of schools. In fact, many of the programs and perspectives in this volume represent this effort.

AT RISK STUDENTS: WHAT CAN AND CAN'T WE DO? Working with at risk students inevitably raises two difficult and essential questions for educators: To what extent can we help these students? and When do we—student, family, and teacher—need additional help? The emotions and thoughts that these questions evoke overlap with the process of SEL for educators that I describe on pages 18–19. In responding to the needs of virtually all students, and more so with at risk students, most educators struggle with very personal questions: What can we do? and What are our limits? Just as self-reflection and recognition-related processes form the basis of social and emotional competencies so, too, do they form the basis of our work with derailed students: What do I recognize in this student? and What is clear about what I can do and should be doing? These questions tend to raise yet more questions: What is the nature of the student's difficulties? What can we and others (e.g., parents, colleagues, consulting health care professionals) do to further clarify the nature of the student's difficulties and strengths? How do we create a plan that addresses the student's difficulties and do so in such a way as to build on his or her strengths? How we will use this information naturally depends on who the child is, what role the child's family plays, who we are, and what the options may be inside and outside school.

When students have been stuck for a long period of time, be it due to a linguistic disability and/or an emotional conflict, teachers can rarely "fix" the problem. Educators cannot be everything for every student. Learning about our limits (and strengths!) is a central and critical facet of our development as educators, just as it is for all children and adolescents.

Educators have developed a range of linguistic, mathematical, artistic, and kinesthetic (athletic- and dance-related) programs specifically designed for various at risk groups. In addition, something that educators do is to further the development of meaningful relationships with their students. Virtually all learning happens within the context of human relationships. So, even if we do not consciously intend to influence our students in this manner, the contacts we have with individual students affect how they feel about themselves and what they are learning. Relationships do not just happen. They are facilitated by what we do. How we structure a classroom, for example, or the extent to which we reach out to students importantly determines the kind of relationship that will ensue: close or distant; caring or cold; primarily focused on academics; or to attuned to other factors in addition to academic functioning.

Schools vary tremendously in the degree to which they value and support teachers forming relationships with students. Too often, daily practice, curriculum, and pedagogy are shaped by anticipated performance on standardized tests. Test scores, not relationships, matter to most administrators and, hence, to teachers themselves. Yet, forming ongoing, caring, and responsive relationships with students makes a profound difference. We all know this intuitively. Think about what you most fondly remember in your own life as a student. For most of us, it was a teacher whom we felt cared about us and helped us in some way, sometimes academically, more often socially and emotionally. And research supports this notion. For example, the extent to which students perceive teachers as caring is found to be predictive of "motivational outcomes" or how much effort students evince; it also strengthens their impulse to act in caring and socially responsible ways with others (see Chapter 6; also see Wentzel, 1997).

A recent evaluation of the "I Have a Dream" program (IHAD)—where a member of the community "adopts" a class and promises financial support of its children, including their college tuition—shows, once again, the fundamental importance of sustained, healthy relationships. It is not only the promise of financial support through college that prompts these children to stay in school or raises the level of their achievement; the opportunity they are given to form a meaningful and supportive relationship with an adult also plays a critical role in opening the door to their future (Kahne & Bailey, 1997).

The extent to which students feel connected to teachers and peers and (in an overlapping manner) the extent to which they feel that their teachers are fair and care about them are significant! For example, a recent groundbreaking study (Klein, 1997) of over 12,000 adolescents found that parent-family connectedness and connectedness to school were protective factors against emotional distress; suicidal thoughts and behavior; violence; use of cigarettes, alcohol, and marijuana; and early sexual experimentation.

Such relationships do not "cure" the problems students present with. But, potentially, they do make a profound difference. What helps or hinders our capacity to relate to, empathize with, and effectively educate students is the essence of SEL for teachers.

Social and Emotional Learning for Educators

How can we, as educators and school specialists, pay attention to and learn about our own experience in ways that further our empathic and educative capacities? Being able to recognize, understand, and learn from our own experience has many powerful implications: It furthers our capacity to experientially convey the process of genuine discovery and its essential value to the children with whom we work. Social and emotional learning for educators enhances our capacity to empathize with and work more effectively with students; it enables us to work more effectively with colleagues; and it increases our ability to work with parents.

In most schools today, there is little or no time set aside for self-reflection. We teach students that learning is a lifelong process. Yet, when it comes to ourselves and the ways that we react to students—responses that are elicited in the classroom every day—we do not practice what we preach. Raffi's ridicule of another student and Maura's insistence that she is "dumb" affect us! These reactions, whatever they are, determine our attitudes in and out of our classrooms.

Knowing ourselves makes a difference. It not only provides us with tools to learn, but also it provides the foundation for all that we do with students. Many of us do this automatically—with our peers, sometimes with our supervisors, and with ourselves. Some educator-centered SEL programs are furthered in group workshops (see, e.g., Chapter 9) and seek to enhance our awareness about how the past influences the present as well as how our experiences and feelings about human diversity helpfully—and unhelpfully— affect our educational work. Other educator-centered SEL experiences may occur in groups or in more individualized, collaborative discussions (see, e.g., Chapter 7). For example, educators may talk with a colleague and/or a consulting mental heath professional to "unpack" what they are experiencing with a given student or class, what personal "buttons" these situations are touching, and how they can actually use these experiences both to learn about themselves and to be more educatively effective.

It is useful to recognize that what we do as teachers is based on our past experiences as well as on the conscious and unrecognized facets of our current lives. When we connect with and care about a Maura, we are making a link that is determined by a multitude of factors: who the student is, who we are, and what the nature of this particular pair or grouping is. Clearly, self-knowledge makes a difference; it provides us not only with the tools to learn but also with a foundation for all we do with students. We must ask ourselves, then, how we can find the time and the community to promote this kind of learning—without which our empathic and educative capacities can scarcely grow.

I believe there is a growing awareness of the importance of creating an environment in which teachers can reflect on their own professional development and their role in enhancing the social-emotional skills of students (e.g., Charney, 1992; Edgcumbe, 1975; Olden, 1953; Wentzel, 1997). This has been an important part of the progressive educational tradition. To the extent that we are invested in understanding students' social and emotional lives, it is essential that we participate in the process ourselves (Adalbjarnardottir & Selman, in press).

A fundamental goal of education is to foster children's ability to learn how to learn. We know that virtually all forms of learning take place within the context of a relationship and that learning won't happen unless a child feels safe—safe enough to listen to the self and others, to be curious, to ask questions, to express what he or she knows and does not know. Educators may differ on how they seek to establish that basic sense of security, but, once there, it has a profound effect on how students feel about themselves and the learning process itself.

CONCLUSION

Today educators are spearheading a number of initiatives to promote SEL in the classrooms, hallways, and playgrounds of our schools. In this chapter, I have described three overlapping approaches to enhancing SEL in schools: for all students, for at risk students, and for educators. All of these endeavors, in one way or another, represent a continuum of the 3,000-year-old quest to "know thyself." An individual's capacity to recognize what self and others are experiencing fosters self-discovery, a spirit of cooperation, and the potential for creative problem solving. By the same token, how young people understand and give meaning to learning, including the frustrations, failures, achievements, and important moments of confusion, determine the degree to which they can learn from the experience. In short, social and emotional competence provides the essential foundation for how children learn—indeed, for how they learn to learn.

REFERENCES

Aber, L. J., Jones, S. M., Brown, J. L., Chaudry, N., & Samples, F. (1998). *Resolving conflict creatively: Evaluating the developmental effects of a school-based violence prevention program in neighborhood and classroom context.* Manuscript submitted for publication.

Adalbjarnardottir, S., & Selman, R. L. (in press). "I feel I have received a new vision": An analysis of teachers' professional development as they work with students on interpersonal issues. *Teaching and Teacher Education.*

Aichhorn, A. (1935). *Wayward youth.* New York: Viking. (Original work published 1925)

Baron-Cohen, S. (1995). *Mindblindness: An essay on autism and theory of mind.* Cambridge, MA: A Bradford Book, MIT Press.

Belenky, M. F., Bond, L. A., & Weinstock, J. S. (1997). *A tradition that has no name: Nurturing the development of people, families, and communities.* New York: Basic Books.

Biber, B. (1961). *Prevention of mental disorders in children* (pp. 323–352). New York: Basic Books.

Caplan, M., Weissberg, R. P., Grober, J. S., Sivo, P. J., Grady, D., & Jacoby, C. (1992). Social competence promotion with inner city and suburban young adolescents: Effects on social adjustment and alcohol use. *Journal of Clinical and Counseling Psychology, 60*(1), 56–63.

Charney, R. S. (1992). *Teaching children to care: Management in the responsive classroom.* Greenfield, MA: Northeast Foundation for Children.

Cicchetti, D., & Cohen, D. J. (1995). *Developmental psychopathology* (Vols. 1 & 2). New York: Wiley-Interscience.

Cohen, J. (1994). On the differential diagnosis of reading, attentional and affective disorders in childhood. *Annals of Dyslexia, 44,* 165–184.

Cohen, J. (1998). *Social abilities and disabilities in childhood: Psychobiological origins and psychological meanings.* Manuscript submitted for publication.

Coie, J. D., Watts, N. F., West, S. G., Hawkins, J. D., Asarnow, J. R., Markman, H. J., Ramey, S. L., Shure, M. B., & Long, B. (1993). The science of prevention: A conceptual framework and some directions for a national research program. *American Psychologist, 48,* 1013–1022.

Consortium on the School-Based Promotion of Social Competence. (1994). The school-based promotion of social competence: Theory, practice, and policy. In R. J. Haggerty, L. R. Sherrod, N. Garnezy, & M. Rutter (Eds.), *Stress, risk, and resilience in children and adolescents: Processes, mechanisms, and interventions* (pp. 268–316). New York: Cambridge University Press.

Cowen, E. L, Hightower, A. D., Pedro-Carroll, J. L., Work, W. C., Wyman, P. A., & Haffey, W. G. (1996). *School based prevention for children at risk: The Primary Mental Health Project.* Washington, DC: American Psychological Association.

Deutsch, M. (1993). Educating for a peaceful world. *American Psychologist, 48*(5), 510–517.

Durlak, J. A. (1995). *School-based prevention programs for children and adolescents.* Thousand Oaks, CA: Sage.

Dryfoos, J. (1990). *Adolescents at risk: Prevalence and prevention.* New York: Oxford University Press.

Edgcumbe, R. (1975). The border between therapy and education. In *Psychoanalytic Study of the Child* (Monograph No. 5). New Haven, CT: Yale University Press.

Elias, M. J., Gara, M., Schuyler, T., Brandon-Miller, L. R., & Sayette, M. A. (1991). The promotion of social competence: Longitudinal study of a preventive school-based program. *American Journal of Orthopsychiatry, 61*(3), 409–417.

Elias, M. J., & Tobias, S. E. (1996). *Social problem solving: Interventions in the schools.* New York: Guilford.

Elias, M., Zins, J. E., Weissberg, R. P., Frey, K. S., Greenberg, M. T., Haynes, N. M., Kessler, R., Schwab-Stone, M. E., & Shriver, T. P. (1997). *Promoting social and emotional learning: Guidelines for educators.* Alexandria, VA: Association for Supervision and Curriculum Development.

Elliot, S. N. (1997). *The responsive classroom approach: Its effectiveness and acceptability in promoting social and academic competence. Year one in a three year study.* University of Wisconsin-Madison.

Fonagy, P., & Target, M. (1997). Attachment and reflective function: Their role in self organization. *Developmental Psychopathology, 9,* 679–700.

Freud, A. (1965). Normality and pathology in childhood. In *The Writings of Anna Freud* (Vol. 6). New York: International University Press.

Freud, A. (1974). Four lectures on psychoanalysis for teachers and parents. In *The Writings of Anna Freud* (Vol. 1). New York: International University Press. (Original work published 1930)

Furman, E. (1987). *The teacher's guide to helping young children grow: The teacher's manual.* Madison, CT: International University Press.

Gardner, H. (1983). *Frames of mind: The theory of multiple intelligences.* New York: Basic Books.

Gilligan, C. (1982). *In a different voice.* Cambridge, MA: Harvard University Press.

Goleman, D. (1995). *Emotional intelligence.* New York: Bantam Books.

Greenberg, M. T., & Kusche, C. A. (1993). *Promoting social and emotional development in deaf children: The PATHS Project.* Seattle: University of Washington Press.

Greenspan, S. I. (1993). *Playground politics: Understanding the emotional life of your school age child.* Reading, MA: Addison-Wesley.

Hamburg, D. A. (1997, June). Toward a strategy for healthy adolescent development. *American Journal of Psychiatry, 154* (Festschrift Suppl.), 7–12.

Hawkins, J. D., Catalano, R. F., Morrison, D. M., O'Donnell, J., Abbott, R. D., & Day, L. E. (1992). The Seattle Social Development Project. In J. McCord & R. Tremlay (Eds.), *The prevention of antisocial behavior in children* (pp. 139–161). New York: Guilford.

Heath, D. H. (1991). *Fulfilling lives: Paths to maturity and success.* San Francisco: Jossey-Bass.

Lantieri, L., & Patti, J. (1996). *Waging peace in our schools.* Boston: Beacon Press.

Kahne, J., & Bailey, K. (1997, November). *The role of social capital youth development: The case of "I Have A Dream."* Paper presented at the University Council for Educational Administration Conference, Orlando, FL.

Klein, J. D. (1997). The national longitudinal study on adolescent health. *Journal of the American Medical Association, 278*(10), 854–859.

Mott Foundation. (1994). *A fine line: Losing American youth to violence—A special report.* Flint, MI.

Nash, P. (1968). *Models of man: Explorations in the western educational tradition.* Malabar, FL: Krieger.

Olden, C. (1953). On adult empathy with children. *Psychoanalytic Study of the Child, 8,* 111–126.

Padel, R. (1992). *In and out of the mind: Greek images of the tragic self.* Princeton, NJ: Princeton University Press.

Pittman, K. (1986). *Preventing adolescent pregnancy: What school can do.* Washington, DC: Children's Defense Fund.

Salovey, P., & Mayer, J. D. (1990). Emotional intelligence. *Imagination, Cognition and Personality, 9,* 185–211.

Salovey, P., & Sluyter, D. (Eds.) (1997). *Emotional development and emotional intelligence: Implications for educators.* New York: Basic Books.

Snell, B. (1982). *The discovery of the mind in Greek philosophy and literature.* New York: Dover.

Sternberg, R. J. (1997). The concept of intelligence and its role in lifelong learning and success. *American Psychologist, 52*(10), 1030–1037.

Valliant, G. E. (1977). *Adaptation to life.* Boston: Little, Brown.

Valliant, G. E. (1993). *The wisdom of the ego.* Cambridge, MA: Harvard University Press.

Weissberg, R. P., Barton, H. A., & Shriver, T. P. (1997). The social-competence promotion program for young adolescents. In G. W. Albee & T. P. Gullotta (Eds.), *Primary prevention exemplars: The Lela Rowland awards.* Newbury Park, CA: Sage.

Weissberg, R. P., & Greenberg, M. T. (1997). School and community competence-enhancement and prevention programs. In W. Damon (Series Ed.) & I. E. Sigel & K. A. Renninger (Vol. Eds.), *Handbook of child psychology: Vol 4. Child psychology in practice* (5th ed., pp. 877–954). New York: Wiley.

Weissberg, R. P., Gullotta, T. P., Hampton, R. L., Ryan, B. A., & Adams, G. R. (Eds). (1997). *Healthy children 2010: Enhancing children's wellness.* Thousand Oaks, CA: Sage.

Weist, M. D. (1997). Expanded school mental health services: A national movement in progress. In T. H. Ollendick & R. J. Prinz (Eds.), *Advances in clinical child psychology* (Vol. 19). New York: Plenum Press.

Wentzel, K. R. (1997). Student motivation in middle school: The role of perceived pedagogical caring. *Journal of Educational Psychology, 89*(3), 411–419.

Yorke, C., Kennedy, H., & Wiseberg, S. (1991). Clinical and theatrical aspects of two developmental lines. In S. I. Greenspan & G. H. Pollock (Eds.), *The course of life: Vol. 3. Middle and late childhood* (pp. 135–160). Madison, CT: International University Press.

2

The Meaning of
Development
in Middle School

William Solodow

In this book about what we can "do" in our classrooms, there is a need to start with how children "do" development. Middle school children are passing into and through adolescence. While there is much that we can teach them about growing up, the "fuel" of development—the force that impels children forward—is within them, not within our programs. There is a biological clock inside us that begins the process on which education has little influence. Teachers in middle school therefore have to contend with some biological givens.

Biology is far from the whole picture, however. We are preprogrammed in our minds to act as though our environment is sending us messages. We assign meanings to all events whether outside or inside us. Our children give meanings to the biological events unfolding within them during middle school. It is this assignment of meaning that we want to channel with our social and emotional learning (SEL) programs. This is where we as educators can have our greatest influence. In shaping what meanings we want to give, however, we have to know development and its biological roots. It is the premise of this chapter that we influence most when our teachings about these deepest emotional matters are in accord with the biological givens of development.

Adolescence is a unique developmental space. Nowhere else in the entire course of individual history is there a more dramatic meeting between biology and mind. New hormones course through the veins of the middle school child. These hormones create emotions never before experienced. Sexual body parts are growing that make for new behavioral possibilities. Neurons in the central nervous system make new connections in the brain that change forever the quality of thought. Old ways of thinking, feeling, and behaving are discarded during middle school and are replaced by radically different modes of operating. The biological changes that produce all this tumult in the body are called "puberty." These biological changes are not the same as the thoughts, feelings, and actions that are precipitated in the mind by them (Blos, 1962). Such mental or psychological events, what we call "adolescence," are not preprogrammed by our genes. These psychological happenings are social and emotional transformations that constitute a story that individuals tell themselves about who they are. Societies and culture and we as educators profoundly contribute to this story.

The difference between puberty and adolescence is important. While there is not much we can change about puberty, there is much we can influence regarding the meanings that get attached to these biological developments. What it means to be "male" or "female" is only one of many biologically prompted stories that children so actively form during these years. We have to be ever focused as educators on the ways we exert powerful influences.

Examining the kind of model we present is an essential first step toward enhancing social and emotional skills. Virtually all our behaviors in the classroom constitute emotional lessons that we teach our students about the meaning of development. We can only avoid having an unintended or unhelpful impact by examining how we the adults behave in reaction to how our children behave during development.

Knowing development is also crucial in that there are pressures that arise during adolescence that seem to reduce our importance as adults. One of the biggest issues in our interactions with middle school children is their growing preoccupation with the influence of the adult world on them and their powerful needs to reject such influences. Powerful emotions of anxiety, anger, and fear can arise both in adults and in our children. These battles over influence can range from stormy to subtle.

Consider Maura and her dad. Maura is a 10-year-old girl who one day, completely out of the blue, announces to her father, a high school teacher, that she wishes he had a different job. Somewhat startled, the father asks why, only to learn that his job must be very boring since he talks all day and doesn't "do" things. Even last year, his daughter would have never said anything like this. He feels evaluated by this remark and by hundreds of others just like it that were never made before. Expressions such as *adolescence* and *stages of development* quickly lose their meaning when applied to the daughter now making these judgments. She is having new thoughts about a no longer idealized parent whose choices she can criticize. He is having feelings never before experienced about needing to defend and explain himself. Their behaviors toward each other change—Maura can be quite rejecting of his efforts to "help," and he in turn can be more distant, at times hurt by this new child.

This short interaction between Maura and her father represents one of the ways middle school children "do" development. It is a story about needing to separate from formerly intense and highly dependent relationships with adults. It is a story about distancing herself from adult influence for the first time. Maura is reinventing her relationships with older people, especially parents and teachers who have been on a pedestal for many years and who now have to be dethroned. Her behavior is increasingly designed expressly to show she is different, that she is not like her parents or teachers. Maura's allegiances shift to the peer group, whose influence is now almost everything. More and more of Maura's emotional life will be invested in people outside the family. The most intense feelings will not be found at home. Peers increasingly occupy center stage.

This process is not at all pleasant to teachers and parents. In this "doing" of development, interactions can be quite charged and explosive, leaving us experiencing a gamut of emotions from slight irritation to fury in spite of our best intentions and efforts to understand growth. How we and our children mutually break away from the older, more comfortable ties of early elementary school and move into these new territories is the stuff of development. It is what we "do" regardless of the theories we tie it to. Looking at the purpose of these interactions from the perspective of our children and seeing these behaviors in terms of the story our children are writing about themselves and their world will hopefully make us better able to influence and shape this story in ways more conducive to our educational goals.

THE BEGINNING OF MIDDLE SCHOOL

In a recent school meeting, several fifth grade teachers were bemoaning a growing lack of status in the eyes of their students. The dialogue was about respect, manners, and the kinds of kids we are raising today. While these are indeed important issues, the hardest one is noticeably absent. These children are in fact preoccupied with who is influencing them. The arguing and questioning of authority that border on rudeness in fact serve a purpose as does the increasing rejection of adults in favor of peer relationships. We can maintain our influence best when we have an explanation of what middle school children are accomplishing with these behaviors.

For parents of middle school children there is keen sense of loss with regard to their child's emotional revolution—Maura's dad, for example, is now more questioned and criticized than idealized and complied with. What has happened to that younger child who saw adults more as heroes than as villains? To a great degree, biology has happened. The arrival of puberty has greatly disrupted the applecart. All the adaptations of earlier grades are thrown to the winds by new, powerful forces that begin to sweep through the bodies and minds of our students. Bodily changes involving hormones and physical maturation redefine how these children see themselves as well as how they see adults and peers, and their minds have to play catch up with this development. To capture this experience, we will look at Maura and Raffi, each a composite of several early middle school students.

Maura

Maura is a happy, bright 10-year-old girl entering the fifth grade of a middle school. She has shifted from having one teacher to having several. She adored her fourth grade teacher and has written several letters to her over the summer. Each letter, however, brings disappointment—the letters are not the same as having her for a teacher. Maura's new teachers do not stack up. They are evaluated unlike any previous teachers for their various quirks and idiosyncrasies. Maura's parents on orientation night note how wonderful some of them are only to find their criteria are now different than those of their daughter. Maura can at times question quite mercilessly the reasons for certain adult decisions and admonitions. Her peer network has arrived at its own assessment of these teachers, which is much discussed among themselves but not entirely shared with parents. The peer relationships are the center of these students' lives. The intensity of Maura's passions lies in these friendships.

Maura has five close friends, two of whom have begun to show beginning signs of puberty. Maura becomes quite silly and giggly when making references to her friends' breast development and the wearing of bras. There is much talk about boys, some of which has a negative tinge—this one is "hated"; various "terrible" behaviors are described. Several girls in the group are teased, however, about which boys "like" them; they deny these connections but seem pleased about the possibility. They go over each interaction with boys in some detail, searching it for meaning. Their relationships with each other remain far more important, however. Maura stands firm about not liking boys but has formed a detective club to gather "clues and signs" regarding the boys' behavior toward the girls in her circle. She is quite indignant about an upcoming "sock hop" with a 1950s theme. She notes that some of the boys think this is about "dating," which is spoiling the dance—"Dances are supposed to be 'fun,' a time to be with my friends, not about 'dating.'" She is insisting she will not go, mildly protesting this new development. Ultimately she goes anyway.

For the past year now, Maura's interactions regarding homework have been dramatically different. Formerly, when she did not understand something, she would stubbornly insist on being shown how to do it, step by step. Not having been "told how to do it" was the worst accusation, summarizing all that was "unfair" about school. She also just wanted the answer—correct answers far outweighing any knowledge of the process about how to do things. Maura now, however, is much less impressed by the mere answer. She is very proud of knowing how to do long division, for example, and sees it as a skill that exists quite independently of how accurately a particular problem is solved. She vociferously denies the importance of having made any careless mistakes because she "knows" how to divide and becomes quite indignant if her parents have the temerity to suggest otherwise.

Most children start the middle school years near the end of what is called the Concrete Operational stage of intellectual development, which covers the age range from 7 to 11 years (Piaget, 1950). For many years now, these children have no longer been "fooled" by the surface appearance of things. Maura observes reality in much closer, more accurate ways. In math, for example, children in this stage know that 10 divided by 2 is the same as 100 divided by 20; they can transform these seemingly different numbers and perform mental calculations on them that will reveal what they "really" are, that is, both expressions equal 5. Maura incorporates such intellectual attainments into her social perceptions and judgments. Not being fooled by the surface appearance of things is not only an intellectual attainment. She sees deeper realities that underlie interpersonal relationships, understanding, for instance, that an angry word or gesture from a friend can be due to a variety of causes, some of which may have nothing to do with her.

The "deeper realities" of boys, in spite of Maura's outward disdain, are similarly becoming evident to her. She desperately loves her friends and would stop them and herself from changing if she could. She has to alter these attachments and make room for new challenges associated with boys. She has begun trying to anticipate the realities of a changing body both within herself and within her peers and is making efforts to integrate her mind's reaction to these processes. She channels her feelings and thoughts about sexuality into the formation of a club, joining with several peers to "detect" clues about the boys.

Maura's increased reality focus and attention to the details of her environment have increasingly created conflict between what her parents have told her and what she herself has observed. With her peers, she has been checking out the real world. Both teachers and parents can no longer simply assert that book reports can be done only one way; they can insist on a particular format, but children at this age make it clear they know there are other ways to do it. Adults can quickly be blamed when any instructions go awry. Maura is indeed giving up some of her emotional dependencies on her parents and teachers and not allowing them to overly color what she sees. She can be critical of her teachers, seeing them as real figures rather than idolized versions of her parents.

Maura is furthermore finding confirmation about what is right and wrong through her peers outside the family. This is an age where children temporarily comply to appease adults while really believing and acting otherwise in nonadult settings. This is not at all a time of wildness, however. At the beginning of middle school, children are particularly focused on rules, if not preoccupied with them. Containment of feelings and structured ways of expressing them have become important to the children themselves. There no longer always has to be an adult present to insist on and enforce fairness. Children have internalized what was formerly a more parent- and teacher-dominated regulation of behavior and made it into their own system of conscience.

These systems of control are based on powerful affects. Where formerly shame and embarrassment in front of parents and teachers almost exclusively motivated control, now fear of shame in front of the peer group and each child's own guilt feelings steer these children toward containment of unacceptable feelings, thoughts, and behaviors. This represents an enormous leap toward independence and autonomy. Even though peer pressure is a powerful external motivator, peers are, after all, much more like oneself, and we also have chosen them on our own. The beginning of middle school is a time of more self-imposed standards, rules we have actively chosen to become involved with. Parents and teachers are increasingly less central. In siding more with peer influences, Maura is separating from early dependencies and becoming more self-reliant.

Some of these processes discussed with regard to Maura do not always begin so smoothly. A look at another child, also a composite sketch, will show a more problematic entry into middle school.

Raffi

Raffi is a boisterous, tall, and skinny 10-year-old, not well liked by either teachers or peers. He does not fit in. On the surface, he is noticeably not as heavily into athletics as are many boys in his class. He has an intense interest in role-playing games almost to the exclusion of all else. His "best friend" has stopped calling, however, due to increasing arguments; Raffi's demands for high levels of involvement, particularly around these games, have become too much for the friend and the friend's parents. Raffi feels angry and excluded by these rejections, not understanding them at all. He is also left out due to not having sports heroes whose exploits are recounted daily as a matter of course. For some, but not for Raffi, this kind of idolization of heroes is like the air one breathes.

In class, Raffi can at times be the bane of his teacher's existence. He is more preoccupied with the teacher's mistakes and instances of injustice (more often imagined) than he is with his peers. In a negative way, he uses his intense involvement with the teacher as a means of relating—he clowns, makes jokes, and calls out during class to get the attention of the other boys who like this challenging of authority. These behaviors leave him constantly entangled with the teacher, however, and not involved with peers. In the clear hierarchies of acceptance in the fifth grade, Raffi does not fit in. He has no real buddies but does have a small circle of two or three boys with whom he occasionally does things.

Raffi is preoccupied with sexual matters; every word or gesture can contain a possible sexual innuendo. He is quick to laugh and smirk in loud and disruptive ways, particularly at teacher comments that Raffi imbues with a sexual slant. He is often unable to let go of his reactions and feels particularly victimized when reprimanded at these moments. His readiness to attribute sexual meaning to the nonsexual stands in stark contrast to actual experiences. Neither Raffi nor any of his immediate group are showing signs of puberty. Only one boy in the class has had a date, a fact that is not discussed at all by Raffi. Few of the boys really talk about dating.

Raffi completes all his schoolwork very quickly and carelessly. He most often has the correct answer, but the product is quite sloppy and it is impossible to know how he arrived at this solution. His favorite expression is "that was easy." He can become noticeably agitated on the rare occasions when the solution does not come to him right away; he is quick to blame any failures or inadequacies on the teacher.

Raffi has not quite given up an emotional investment in parentlike forms of control. He is consequently not fully integrated into the peer group and seems locked in a struggle with his teacher and presumably his parents. He looks backward to his older ties rather than forward to new ones within the peer group. On the surface, Raffi rejects adult authority, but his behaviors in truth keep him tied up with these parental figures, albeit in negative ways. It is an enmeshment that powerfully causes his thought to still be "fooled" by the surface appearance of things. Outwardly he is separating. His constant railing at control by parents or teachers is "independence" from these adults. His attacking and criticizing "prove" he no longer needs them. He lacks, however, the positive piece of this emotional transformation. What would truly separate Raffi is connections to peers outside the family.

In truth, Raffi's preoccupation with mistakes and instances of injustice expresses his wish that everything the teacher does be focused on him. His emotions and storms surrounding "separation" are more extreme than those of his classmates. His actions court the negative responses of authorities in ways that smash the space that should be reserved for peer interactions. His oppositional, "class clown" persona has a deeper reality of being an inappropriate dependency on adults. His peers see this. They have learned how to "render unto Caesar what is Caesar's" so that they can be left alone with friends for ever growing amounts of time with less and less supervision. Raffi's behavior will not lead to independence from adult control and more room for peer interactions.

Raffi is at an earlier stage of moral development where parental and teacher authority is almost all there is. His sense of right and wrong is still highly motivated by whether or not he will be caught by adults. It is a very shame-based morality, externally focused, and not entirely located within him. In not giving up the importance of parents and parentlike figures, Raffi is not yet emphasizing self-control with regard to his actions; he is in fact angrily demanding that adult controls be imposed by his oppositional stance. His preoccupation with role-playing games reflects an effort to establish shared rules with peers, but Raffi clings to these games much like he clings to his parents, alienating peers who operate within ever expanding horizons. Others move on. Raffi remains "stuck."

Raffi demonstrates an important point about separation and the emotional revolution associated with it. While for most children, the thrust is forward, away from parents and into the peer group, all children feel a backward pull. They also all use the very behaviors employed by Raffi to periodically reestablish ties to parents. They do it in a much more transitory fashion than Raffi does. Children can readily push their independence too far when they feel too threatened by their separateness. All children do experience this threat from time to time. These moments are a test to see if parents and teachers are still there and capable of providing that kind of all-pervasive care of the earlier years. For most children such needs are temporary. They are reassured by being "grounded" and even wear these episodes like badges of courage within the peer community. Most are soon able to resume their strivings for autonomy, having been "emotionally refueled" by a firm parental hand.

The tasks of the middle school child are not only with regard to their feelings about adults and peers. These children are also self-preoccupied in powerful ways and focus many emotions on themselves. Somewhere during the middle school years, the biological engine that has pushed forward the emotional transformation of separation starts to take a different role, producing an intense focus on the body and how acceptable one looks based on body changes associated with puberty. Whereas separation involves feelings toward others, the emergence of bodily concerns involves feelings about oneself. Self-images especially need to be created by these young adolescents who no longer exclusively define themselves in relation to what parents and teachers think.

THE MIDDLE YEARS OF MIDDLE SCHOOL

The impact of biology on the children just described is immense. Biology directly forces itself into our awareness by creating new somatic events that our minds then have to deal with.

Puberty results primarily in physical development of the genital sex organs. There are also changes in height, weight, and musculature as well as a number of secondary sexual characteristics that appear for the first time: for boys facial hair and voice change; for girls breast development and menstruation. Perhaps as adults, having grown used to all these physical and somatic aspects of ourselves, we tend to forget what a big impact they had when they first appeared. Maura has changed dramatically due to puberty.

Maura

At 12 years old, now in the seventh grade, Maura has fully entered puberty as have most of her friends. Getting ready for school is now an hour and a half process. Emotional storms regularly arise over any perceived inadequacy of outfit or appearance. She alternates between angrily blaming her parents for little things that go wrong—an unwashed blouse, a forgotten errand—and at times raging at their "interference" in her life when they try to help her plan or anticipate events—a simple parental question such as, "Don't you need some clothes for tomorrow?" will cause explosions. When not in school, she spends enormous amounts of time in her room, listening to "alternative" rock music.

Long hours are spent on the phone. When boys are discussed, there is now the added element of analyzing the impressions one has created with various efforts and behaviors directed toward specific boys. Interactions are everything. The pursuit is very active across many arenas carved out of the school day. The boys are much more the pursued than the pursuers. Even though sounds of animated discussion among Maura and her friends can be heard through closed doors, profound silences descend when adults enter. Her teachers are clearly divided into the "okay" ones and the ones she "hates"—there are no shades of gray. Parents and teachers can be harshly judged for various shortcomings. Although many of Maura's observations are quite true, the vehemence of her condemnation seems to far outweigh the "crimes" these adults have committed.

From the beginning, boys and girls have a very different experience. Maura and her friends are likely to mature much earlier than Raffi and his. On the average, girls are two years ahead of boys. There is a wide window of time during which these changes can occur—children can experience the beginning of these changes as early as age 8 or 9, but they can also begin puberty at 12 or 13 and still be considered within a normal or expectable range. Each individual is different. A further complication is that the various systems within the body do not mature at the same rate. There are also great variations in how long these changes take and at what age the physical maturation is fully accomplished. To adults this suggests that we not worry so much about what is normal because there is such a wide range of possibilities. For each child in the midst of the peer group at school, however, matters are quite otherwise.

Maura cannot help but notice her friends who are wearing brassieres. The individual differences in the rate of maturation create a charged, "everybody watching everybody else" tableau. The children within each grade, placed together largely by chronological age, are not at all the same in terms of their physical development. They interact, compete, and cooperate on a playing field that is far from level. This is the atmosphere in middle school, precipitated by these biological changes, that generates two related characteristics of adolescent children—their intense self-preoccupation and their enormous struggle to maintain self-esteem.

Maura is painstakingly piecing together an image of herself each morning with her preoccupation with clothing and appearance. She is literally looking in the mirror to both create and find how she wants to see herself. The image she seeks may change from day to day. She is experimenting and trying on identities all in the name of finding a reality about herself that suits her. Nothing is settled at this point.

The contradictory states of needing her parents and angrily pushing them away reflect the enormous vulnerability of Maura's self-esteem, which is ready to be punctured at any moment. When these images she tentatively forms begin to shatter, as all of them at this age do, she will reach out desperately to parents and teachers for something safe to hold onto—someone who does have a stable image of her that she can count on. This kind of contact can have either a needy, dependent quality or be a moment of rage that conceals the underlying need. Parents and teachers can be especially misled by these bursts of anger in response to their best intentions. Seeing that adults in fact can survive her moments of fury is crucially important to Maura.

Puberty has both a disorganizing side, creating an enormously unstable sense of self-esteem, and a positive, forward-looking side, generating forces that impel Maura to try new behaviors and ways of being that will ultimately make her an adult who will be fully accepted into the larger community. Her preoccupation with alternative rock music is not an idle pursuit. It is a music she is making her own. Initially it is in fact much better that adults "cannot stand it." This process of first separating herself from parents and teachers and making something truly her own will repeat itself over and over during the years of middle school.

Not everyone takes on the struggles as fully as Maura seems to. Puberty for some can be more a retreat than a time of meeting new challenges and trying out new ways of being. Raffi is a case in point.

Raffi

Raffi at 12 years old has only recently begun to show signs of puberty. He can be extremely angry and hostile to his parents, at times blowing up for no apparent reason. He is particularly harsh with his mother, who at times refuses to talk to him for days at a time due to his behavior. Increasingly, stories about sex make him anxious, silly, and out of control in the telling. Raffi has at times become alarmed at any signs of interest shown in him. Although many of his peers can be tongue-tied, not knowing what to say or do when girls talk to them, Raffi can become verbally abusive, if not aggressive, calling them names and on one occasion slapping a girl in the face when she pushed him out of the way.

Raffi is no longer engaged by role-playing games. He has taken up chess with a vengeance. He feels increasingly lonely and isolated from his peers; very few of them play chess. Raffi is somewhat less angry and oppositional with those in authority. He especially likes his science teacher, for example. He seems to be absorbing his science teacher's views of life and current events as though these thoughts provide a welcome structure for an otherwise confusing world. He is better able to contain behaviors that used to alienate adults. He has stopped being the class clown and is more preoccupied with internal matters.

With puberty have come a variety of somatic concerns and worries for which he is often taken to the doctor. His parents, like Raffi, remain anxious that something might be wrong medically. Raffi is not prompted by physical changes inside him or by noticeable maturation on the outside to take on new roles. He angrily rejects any such images. Though he is like most boys in not actively pursuing girls, he does not belong to any peer group where there are arenas within which to develop ways of seeing himself that are more in accord with the biologicial changes associated with being male. He does try out and experiment with new roles, new self-views that he can try to make his own. The feelings and urges associated with puberty that normally impel social interaction for his peers stay bottled up inside Raffi, emerging in explosive ways toward his parents, his only available outlet. The inner turmoil will be defined as a "medical problem" rather than as a developmental challenge of establishing an image of himself he can feel good about.

As students near the end of middle school, adolescence is far from over. We have described several arenas of social and emotional functioning that these students have entered. What they "do" is establish their separateness from adults, form their connections to peers, and create images of themselves they can feel good about. The "doing" in all these areas is still ongoing and by no means fully resolved. Raffi has advanced much less in any of these arenas than Maura has. For both, however, the reaction by parents and teachers to their efforts has been the key. The kind of welcome that their efforts receive is central. Near the end of middle school and even much earlier, Maura and Raffi have often reached a point where what they incorporate into their story about themselves is what has been validated by the larger community. Parents, teachers, peers, and schools are the most immediate representatives of society and culture with which Maura and Raffi have powerfully interacted.

THE END OF MIDDLE SCHOOL

Although one central issue has been autonomy, Raffi and Maura "do" nothing in isolation. Development from the beginning is always about interaction. Parents and teachers initially act as a buffer between the child and pressures from society. It is this protective, sheltering role that children increasingly give up as they move into middle school. They separate themselves from these early emotional dependencies. The peer group is the first of many larger forces in society that they come to terms with. There is a need to connect here with the same intensity of emotions that was formerly associated with parents. With the maturation of full sexual capacities and the growth in brain cells that now allows full abstract reasoning, the last physical characteristics that separate children from adults have disappeared. They are physically like adults but still far away in terms of their social and emotional development. They now need to deal with their connections again but this time in larger ways than they have done within their immediate peer group. They have to find an acceptance within the greater community.

We do not have many institutions or rituals by which we welcome adolescents into our adult world. Some of our "welcomes" such as TV and movies can in fact have a devastating impact in terms of the symbols we convey regarding what it takes to gain acceptance. In many cases we largely ignore certain groups and their needs and strivings. It is these issues that make SEL programs so important. In our schools we can add some necessary channels and paths to teach children to better accept all that is in themselves, a process that invariably leads to more respect for all that is in others around them.

Maura

Maura is now 14 years old and in the ninth grade. She has gone on her first date but does not have a boyfriend. A distinction between being "just friends" and "dating" has increasing importance to her. The former category is somewhat of a safety valve. When any interaction with a boy becomes too charged, she and he can quickly become "just friends" to retreat from the more serious implications of "dating." This actually works reasonably well. She is much more comfortable with herself. There are many moments where she starts to explode with her parents and then visibly contains it, making herself calm again and seeing the point of what she is being asked to do. She is working hard in school. Difficulties with the work itself have largely replaced difficulties with the teacher—moments of stress still lead to angry denunciations of particular instructors but these lapses serve to make the point that learning has become more objectified and much, much less a function of the personalities involved.

The mind itself is also growing. While bodily development and new images that result from it understandably preoccupy students and make them less available for academics, when properly engaged, intellectual functioning also starts to really take off. Around the time of puberty, abstract reasoning begins to emerge. Our students no longer need the object to be there in reality before they can experiment, perform actions, and reach conclusions; they can do all these things mentally. They develop hypotheses about people and the world that can then be evaluated for their usefulness. For the first time, the student sees that many interpretations of data are possible and that a particular course of events is but one of many possible alternatives. These cognitive capacities set the stage for relentless experimentation with roles and ways of behaving in order to find a place in the larger society, as Maura so actively demonstrates and Raffi does not.

One remaining story characterizes the emotional changes that have occurred. Maura has been into alternative rock music for many years. She and her peers avidly follow events in the lives of many of their favorite performers. Adults were by definition hopelessly outside the loop. Four years ago, Maura was startled to see her science teacher with a CD of one of her favorite groups. She could not believe it was the same singer and even had to hear the CD played after school to verify it. This remained so unbelievable to her that she told none of her friends.

This year Maura has an English teacher whom she knows likes her kind of music. She is no longer startled by this. She in fact quite proudly takes every opportunity to let her friends in on the teacher's shared knowledge about these rock bands. The intensity of peer culture as apart from the adult world has started to shift. Over the years of middle school, autonomy has been firmly established. Now at the end of this period, Maura is letting adults back in, but this time from a position of strength—Maura knows what she likes in the world of music and now welcomes having this validated by adults. She in fact increasingly needs this acceptance and validation of who she has become.

Raffi

Raffi at 14 years old is now in the ninth grade. He has become more depressed and withdrawn rather than being caught up in any excitement about pursuing girls. He has one close female friend toward whom he has an "utterly secret" sexual interest. He has preoccupying fears that revealing anything about these urges either to her or anyone else will destroy the friendship. To some degree he prefers to stay within the safety of being friends, not seeing himself as a player in the sexual arena. Fantasies about winning over girls by being a famous chess player have been replaced by sadness about not feeling at all liked by others. Any story he tells himself or others about his future has a very negative cast.

Raffi is much quieter in school. He is increasingly aware that his sense of isolation comes from his negative position in the peer group. He no longer blames the adults for this. He is often angry with other students about being excluded from parties and discussions but tends to keep his upset to himself. On one occasion he found a cause to pursue at school. He organized a petition drive regarding a particular teacher's harsh stand about being late for class. The school administration did force the teacher to make some changes. Certain teachers were outraged, but others supported Raffi's move. Although this won Raffi some momentary respect in the peer community, it did not really lead to any new personal connections.

The stories Maura and Raffi are telling themselves are vastly different because of the different ways Maura and Raffi have handled the steps leading up to this moment. The first step was in managing anxiety that their choices had been unduly influenced or controlled by the "authorities." They had to be and feel separate enough to do things for themselves. The second step was to have had enough room to experiment and try out different choices so that they knew the range of possibilities from which they were choosing. Maura received peer support in exploring this developmental space, but Raffi failed to get it. The last and final piece was to have this experimentation and the choices that resulted from it affirmed and accepted by those in power. Raffi had clear difficulties with all these steps.

Toward the end of middle school, a sense of acceptance into the larger culture and encouragement to proceed with various chosen roles become more central. All of these processes of acceptance by the powers that be can go awry. Failures here can result in what Erikson (1956) has called "negative identity"—a definition of self that exists largely in defiance of prevailing norms and values and where there has been no place in the larger culture for one's strivings. This seems to be the most relevant dimension by which to understand the experience of many minorities in our society. It is also a way of conceptualizing the loss of voice in females that Gilligan (1982) has described. In the case of Raffi, it is more a matter of undeveloped emotional transitions that have not allowed him to reach out and make connections. One of the challenges to be addressed in our schools is to create a climate where cultural diversity, gender awareness, and sensitivity to individual differences maximize the chance for children to "do" development in optimal ways. We need to include rather than exclude all members of our community. Such acceptance is crucial to the formation of positive stories about who our students say they are and what the community is within which they live.

While Maura is humming with a biological clock ticking away inside her, Raffi is sputtering and lurching in fits and starts toward adulthood. While it is biology that is changing their internal landscape, it is the different stories and meanings they are attaching to these events that will determine the man and the woman who will emerge. Theirs are but two stories about separation from early bonds of dependency. So far we have described only highly personalized meanings—for Maura, one of hope and possibility; for Raffi, one of loneliness, suspicion, and failure of connection to the larger group.

Both Maura and Raffi have been highly aware of and attuned to the meanings their parents, their teachers, and their society have assigned to these occurring developmental changes. Some of these meanings should be struggled with. Raffi, for example, needs a positive thrust to internal changes, not the almost exclusively medical one being assigned to him by parents and doctors. His suspicion and mistrust of peers, a story about not being wanted, also needs modification. Maura, with her more positive personal story, has nonetheless many social meanings attached to growing up as a female. Other children face social meanings about race, ethnic background, and economic class. Raffi could well have all these other factors added to his more personal issues. Where Maura, Raffi, and these others choose to battle and where they submit is a matter of some concern.

CONCLUSION

This chapter is about the meanings middle school children choose to struggle with, some of which we might very much want them to own. We cannot help but provide models and be active agents in shaping such choices. To think we are not so important due to these students' need to separate from adults is to miss the main point of development during the middle school years. We can be more or less aware of how we are shaping Maura and Raffi by the way we run our classrooms. We need to be especially aware of our role as validators of their emerging stories. We can validate both positive and negative meanings. We need to more actively define and choose the meanings that will best serve our social and emotional goals, both at school and in the larger community. We are in fact helping our children write a story that is indelibly printed in their minds by the kinds of classrooms we run and the kinds of interactions we have with these former children now in middle school. This is a story they will tell themselves for the rest of their lives, and it will determine how active or passive an agent they can be in shaping their surroundings in ways that are chosen rather than imposed in negative ways.

REFERENCES

Blos, P. (1962). *On adolescence.* New York: Free Press.

Erikson, E. H. (1956). The problem of ego identity. *Journal of the American Psychoanalytic Association, 4,* 56–121.

Gilligan, C. (1982). *In a different voice.* Cambridge, MA: Harvard University Press.

Piaget, J. (1950). *The psychology of intelligence.* New York: Harcourt, Brace.

Programs, Strategies, and Perspectives

Part II of this volume presents a representative range of SEL programs and perspectives that educators can consider using in their work with the middle school child. Some of the chapters present programs that are quite structured; for example, Chapter 3 presents a K through 12 curriculum-based program that is a "stand-alone" course. Other chapters present perspectives on the social and emotional life of students and educators that we can integrate into all that we do in school without creating a new "space" in the curriculum. In this line, Chapter 7 describes a point of view about social and emotional life and child development that can inform all of our work with students. Other chapters offer programs and/or perspectives that are between these two end points: for example, both Chapter 5 and Chapter 6 present programmatic effects that have a clear philosophy and set of methods that educators can integrate into whatever they are doing in school. Still other chapters focus on the essential importance of conflict resolution (Chapter 8) or self-esteem (Chapter 4) and how we can further learning in these fundamental social and emotional realms. Chapter 10 presents ideas about how we can promote empathy and prosocial behaviors in the classroom in the context of Comer's groundbreaking School Development Project. Finally, not all SEL programs are directed at our students; some focus on how educators can also develop in these areas. Chapter 9 describes one important perspective (with related methods) that can further social and emotional learning for educators.

3

Why SEL Is the Better Way

The New Haven Social Development Program

Timothy P. Shriver, Mary Schwab-Stone, and Karol DeFalco

Recently a middle school principal was venting the frustration he felt about his school not being able to raise its standardized test scores. "We've moved reading class to first period because students seem to be more alert at that time of day. We've lengthened the reading time from one period to two periods a day. We've purchased a new math series and provided teachers with staff development opportunities to learn best how to use the new text. We've reassigned teachers so that those who are strongest in reading, teach reading, and those who are strongest in math, teach math. Still, our scores haven't gone up. There's got to be a better way."

School district personnel, upset by lack of improvement on test scores, usually resort to strategies such as increasing the amount of time spent in class, choosing new texts, reassigning teachers, and providing staff development. Each of these responses can provide benefits, but they alone are not enough. These strategies don't meet the needs of students like Maura and Raffi. A new math text doesn't help 10-year-old Maura manage stress, yet her inability to handle stress may be having an impact on her academic abilities. Raffi's poor attention span, caused by feelings of anxiety, affects his schoolwork but is not helped by increasing the amount of time spent in reading class. Maura and Raffi can learn, but for them to learn optimally, the school must find a different strategy—a better way.

THE CRISIS

An unprecedented adolescent health crisis is facing our nation (National Commission on the Role of the School and the Community in Improving Adolescent Health, 1990). Research suggests that 25% to 50% of U.S. youth engage in high-risk behaviors such as drug use, early and high-risk sexual activity, and violence. Behaviors such as these frequently interfere with the capacity to learn in school, as well as with the ability to become constructive family members and citizens (Dryfoos, 1990). It is not difficult to brainstorm a list of the causes of this social-emotional-health crisis.

Single parents who work outside the home, two-career couples, lack of contact with extended family, mobility, and poverty would make it to the list. These causes have made it more difficult for family members and other adults to act as positive role models for children, to monitor children's behavior, and to create nurturing environments. The combination of these changing family/societal conditions and the prevalence of high-risk behaviors among our youth have prompted calls for effective school-based prevention programs to address children's social and health needs (DeFriese, Crossland, Pearson, & Sullivan, 1990; National Mental Health Association, 1986).

However, everyone has a different opinion about how this prevention programming should be implemented. To prevent at risk behaviors, some educators and other child advocates want to strengthen students' basic skills. Some want more information on drugs, sex, and violence in the curriculum. Some want to promote citizenship and character. Some want more parental involvement. Some want an emphasis on morals and values. Some call for more diversity. Whatever the opinion, there is growing consensus about the central role of schools in developing the whole child—academically, socially, and emotionally—to make our next generation of adults knowledgeable, responsible, and caring.

If schools are to be responsive to the needs of the whole child, then the social and emotional needs of children will have to be a more integrated and central focus of classroom teachers and school communities. Of central importance is the understanding that social and emotional factors are central parts of learning—that stability, motivation, and even attention are essentially social and emotional components of the individual. Without a stable, motivated, and attentive learner, every teacher knows that instruction is futile. So learning itself is at risk if schools fail to understand the social and emotional development of children.

While knowledge acquisition is the core task of education, schools are central institutions in communities and play many roles in helping young people develop. In *Promoting Social and Emotional Learning* (Elias et al.,

1997), the concept of promoting the three values of knowledge, responsibility, and caring is suggested as a way of navigating the polarized environment of educational reform while being responsive to learners' needs.

> Knowledgeable. Responsible. Caring. Behind each word lies an educational challenge. For children to become *knowledgeable,* they must be ready and motivated to learn, and capable of integrating new information into their lives. For children to become *responsible,* they must be able to understand risks and opportunities, and be motivated to choose actions and behaviors that serve not only their own interests but those of others. For children to become *caring,* they must be able to see beyond themselves and appreciate the concerns of others; they must believe that to care is to be part of a community that is welcoming, nurturing, and concerned about them. (Elias et al., 1997, p. 1)

From this vantage point, social and emotional learning (SEL) becomes more than a fad or an add-on. Instead, the social and emotional development of the child becomes the foundation for learning, responsibility, and caring. Although the concepts of SEL have existed in one form or another in classrooms all across the country, they have been used sporadically and SEL has been done on a hit-or-miss basis. In some cases, teachers have enjoyed doing SEL lessons as supplemental activities or add-ons as a way of utilizing extra time in the day. SEL has not been part of the core curriculum of schools in the past, but with new knowledge and new methods, many educators are recognizing the need for a shift. The hit-or-miss and the supplemental are becoming more central in meeting the needs of students, and opportunities for a renewed school reform movement are upon us.

Although many educators attempt to provide instruction that enhances SEL, their attempts are frequently based on intuition. They are left to manage the social and emotional lives of their students independently, with little support. Moreover, programs that address these issues too often are relegated to second-class status. Systematic, well-designed programs are needed and these must be implemented by trained staff members in supportive educational contexts (Shriver & Weissberg, 1996).

THE NEW HAVEN SOCIAL DEVELOPMENT PROGRAM

One of the most ambitious social and emotional learning programs in the country was developed over a six-year period in New Haven, Connecticut. While the program continues to evolve, its fundamental features should capture the attention of parents, teachers, and administrators.

The New Haven Social Development Program was launched to incorporate all prevention efforts into one comprehensive strategy, with the goal of building a K–12 curriculum and activity sequence that would nurture the development of each child's learning, responsibility, and caring potential. While its focus is partially preventive, it is equally focused on enhancing the learning environment and the full development of all students. The program has been implemented through broad collaboration among teachers, parents, administrators, and community leaders who make it possible for children to receive the support, guidance, and nurturing that make positive development a reality. As such, the program has sought the support of all of the key caretakers in the life of the child and in the operation of the school.

The New Haven program began when several school system committees—separately responsible for substance abuse, dropout, delinquency, teen pregnancy, and violence—noted that the prevalence of these problems was too high, that existing prevention efforts were piecemeal, and that a long-term, comprehensive program was needed. As various recommendations were reviewed, it became increasingly clear to the system's leaders that prevention programs would be more effective if they were less focused on behavior problems after they had already started and more focused on helping children protect themselves from becoming involved in those behaviors in the first place.

In response, the superintendent of schools created a new department with a supervisor and staff. This department—similar to the math and reading departments—was given the responsibility of coordinating, implementing, and evaluating a K–12 program that would focus on the promotion of social and emotional development. Teachers, parents, administrators, and community leaders chose a program name that emphasized the positive development of children, rather than accentuating bad things that children should not do. Instead of using the title "Department of Prevention Services," they called the new entity the "Department of Social Development."

Over the next few years, the department established three components of the Social Development Program that continue to mark it as distinctive among SEL and prevention initiatives nationwide. First, over a five-year period, it developed a K–12 social and emotional learning curriculum. At each grade level, teachers chose the curriculum from a selection that met the Social Development Program's criteria in terms of skills, attitudes and values, and content that should be taught (Figure 3.1). The K–12 curricula emphasized self-monitoring, problem-solving, conflict-resolution, and communication skills; values such as respect for self and others, character, and personal responsibility; and content about substance abuse, health, sexuality, culture, and citizenship. Teachers received 10 hours of training before implementing the curriculum specific to their grades. Staff from the social development department conducted the training and continued to coach and support teachers throughout the year.

The K–12 curriculum was implemented gradually over a four-year period, thus enabling the school district to learn from the implementation process. For each grade level, surveys were conducted of teacher, parent, administrator, and student satisfaction, and, at the same time, representative committees were planning implementation of the next grade's curriculum. This combination of factors—the involvement of multiple constituencies in curriculum selection, provision of significant training opportunities, and the regular evaluation of satisfaction—made curriculum implementation more likely to be both supported and institutionalized by the key stakeholders within each school.

Second, members of the department created school and community activities that offered children educational, recreational, and health-promotion opportunities outside the classroom. These activities reinforced the mission of the department in that they offered students positive, prosocial opportunities that nurtured their social and emotional development and, at the same time, reduced the likelihood of involvement in troublesome behaviors. The activities included programs such as mentoring, an extended day academy with after-school clubs, an outdoor adventure class, peer-mediation programs, and student leadership groups.

Third, each school's mental health team—composed of school personnel such as administrators, psychologists, and social workers—became the group responsible for ensuring that the climate of the whole school would support positive SEL. The teams were trained in the key features of the curriculum and worked to ensure that each school's staff understood the implications and likely results of the curriculum. In some cases, the teams focused on providing teachers with adequate support in dealing with students who needed specialized help. In other cases, the teams focused less on individual needs and more on schoolwide issues, such as attendance, retention, and relationships between staff and students, and on activities such as assemblies, workshops for parents, and outreach to community groups. This three-pronged approach—curriculum, activities, school climate—created a comprehensive, coordinated program to address the needs of the whole child and avoided the error of creating reactive campaigns to fight one or another behavior problem.

The cornerstone of the Social Development Program is the highly structured classroom instruction of 25–50 hours at each grade level. Table 3.1 shows the K–12 curriculum sequence. For the purpose of this book, we only discuss the middle school curriculum.

New Haven Social Development Program
CURRICULUM SCOPE
Preschool through 12th Grade

Attitudes and Values

About Self
Self-respect
Feeling capable
Honesty
Sense of responsibility
Willingness to grow
Self-acceptance

About Others
Awareness of social norms and valuesÑpeer, family, community, and society
Accepting individual differences
Respecting human dignity
Having concern or compassion for others
Valuing cooperation with others
Motivation to solve interpersonal problems
Motivation to contribute

About Tasks
Willingness to work hard
Motivation to solve practical problems
Motivation to solve academic problems
Recognition of the importance of education
Respect for property

Skills

Self-Management
Self-monitoring
Self-control
Stress management
Persistence
Adaptability
Emotion-focused coping
Self-reward

Problem Solving and Decision Making
Problem recognition
Feelings awareness
Perspective taking
Realistic and adaptive goal setting
Awareness of adaptive response strategies
Alternative solution thinking
Consequential thinking
Decision making
Planning
Behavioral enactment

Communication
Understanding nonverbal communication
Sending messages
Receiving messages
Matching the communication to the situation

Content

Self/Health
Alcohol and other drug abuse
    education and prevention
AIDS and STD prevention
Growth and development and teen
    pregnancy prevention
Nutrition
Exercise
Personal hygiene
Personal safety and first aid
Understanding personal loss
Use of leisure time
Spiritual awareness

Relationships
Understanding relationships
Multicultural awareness
Making friends
Developing positive relationships
    with peers of different genders,
    races, and ethnic groups
Bonding to prosocial peers
Understanding family life
Relating to siblings
Relating to parents
Coping with loss
Preparation for marriage and
    parenting in later life
Conflict education and violence
    prevention
Finding a mentor

School/Community
Attendance education and truancy
    and dropout prevention
Accepting and managing
    responsibility
Adaptive group participation
Realistic academic goal setting
Developing effective work habits
Making transitions
Environmental responsibility
Community involvement
Career planning

FIGURE 3.1. New Haven Social Development Program: Curriculum scope, preschool through 12th grade. © 1991 Jackson and Weissberg.

49

TABLE 3.1. New Haven Public Schools Social Development Program
Curriculum Sequence

K–3rd Grade	*4–5th Grade*	*6th Grade*
36–55 lessons taught in each grade 2–3 times a week for the school year	25 lessons taught 2–3 times a week for the school year	45 lessons taught 3 times a week for 2 marking periods as a Life Skills Class

<table>
<tr><td valign="top">

Project Charlie

- Self-awareness
- Relationships
- Decision making
- Chemical use in society
- Violence prevention

Building Blocks: An AIDS Curriculum for Early Elementary Educators
(4–6 lessons taught with Project Charlie)

- Germs
- Communicable diseases
- Staying healthy
- Sickness and medicine
- Immune system
- Seeking health information
- Being different
- HIV/AIDS

</td><td valign="top">

Second Step

- Violence prevention
- Empathy training
- Impulse control
- Anger management

Human Sexuality and AIDS Education
(1–2 lessons)

- Video about puberty with question and answer sessions
- Teachers trained to feel comfortable answering questions about sex and AIDS
- Parent meetings held on "How to Talk to Your Children about Sex and AIDS"

Substance Use Prevention
(4 Project Charlie lessons)

- Chemical use in society

</td><td valign="top">

Social Problem Solving

- Self-control
- Stress management
- Problem solving
- Decision making
- Communication
- Violence prevention

Substance Use Prevention

- Peer pressure resistance

Human Growth and Development, AIDS Prevention, and Teen Pregnancy Prevention

- Puberty
- Reproduction
- Relationships without sex
- HIV/AIDS

(continued)

</td></tr>
</table>

Fifth Grade

In New Haven, middle schools begin with fifth grade. The fifth grade social development curriculum focuses on empathy training, impulse control, anger management, and puberty. As fifth graders, both Maura and Raffi would benefit from developing these skills and knowledge. Lessons from the impulse control unit would help decrease the number of times Maura strikes out at others. Rejections have made Raffi feel angry and excluded. His empathic capacity to "read" others is seriously impaired. He would benefit

TABLE 3.1. Continued

7th Grade	8th Grade	9th Grade
24 lessons taught 3 times a week for 1 marking period as a Life Skills Class	20 lessons integrated in Math throughout the year and 10 lessons taught in Physical Education	47–57 lessons taught 5 times a week for 2 marking periods as a Life Skills Class
You and Your Relationships	*Making the Most of School* (taught in Math)	*Crossroads: A Program to Promote Responsible Decision Making*
• Review of social problem solving • Communication skills • Peer relationships • Violence prevention • Substance use prevention • Review of puberty, teen pregnancy, and AIDS prevention • Evaluating risks • Checking accuracy of information	• Self-monitoring and self-management skills • Academic goal setting • Attendance • Substance use prevention	• Self-control • Stress management • Making transitions • Problem solving • Decision making • Communication • Violence prevention
	Values and Choices (taught in P.E.)	*Protecting Oneself and Others*
	• Values and human sexuality • Puberty: physical and emotional changes • Decision making and consequences • Recognizing sexual pressure • Refusal and assertiveness skills • Teen pregnancy • Effects of drugs in pregnancy • STDs • Sexual assault	• Substance use prevention for smoking, drinking, and drugs • Violence prevention *AIDS Education and Prevention Week* • Review of basic facts about HIV • Barriers to prevention • Living with AIDS

(continued)

from both the empathy training and the anger management lessons. Additionally, both need information on puberty.

Sixth Grade

At the sixth grade level there are modules for social problem solving, substance use prevention, and human growth and development, with an

TABLE 3.1. Continued

10th Grade	*11th Grade*	*12th Grade*
47 lessons taught 5 times a week for 2 marking periods as a Life Skills Class	37 lessons integrated in U.S. History II throughout the year and 3 lessons taught in English	16 lessons taught 1 time a week for 2 marking periods as a senior guidance class and 5–10 lessons taught in English

10th Grade

Violence Prevention

- Understanding violence
- Substance use prevention

Conflict Resolution

- Communication
- Conflict cycle
- Review of social problem solving
- Communication and human sexuality
- Violence prevention

Strengthening Relationships with Family and Friends

- Application of problem solving and conflict resolution to situations with family and friends
- Accepting individual differences

11th Grade

A World of Difference (taught in History)

- Beliefs and values
- Prejudice, stereotyping, and discrimination
- Scapegoating and racism
- Violence prevention

Substance Use Prevention (taught in History)

- Effects of drug use in pregnancy and video *Innocent Addicts*

HIV/AIDS Education and Prevention (taught in English)

- Review of basic facts about HIV
- Barriers to prevention
- Living with AIDS

12th Grade

Transition Skills for Life

- Planning for transitions
- Coping with stress and anxiety
- Help seeking and social support
- Service learning

Substance Use Prevention (taught in English and Senior Seminars)

- Legal, social, health, and peer resistance issues surrounding substance abuse
- Violence prevention

HIV/AIDS Education and Prevention (taught in English)

- Review of basic facts about HIV
- Barriers to prevention
- Living with AIDS

emphasis on puberty, reproduction, relationships, and AIDS. The problem-solving module is the basis for the middle school social development curriculum. The module has 27 lessons that teach a six-step problem-solving process (see Figure 3.2) through which students learn stress management, problem identification, feelings identification, goal setting, solution generating, consequential thinking, and planning.

Once the students are able to apply the steps in hypothetical situations, it is important to provide practice in real-life situations as well. Maura can

WHEN YOU HAVE A PROBLEM:

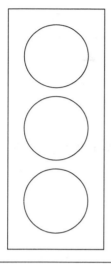

STOP, CALM DOWN, and THINK
                    before you act

say the **PROBLEM** and how you **FEEL**
set a **POSITIVE GOAL**
think of lots of **SOLUTIONS**
think ahead to the **CONSEQUENCES**

GO ahead and **TRY** the **BEST PLAN**

FIGURE 3.2. Six-step problem-solving process. © Roger P. Weissberg and M. Z. Caplan.

be encouraged to use the steps in the conflicts with her parents. Raffi could use the process with the problem involving his best friend who doesn't call anymore. One way of assisting students in applying the process to real situations is to provide "Becoming a Successful Problem Solver" sheets for students to fill in (Figure 3.3).

In one New Haven classroom, the girls were upset about a problem in the cafeteria. Each lunch table had 12 attached seats. Because there were 13 girls in the class, one girl had to sit at the boys' table each day. The girls were upset, and the teacher helped them put the problem through the process. Their goal was "to fix it so that the girl doesn't have to sit at the boy's table." The group came up with many solutions.

1. A different girl could sit at the boys' table each day.
2. The girl could invite a friend to sit with her at the boys' table.
3. The girl could sit at the girls' table from another class.
4. The class could end its gender-specific seating assignment, mixing girls and boys at the two tables.
5. The entire cafeteria could end its gender-specific seating.
6. The cafeteria could have open seating rather than tables assigned to classrooms.

BECOMING A SUCCESSFUL PROBLEM SOLVER

Name: _____

1. *My problem* is _____

   _____

2. The people involved were _____

   _____

3. *Before* the problem was solved:

   a. My *stress level* was _____ on a 1 (low) to 10 (high) scale.

   b. I felt _____ and _____.

   c. The other people felt _____ and _____.

4. My goal is _____

5. My solution was (what I did or said) _____

   _____

6. Was the problem solved? _____

7. If the problem was not solved, what are some different solutions you could have tried? Think ahead to the consequences of each solution.

   　　　　　Solution　　　　　　　　　　Consequence

   a. _____ → _____

   b. _____ → _____

   c. _____ → _____

8. Which solution do you think is best? _____

9. Why do you think it is best? _____

10. When are you going to try it? _____

FIGURE 3.3. Becoming a successful problem solver. © 1990 Weissberg, Caplan, Bennetto, and Jackson.

After considering the consequences of each solution, the group decided on solution 4 and developed a plan to implement it. This experience of applying the process to a real-life situation not only gave the group a chance to practice the problem-solving process but also empowered the students. It helped them realize a stronger sense of internal control over their lives.

Once the skills are mastered, problem solving can be applied to situations in several content areas. It is a framework that is particularly useful for topics such as the prevention of substance use and high-risk sexual behavior.

Seventh Grade

When Maura is in seventh grade, she blames her parents when things go wrong and rages at their interference in her life. Interactions with her peers are everything. Raffi still has no good peer relationships, and his feelings stay bottled up inside. The seventh grade module, "You and Your Relationships," focuses on communication skills and thinking about relationships with friends and family, areas in which our two adolescents both need help. The 24-lesson program also reinforces the problem-solving, substance use prevention, and human growth and development skills taught in sixth grade. The sixth and seventh grade programs are taught as subjects for which students receive grades.

Eighth Grade

There are two modules in the eighth grade curriculum. "Making the Most of School" is designed to be integrated into the mathematics program. It focuses on self-management skills as well as substance use prevention. The lessons reinforce problem-solving and communication skills and provide opportunities to use mathematics skills as tools to help students monitor and understand themselves and their behavior. The second eighth grade module is "Human Sexuality: Values and Choices." It includes self-awareness and acceptance of the physical, emotional, and social changes that take place during adolescence; decision-making and relationship-building skills; and consequences of sexual activity. The curriculum introduces the concept of homosexuality. It also promotes an understanding of the difference between positive touch and abusive touch. Because of Raffi's preoccupation with sexual matters, his anxiety over stories about sex, and his alarm at any signs of interest in him, the lessons in this portion of the curriculum would be beneficial to him. In particular, the lessons through which students learn that the victim is never at fault, that there are strategies one can use to stay safe, and that resources are available could help Raffi deal productively with his challenges.

EVALUATION OF THE SOCIAL DEVELOPMENT PROGRAM

The Social Development Program has been evaluated over the years, using a number of complementary strategies. These include the following:

(a) reactions to the Social Development Program as assessed through surveys of teachers, students, administrators, and social development staff; (b) evaluations of elementary school students' academic, social, and behavioral functioning; and (c) evaluations of middle and high school students' attitudes, values, daily activities, and problem behavior involvement. This evaluation process is coordinated through collaboration between the Social Development Program and an evaluation research group at Yale University that designed the evaluation plan, developed and selected the assessment tools, and analyzed the results.

Over 200 teachers from elementary, middle, and high schools were surveyed about their opinions on the curricula they taught and on their overall reactions to the Social Development Program. More than 95% of the teachers thought that the social development curriculum addressed issues that were important for their students. Approximately 80% of teachers at all grade levels found the curriculum helped them communicate better with their students. Over three-quarters of the elementary teachers reported that their students applied what they had learned in class.

A representative sample of over 1,200 students provided their reactions to the social development curriculum. Most students indicated that they learned from their social development classes and thought that all New Haven students should have such classes. It was clear from both survey results and written comments that students saw the link between skills learned in social development classes and the goals of reducing violence, AIDS, and substance use in youth.

Teachers of a large sample of students (2,611) in grades K–5 completed the Teacher-Child Rating Scale (T-CRS; Hightower et al., 1986), a measure developed to provide reliable information about child problem behaviors (acting out behavior, shy-anxious behavior, learning problems) and social competencies (frustration tolerance, assertive social skills, peer social skills). On the T-CRS, boys were rated as having more problems than girls, and there were generally no differences on problems or competencies as a function of grade. A subsample of 1,869 students was rated in two consecutive years. As is common when students progress to higher elementary grades, reports of learning problems increased; however, these same students showed significant improvement in the areas of acting out behavior and frustration tolerance over the two-year period.

The social development of middle and high school students has been assessed on a regular basis through a comprehensive survey, the Social and Health Assessment (SAHA) Survey (Barone et al., 1995; Weissberg et al., 1991). The SAHA is a 23-page survey designed to assess the high-risk behaviors and positive school and community involvements of students. The SAHA was administered to all students in grades 6, 8, and 10 in the New

Haven Public Schools in 1992 and every two years subsequently. The SAHA collects a variety of self-report information about school and academic performance, substance use, aggressive and delinquent behavior, and AIDS and high-risk sexual behavior (Barone et al., 1995). Information on environmental influences concerning these four problem areas, including peer and parental attitudes, is also collected.

Findings from the SAHA have supported program concerns of the Social Development Program staff and have served as a valuable source of information on the behavioral and attitudinal outcomes that are the goals of the program. Especially compelling has been an analysis of trends in behaviors and attitudes from 1992 to 1996. There have been important positive changes in many areas, including substantial increases in percentages of students who feel that school is a safe place (e.g., an 18% increase among 10th graders) and major reductions in participation in gang fights and in weapon carrying. In terms of race relations, there have been significant improvements in the perception that people of different races are treated respectfully at school (e.g., a 20% increase among 10th grade students reporting this perception). In terms of emotional adjustment, in 1996 many fewer students reported frequent worries and feelings of hopelessness.

Many complex forces and diverse interventions shape the development of youth in New Haven. Thus, in assessing the efficacy of a program such as the Social Development Program, it is difficult to demonstrate links between specific program components and their intended outcomes. Nevertheless, there have been marked improvements in attitudes and behaviors that reflect positive social development, as well as changes in particular areas after expansion or modification of an aspect of the program. Taken together, high levels of satisfaction with the curriculum and program overall, improvement in competencies with exposure to the program, and striking positive changes over time for middle and high school students all provide support for the effectiveness of the Social Development Project for students across the K–12 grade range.

HOW TO GET STARTED

Many teachers, parents, and administrators have become interested in learning more about the New Haven program in particular and about how to incorporate SEL principles into their schools and school districts. There are many ways to go about getting started and insuring the best possible outcomes. First, consider the principles in Figure 3.4. These principles suggest a daunting challenge, but they are designed to help individual teachers—

GUIDELINES FOR SOCIAL AND EMOTIONAL LEARNING PROGRAMS

- SEL programs should simultaneously—and seamlessly—address students' mental, emotional, social, and physical health, rather than focus on one categorical outcome.

- SEL programs should be based on developmentally appropriate, sequential preschool to high school classroom instruction.

- Competence-enhanced programs must address students' cognitive, affective, and behavioral skills; their attitudes and values about themselves and others; their perceptions of social norms; and their understanding of information about targeted social and health domains.

- Effective instruction requires teaching methods that ensure active student engagement, emphasize positive behavior, and change the ways in which children and adults communicate about problem situations.

- Multilevel interventions in which peers, parents, the school, and community members create a learning climate and reinforce classroom instruction are most effective in addressing the widespread social problems of children.

- System-level policies and practices to support program implementation and institutionalization should be developed.

FIGURE 3.4. Guidelines for social and emotional learning programs.

as well as entire school districts—establish programs. No initiative would be responsible if it did not first consider the broader implications of SEL, and so we suggest these principles as important factors.

Then, get started! We suggest a few ideas, depending on whether you are a parent, a teacher, or an administrator.

Parents

- Work with the school governance team to determine what is already in the curriculum in the area of social and emotional skill development. Then develop goals for strengthening existing efforts and develop strategies for implementing these goals.
- Work to be part of a curriculum committee that looks into SEL issues.
- With the PTA, plan a workshop for parents to raise their awareness of SEL.
- Follow up the workshop by providing the parents with activities they can use at home to foster their children's social and emotional intelligence.
- Develop a selection of SEL resources for parents.

Teachers
- "Talk it up" with colleagues.
- Attend workshops on SEL.
- Assess your curriculum to determine which SEL skills, information, and attitudes are already being addressed in your grade level/subject.
- Work with the school governance committee to assess the SEL skills already in the building-wide curriculum and to determine what is missing.
- Develop a plan for one or more grade levels that would systematically enhance the social and emotional development of the students.
- Borrow curricula from various companies for preview.
- Visit schools that have a SEL emphasis.

Administrators
- Create a partnership among university personnel, parents, educators, business leaders, social service providers, and religious leaders to develop and support the concept of SEL.
- Provide staff development activities to raise awareness of SEL.
- Assist in planning workshops on SEL for parents.
- Identify resources, including the Collaborative for the Advancement of Social and Emotional Learning (CASEL); telephone (312) 413-1008 for information.

CONCLUSION

For any concerned educator, SEL issues are important. The New Haven program, although still early in its development, demonstrates that a comprehensive and coordinated approach can be implemented. But more importantly, it points to the importance of developmental approaches to all the complex social and environmental challenges facing young people today. Every child needs rich and supportive social and emotional experiences in order to learn and grow. Perhaps Maura's and Raffi's most important lesson is the one they will teach educators—that they can indeed learn if only the school will give them the learning experiences they most need.

REFERENCES

Barone, C., Weissberg, R. P., Kasprow, W. J., Voyce, C. K., Arthur, M. W., & Shriver, T. P. (1995). Involvement in multiple problem behaviors of young urban adolescents. *Journal of Primary Prevention, 15*(3), 261–283.

DeFriese, G. H., Crossland, C. L., Pearson, C. E., & Sullivan, C. J. (1990). Comprehensive school health programs: Current status and future prospects. *Journal of School Health, 60,* 27–190.

Dryfoos, J. G. (1990). *Adolescents at risk: Prevalence and prevention.* New York: Oxford University Press.

Elias, M. J., Zins, J. E., Weissberg, R. P., Frey, K. S., Greenberg, M. T., Haynes, N. M., Kessler, R., Schwab-Stone, M. E., & Shriver, T. P. (1997). *Promoting social and emotional learning.* Alexandria, VA: Association for Supervision and Curriculum Development.

Hightower, A. D., Work, W. C., Cowen, E. L., Lotyczewski, B. S., Spinell, A., Guare, J. C., & Rohrbeck, C. A. (1986). The teacher child rating scale: A brief objective measure of elementary children's school problem behaviors and competencies. *School Psychology Review, 15,* 343–409.

Langdon, C. A. (1996). The third annual Phi Delta Kappan poll of teachers: Attitudes toward the public schools. *Phi Delta Kappan, 78*(30), 244–250.

National Commission on the Role of the School and the Community in Improving Adolescent Health. (1990). *Code blue: Uniting for healthier youth.* Alexandria, VA: National Association of State Boards of Education.

National Mental Health Association. (1986). *Report of the NMHA Commission on the prevalence of mental-emotional disabilities.* Alexandria, VA: Author.

Shriver, T. P., & Weissberg, R. P. (1996). No new wars! *Education Week, 33,* 37.

Weissberg, R. P., Voyce, C. K., Kasprow, W. J., & Shriver, T. P. (1991). *The Social and Health Assessment.* New Haven, CT: Authors.

4

Creating a Positive School Climate

Strategies for Fostering Self-Esteem, Motivation, and Resilience

Robert B. Brooks

During the past 20 years, I have had the opportunity to offer many workshops for educators about the school's role in nurturing a student's social and emotional growth. Although many teachers and school administrators believe as I do that focusing on a student's social and emotional development may be as important as teaching specific academic skills and content, there are other educators who have questioned this focus.

Some teachers have told me that they do not have the training or expertise to deal with the social and emotional life of students, while others have said that they do not believe that it is their responsibility to work with this facet of a student's life. Still others have observed that they would like to spend more time "getting to know students" and supporting their emotional growth but are unable to do so because of a prescribed curriculum that fills the class time. Not surprisingly, middle school and high school teachers are more apt to voice these concerns than their elementary school counterparts who spend more time with the same students each day.

It is unfortunate that some educators perceive bolstering a student's emotional and social well-being as interfering with or taking precious time away from teaching academic skills. In fact, in addition to my own experience, the feedback I receive from many educators has convinced me that strengthening a youngster's self-esteem and self-confidence need not be an "extra" curriculum; if anything, a student's sense of security and self-worth in a classroom provides the scaffolding that supports increased learning, motivation, self-discipline, realistic risk-taking, and the ability to deal effectively with mistakes (Brooks, 1991, 1997a).

THE MIND-SET OF THE EDUCATOR

Before reviewing a framework that articulates the components of self-esteem and motivation and detailing specific strategies for reinforcing the social and emotional growth of students in the school setting, it is important to examine the mind-set that is most helpful for teachers to possess if they are to be successful in creating a positive school climate, a climate that is permeated with a feeling of security and respect. Strategies will not be as effective if they are implemented by teachers who are burdened with a negative mind-set and who do not truly appreciate their own worth and the lifelong impact they have on students.

Topics such as (a) the significance of empathy; (b) the educator's role in promoting motivation, hope, and resilience; (c) the importance of accommodating to the unique temperament and learning style of each student; (d) the need to recognize that whether a student thrives in a classroom may have as much to do with a teacher's approach as it does with the attitudes a child brings into the classroom; and (e) specific strategies that teachers can implement to reinforce self-esteem and emotional development should have a prominent place in a teacher's early and ongoing training, but unfortunately they often do not. I have been told by teachers both new to the field and with years of experience that they have had little, if any, exposure to these topics or to related theories pertaining to different theories of motivation (Adelman & Taylor, 1990; Deci, Hodges, Pierson, & Tomassone, 1992; Ford, 1995), multiple intelligences (Gardner, 1983), emotional intelligence (Goleman, 1995), or temperamental differences in children from birth (Chess & Thomas, 1987). The following are several of the topics that I believe serve as underpinnings for a positive school climate and should have a prominent place in a teacher's approach.

Empathy

A basic skill in any relationship—husband-wife, parent-child, teacher-child—concerns the ability to be empathic, to truly see the world through the eyes of the other person (Brooks, 1991, 1997b). While empathy is an essential skill, it is far more difficult to achieve than most people realize. Many of us judge ourselves to be empathic, but are we? How often do we stop to consider how our children, our students, or our colleagues would describe us? How often at the end of a school day do we reflect upon how the students in our classrooms would describe what occurred in class that day and how they felt we treated them? When we are empathic we not only ask ourselves what we hope to accomplish when we say or do things, but as importantly, we think about the following question: Am I saying or doing things in a way that will help my students to be most responsive to listening to me?

Typically, it is most difficult to be empathic toward those students who challenge us, who question our authority, who fail to do their homework, who act up in class. Yet, it is precisely with these students that we must expend much energy to be empathic. Unless we understand the developmental issues of middle school children such as Maura and Raffi, unless we have a sense of what their words and actions represent, unless we appreciate both the middle school child's anxieties about growing up and the child's strong quest for separation and independence (a quest often expressed in ways that push adults aside and even seem to belittle adult values), it can become easy to lock horns with them and respond to them in negative ways.

The Central Role of Self-Esteem and Hope

As I struggled in the early part of my career to be more empathic and to understand the experiences of children in school, especially those with learning, attentional, and behavioral problems, I invited them to write stories about their lives. What impressed me was a powerful theme that emerged in these stories, a theme dominated by feelings of low self-esteem and a loss of hope. Not only were many of these students burdened by a negative self-image, but as they thought about their futures, they could imagine only continued failure—in essence, they had lost hope (Brooks, 1997a, 1997b). Consequently, I began to reflect upon interventions that would reinforce self-esteem, motivation, and realistic hope in all students, interventions that could become an integral part of the fabric of a school. Consideration of such interventions led to another key role that schools can play, namely, to promote resiliency in their students.

Self-Esteem and Resilience

It is important to note that many researchers and clinicians have emphasized self-esteem as a key variable in determing resilience (Rutter, 1985; Werner, 1993). Others, however, have viewed the concept of self-esteem from a very different perspective, contending that many people who advocate fostering self-esteem are doing so at the expense of teaching children responsibility, discipline, and compassion (Baumeister, 1996; Lerner, 1996). One basis for the existence of these different perspectives may be the confusion between what Lerner calls "feel-good-now" self-esteem in contrast with "earned self-esteem." Lerner notes:

> Earned self-esteem is based on success in meeting the tests of reality—measuring up to standards—at home and in school. It is necessarily hard-won and develops slowly, but it is stable and long-lasting, and provides a secure foundation for further growth and development. (p. 12)

In striking contrast, "feel-good-now" self-esteem is seen as an approach to strengthening self-esteem that does not challenge children, nor set realistic expectations and goals, nor teach them how to deal with frustration and mistakes.

The concept of self-esteem that I subscribe to, which is linked to resilience and which I believe a school can reinforce, may be understood as including the feelings and thoughts that youngsters have about their competence, about their abilities to make a difference, to have control over their lives, to develop self-discipline, to confront rather than retreat from challenges, to learn from both success and failure, and to treat themselves and others with respect. I believe that self-esteem guides and motivates our actions, and, in turn, the outcome of our actions influences our self-esteem so that a dynamic, reciprocal process is constantly in force (Brooks, 1994).

Resilience: The School's Role

In the past 15 to 20 years there has been an increased effort to understand not only the risk factors that contribute to the emergence and maintenance of cognitive, emotional, and behavioral disorders in children but also the protective factors that serve to buttress the resources of these children and help them to become more resilient (Brooks, 1994; Katz, 1997; Rutter, 1985, 1987; Werner, 1993; Werner & Smith, 1992). Different variables have been delineated that contribute to resilience, including a child's inborn temperament, problem-solving and interpersonal skills, self-esteem, family climate (e.g., family warmth, affection, clear-cut and reasonable expectations and limits), and support from outside the family (Hechtman, 1991).

Given the focus of this chapter on the influence of educational institutions on a child's emotional and social development, it should be emphasized that schools have been spotlighted as environments that can provide children with experiences that enhance their self-esteem and competence, thereby reinforcing resilience (Brooks, 1991; Rutter, 1980, 1985). For example, psychologist Julius Segal (1988), in describing resilient children, writes:

From studies conducted around the world, researchers have distilled a number of factors that enable such children of misfortune to beat the heavy odds against them. One factor turns out to be the presence in their lives of a charismatic adult—a person with whom they can identify and from whom they gather strength. And in a surprising number of cases, that person turns out to be a teacher. (p. 2)

I believe that the time has arrived for us to expend less energy debating whether or not educators should attend to the emotional and social needs and growth of students. Instead, we should be focusing on how best to address these needs in the classroom. We must recognize that students will learn most effectively in an atmosphere in which they feel safe and do not fear being ridiculed or humiliated, in which they are challenged and assisted to meet realistic goals, in which they feel teachers genuinely care about them and respect their individuality, and in which learning is seen as an exciting adventure rather than as drudgery. It is within such an atmosphere that resiliency and hope are reinforced.

A FRAMEWORK FOR UNDERSTANDING THE COMPONENTS OF SELF-ESTEEM AND MOTIVATION

Recognition of the importance of self-esteem and the social and emotional factors involved in the educational process has generated efforts to articulate the main components that are associated with a classroom climate that nurtures the whole child. Various theories have been advanced as part of this effort. One framework that I find particularly useful in designing a positive school climate has been proposed by psychologist Edward Deci (Deci & Chandler, 1986; Deci et al., 1992). Deci's model, which contains many similarities to Glasser's (1997) "choice theory" (formerly called "control theory"), suggests that children and adolescents will be more motivated to confront and persevere at tasks in school when the staff has created an environment in which certain basic needs are satisfied. Deci articulates three such needs that provide direction for fostering self-esteem, motivation, and resilience in students. They are as follows.

TO BELONG AND FEEL CONNECTED. Students are more likely to thrive when they are in school environments in which they feel they belong and are comfortable, in which they feel appreciated by teachers. Many adolescents join gangs to satisfy this need for connectedness and a sense of identity. Related to this feeling of belonging is the importance of helping each student to feel welcome, thereby lessening feelings of alienation and disconnectedness. A teacher's small gestures—a warm greeting, a smile— can have a major impact in helping middle school students to feel welcome in the school setting.

TO FEEL AUTONOMOUS AND HAVE A SENSE OF SELF-DETERMINATION. The concept of a sense of ownership and self-determination is at the heart of many theories of self-esteem and motivation, and the development of this concept is a major developmental task of young adolescents. Motivation is heightened when students feel they are heard and respected, when they feel they have some control over what is transpiring in the school milieu. If students believe that they are always being told what to do and how to behave, they are less likely to be enthused about engaging in activities that they feel are being imposed upon them. In such a situation, their main motivation may be to avoid or oppose what others wish them to do and a power struggle is likely to ensue. As I will outline in greater detail in the discussion of strategies, reinforcing self-determination requires educators to teach students how to set realistic short-term and long-term goals and how to solve problems and make wise decisions.

TO FEEL COMPETENT. Students need to have areas in their lives in which they feel competent and accomplished, areas that generate a sense of pride. We must remember that feelings of incompetence prompt students to retreat from challenges and to engage in avoidant behaviors that often exacerbate their problems. Students require positive feedback and encouragement from their teachers. A focus on encouragement should not be confused with false praise or inflated grades since students are very perceptive in knowing when they are receiving undeserved positive evaluations. Positive feedback about a child's competencies must be predicated on actual accomplishment, which requires that teachers provide ample opportunities for children to succeed in areas that are judged to be important. It is also important to emphasize that a focus on competencies is not incompatible with offering feedback to correct a student's performance or behavior as long as this feedback is done in a nonaccusatory, nonjudgmental manner that does not humiliate the child.

There is a metaphor I use to capture a child's areas of strength. Many at-risk students seem to feel that they are swimming or drowning in what I call an "ocean of inadequacy." To counteract this image of despair we must remember that every child possesses "islands of competence," that is, areas that are (or have the potential to be) sources of pride and accomplishment. If we are to serve as the "charismatic adults" in the lives of students, we have the responsibility of identifying, reinforcing, and displaying these "islands of competence"; in so doing, a ripple effect may be triggered that provides students with the courage, strength, and motivation to venture forth and confront learning tasks that have been problematic for them in the past.

STRATEGIES FOR REINFORCING SELF-ESTEEM, MOTIVATION, AND THE SOCIAL AND EMOTIONAL FEATURES OF A STUDENT'S LIFE

There are a number of interventions that educators can use to create a positive school climate that strengthens a student's social and emotional growth and development and establishes a classroom atmosphere in which students are excited and motivated about learning. It is important to emphasize again that if these strategies are to be effective, teachers must have a positive mind-set, a mind-set that avoids blaming students, that focuses on and uses the unique gifts of each student; it is also a mind-set that recognizes that whether or not students are successful has as much to do with the classroom environment we create as with the attitudes the student brings into this environment. In order to enhance this mind-set, I advocate an orientation period at the beginning of the school year (although it may be implemented later in the year as well).

The Orientation Period

The orientation period I envision is divided into two parts. The first takes place a day or two before the students arrive and involves having teachers as a staff reflect upon why they became teachers, what they believe is their essential role (information about resilience should be considered), what factors they believe are most important in creating a positive school climate, how they would like their students to describe them (this involves the concept of empathy), and what support they need from each other during the year to minimize cynicism and burnout. When I conduct workshops with educators several days before the start of the school year and address these various themes, I find that it produces greater staff cohesion and support and helps teachers to remember and appreciate the enormous lifelong impact they have on students.

The second part of the orientation period that I advocate is implemented during the first two or three days of school, but it is important to emphasize that the activities used are refined and reinforced throughout the school year. I recommend that during the initial few days teachers refrain from taking out any books or covering any academic content. Instead I believe the time should be used to begin to create a classroom climate in which students will thrive. Although some might argue that this is a waste of several days of classroom teaching time, it has been my experience that when the first few days are used to address the needs of students, the students will be much more motivated to learn, much more involved in their own education, much more capable of dealing with frustration and mistakes, and much more self-disciplined. This can be best illustrated by describing several interventions or strategies for meeting the social and emotional needs of students, interventions that begin as part of the orientation period and continue as a integral feature of the class atmosphere for the entire school year.

HELPING STUDENTS TO FEEL WELCOME. One major factor that helps students to feel connected to and welcome in a school is the personal relationship they develop with a teacher. Quickly learning the names of students, calling them at home, or writing a brief, positive note can serve as powerful forms of acceptance and caring that help students feel connected to the school setting (Brooks, 1991).

Another way to make students feel welcome is for teachers to develop realistic expectations and goals and to make appropriate accommodations, given a student's unique makeup and learning style. We now have impressive research findings that highlight the temperamental differences that exist in children from birth (Chess & Thomas, 1987), the multiple intelligences that children possess (Gardner, 1983), and the different learning styles and learning differences in each student (Goldstein, 1995; Levine, 1994). Unfortunately, despite this research, we often give lip service to differences in children, responding to students as if they were a homogeneous group. For example, I continue to hear teachers question the fairness of making accommodations for some students, arguing that other students would be offended and upset by a situation they perceive as unfair. I can appreciate the concern that these educators are voicing, but I also believe that if children are different from birth, the least fair thing we can do is to treat them all alike.

In the school environment, one of the most effective ways to address the issue of fairness is during the orientation period. For instance, to lessen the possibility of students perceiving a teacher as unfair because of different expectations for different students, the teacher could discuss with students on the first day of school how each one of them is different, how some students are better at sports than others, how some can read more rapidly, how some can solve math problems more efficiently. The teacher can then say that given these differences, there will be different expectations for the amount and kind of work done by each student. Most importantly, the teacher can then add, "One of my concerns is that because of different expectations, some of you may begin to feel that I am not being fair. If any of you begin to feel that way, please let me know so that we can discuss it."

This is important since if students believe that things are not fair in a classroom, it can interfere with learning.

Feedback I have received indicates that when a teacher brings up fairness before it becomes an issue, it basically remains a nonissue and permits the teacher to accommodate more easily to each student's unique needs without generating negative feelings (teachers must also inform parents of this approach to fairness in order to obtain parental support). Another benefit of such a discussion is that it educates students about individual differences, resulting in an atmosphere of greater tolerance. We must remember that students will feel most welcome when our expectations are in keeping with their unique makeup. Students in middle school are especially sensitive to appearing different from their peers, and so handling this issue with care and empathy will more easily permit students to accept accommodations in their programs.

The kinds of accommodations I typically recommend do not require major modifications in a child's program, nor do they demand a vastly different educational plan for each student. They involve such interventions as a maximum amount of time for homework even if a student does not complete all of the assigned work, untimed tests, two sets of books—one at home and one at school—for those children prone to lose things, a syllabus for students who have difficulty copying assignments from the board, and more physical activity for those students who are hyperactive.

DEVELOPING RESPONSIBILITY. I asked approximately 1,000 educators to complete an anonymous questionnaire, which included an item asking them to recall a positive memory of school involving a teacher who had reinforced their self-esteem when they were students. A vast number of their responses had an interesting common theme: They remember being asked to help out in some fashion in the school (Brooks, 1990, 1991). If students are to develop a feeling of ownership and accomplishment, educators must provide them with many opportunities for assuming responsibilities, especially responsibilities in which they are helping others. I find that enlisting students to use their "islands of competence" in such activities as tutoring or writing stories for younger children, painting murals on the walls of the school, watering plants, assisting the custodian or secretary, and taking messages to the office reinforces their motivation and self-esteem as they witness concrete examples of their achievements (Brooks, 1991; Werner, 1993). They also develop a more positive attachment to school. Obviously, many of these kinds of activities can be delegated to students during the orientation period.

TEACHING DECISION-MAKING AND PROBLEM-SOLVING SKILLS. An integral component of high self-esteem and resilience that is associated with a feeling of self-determination and autonomy is the belief that one has some control over what is transpiring in one's life. Although it is important for all students to develop this belief, it may be even more so for students during the middle school years when they are grappling with issues of independence. The classroom is an environment in which the skills of problem solving and decision making—skills that are a vital part of a sense of ownership—can obviously be taught and reinforced.

Teachers can accomplish this task in various ways, such as involving students in discussions of how best to solve academic and social problems; or having them decide which six of eight problems on a homework sheet to do; or responding to an incorrect answer not by calling on other students until the correct answer is given but by reviewing the process of solving the problem (a teacher whose main style is to call on student after student until the correct answer is obtained is basically conveying the message that "I am not interested in how you solve the problem but rather just in the correct answer"); or by developing educational goals with each student, goals that can be periodically reviewed with the input of the student. As Shure (1994) notes, we must involve students in developing their own solutions to problems rather than constantly telling them what they should do.

USING DISCIPLINE TO CREATE SELF-DISCIPLINE AND SELF-CONTROL. It is difficult to conceive of children developing high self-esteem and resilience if they do not possess self-control. A major goal of discipline, in addition to establishing a safe school environment, is to have students develop self-discipline, which requires that we teach and educate children rather than humiliating or intimidating them (Curwin & Mendler, 1988; Mendler, 1992). If students are to assume ownership of their actions and not perceive rules and limits as arbitrarily imposed by adults, they must understand the purpose of the rules and contribute within reason to the formation of rules, guidelines, and consequences. For this reason I advise teachers to ask students during the orientation period what rules they think are necessary for the classroom to run smoothly, what the best way is to remember rules so that the teacher is not "nagging" the students or the students "nagging" the teacher, and what the consequences should be if someone forgets a rule.

Some teachers in hearing this recommendation for student involvement in the establishment of rules and consequences have wondered if students would attempt to take advantage of the situation or create silly rules. Actually, the feedback received is that one of the main problems encountered by teachers is that the rules and consequences of the students are often more restrictive and more severe than those of the teachers. Many teachers have told me that one of their main tasks is to help students create less harsh, more reasonable rules. Students have also developed some interesting ways of remembering rules, including drawing signs that are posted. Rather than take advantage of a teacher who involves them in the formation of class rules, most students appear to develop self-discipline or ownership of these rules.

Educators should especially focus on ways to prevent the emergence of misbehavior rather than struggling primarily with what action to take and what form of discipline to use once the misbehavior has occurred. Meeting the needs of students (as outlined by Deci) from the beginning of the school year, and anticipating situations that are likely to prove problematic for students so that we can help them to develop alternative ways of responding to these situations, will lessen the discipline problems that emerge in a classroom.

PROVIDING POSITIVE FEEDBACK AND ENCOURAGEMENT. While positive feedback and encouragement fall within the rubric of discipline, I am placing them in a separate section to emphasize their importance. Self-esteem and resilience are strengthened when we communicate realistic appreciation to children and help them to feel special in our eyes. Writing brief notes on a student's paper, calling students at home to find out how they are doing, being available to them, and having a school assembly in which students are recognized for various accomplishments (not just academic achievements) are but a few examples of conveying to students that we genuinely care about them. In so doing, we become the "charismatic adults" in their lives. In this regard, there are times I wonder about changing the words *special needs* to *every student needs to feel special.*

TEACHING STUDENTS TO DEAL EFFECTIVELY WITH MISTAKES. The fear of making mistakes and looking foolish is one of the strongest obstacles to developing high self-esteem and motivation. Students with a positive self-image view mistakes as experiences to learn from while those with low self-esteem perceive mistakes as failures that cannot be corrected easily (Brooks, 1991). The latter group of students are likely to retreat from school tasks that they believe will lead to further failure and frustration. I believe that minimizing the fear of mistakes is one of the most important challenges faced by educators.

One intervention for minimizing this fear can take place during the orientation period. Before any academic work has been introduced, teachers can ask their class, "Who in this class thinks that they will make mistakes and not understand something the first time this year?" Before any student can respond, teachers can raise their own hands and share memories of their own anxieties when they were students. Teachers can then involve the class in a discussion about the best ways to insure that no student will be worried about being called upon, about not understanding material, about making a mistake. Placing the fear of making mistakes in the open typically serves to minimize its potency, thereby helping the class-room environment to feel safer. This sense of safety promotes a student's social and emotional growth.

Teachers can also lessen the fear of failure by avoiding such comments as "Have you been paying attention?" or "Why don't you try harder!" or "You have to listen more closely!" Instead, a student's not understanding academic material should be seen as an opportunity to review the material (obviously, some students will require more assistance outside the class-room). I visited a school in which tests were scored by adding points for a student's correct answers rather than deducting points for incorrect answers and this was done in green rather than red ink. The teachers reported that this method of scoring tests helped to create a more positive atmosphere in which students perceived mistakes as part of the learning process.

CONCLUSION

Educators must realize that they have a major impact on students, not just concerning what occurs on a particular day but for the rest of the students' lives. We must move away from the simplistic view that teaching academic skills and content is separate from promoting the growth of a student's emotional and social well-being. Focusing on the whole child does not detract from teaching academic material. Rather both domains are parts of the same fabric and are inextricably interwoven. If any part of the fabric is weakened, the entire fabric may unravel; if all of the fibers are strong, the total fabric will be resilient.

The implications of this view are far-reaching and require that teachers be exposed to ideas that focus on empathy, motivation, "charismatic adults," and resilience. I believe that rather than adding to the many responsibilities a teacher already has, this broader perspective of a teacher's role will provide greater meaning and purpose to what a teacher can accomplish in the classroom every day. This meaning—this purpose—can serve as the catalyst for a more positive school climate, a climate filled with a sense of security, excitement, and fun.

REFERENCES

Adelman, H., & Taylor, L. (1990). Intrinsic motivation and school misbehavior: Some intervention implications. *Journal of Learning Disabilities, 23,* 541–550.

Baumeister, R. F. (1996). Should schools try to boost self-esteem? *American Educator, 20,* 14–19.

Brooks, R. B. (1990). Indelible memories of school: Of contributions and self-esteem. *School Field, 1,* 121–129.

Brooks, R. B. (1991). *The self-esteem teacher.* Circle Pines, MN: American Guidance Service.

Brooks, R. B. (1994). Children at risk: Fostering resilience and hope. *American Journal of Orthopsychiatry, 64,* 545–553.

Brooks, R. B. (1997a). *Learning disabilities and self-esteem. Look what you've done! Stories of hope and resilience.* Videotape and educational guide produced by WETA in Washington, DC. Distributed by PBS Video, Arlington, VA.

Brooks, R. B. (1997b). A personal journey: From pessimism and accusation to hope and resilience. *Journal of Child Neurology, 1997,* 387–395.

Chess, S., & Thomas, T. (1987). *Know your child.* New York: Basic Books.

Curwin, R. L., & Mendler, A. N. (1988). *Discipline with dignity.* Reston, VA: Association for Supervision and Curriculum Development.

Deci, E. L., & Chandler, C. (1986). The importance of motivation for the future of the LD field. *Journal of Learning Disabilities, 19,* 587–594.

Deci, E. L., Hodges, R., Pierson, L., & Tomassone, J. (1992). Autonomy and competence as motivational factors in students with learning disabilities and emotional handicaps. *Journal of Learning Disabilities, 25,* 457–471.

Ford, M. E. (1995). Motivation and competence development in special and remedial education. *Intervention in School and Clinic, 31,* 70–83.

Gardner, H. (1983). *Frames of mind.* New York: Basic Books.

Glasser, W. (1997). A new look at school failure and school success. *Phi Delta Kappan, 78,* 597–602.

Goldstein, S. (1995). *Understanding and managing children's classroom behavior.* New York: Wiley.

Goleman, D. (1995). *Emotional intelligence.* New York: Bantam Books.

Hechtman, L. (1991). Resilience and vulnerability in long term outcome of attention deficit hyperactivity disorder. *Canadian Journal of Psychiatry, 36,* 415–421.

Katz, M. (1997). *On playing a poor hand well.* New York: Norton.

Lerner, B. (1996). Self-esteem and excellence: The choice and the paradox. *American Educator, 20,* 14–19.

Levine, M. D. (1994). *Educational care: A system for understanding and helping children with learning problems at home and in school.* Cambridge, MA: Educators Publishing Service.

Mendler, A. N. (1992). *What do I do when ...? How to achieve discipline with dignity in the classroom.* Bloomington, IN: National Educational Service.

Rutter, M. (1980). School influences on children's behavior and development. *Pediatrics, 65,* 208–220.

Rutter, M. (1985). Resilience in the face of adversity: Protective factors and resistance to psychiatric disorder. *British Journal of Psychiatry, 147,* 598–611.

Rutter, M. (1987). Psychosocial resilience and protective mechanisms. *American Journal of Orthopsychiatry, 57,* 316–331.

Segal, J. (1988). Teachers have enormous power in affecting a child's self-esteem. *Brown University Child Behavior and Development Newsletter, 4,* 1–3.

Shure, M. (1994). *Raising a thinking child.* New York: Holt.

Werner, E. E. (1993). Risk, resilience, and recovery: Perspectives from the Kauai Longitudinal Study. *Development and Psychopathology, 5,* 503–515.

Werner, E. E., & Smith, R. S. (1992). *Overcoming the odds: High risk children from birth to adulthood.* Ithaca, NY: Cornell University Press.

5

Social Decision Making and Problem Solving

Essential Skills for Interpersonal and Academic Success

Maurice Elias and Linda Bruene Butler

"As children grow and face situations of increasing complexity and challenge, it is beneficial to provide a developmentally appropriate combination of formal, curriculum-based instruction with ongoing informal and infused opportunities to develop social and emotional skills from preschool through high school" (Elias et al., 1997, p. 33). This is not a mere suggestion. This is the first empirically supported Guideline for Promoting Social and Emotional Learning, published by the Association for Supervision and Curriculum Development. It marks a transition in thinking about educational necessity and responsibility. This chapter describes a research-validated approach to accomplishing this objective that has been carried out in hundreds of schools across the United States and elsewhere for over two decades. It is not experimental or hypothetical. Educators can carry it out, students enjoy it and learn from it, and parents support it.

SOCIAL AND EMOTIONAL LEARNING AND THE MIDDLE SCHOOL YEARS: THE CONTEXT

The middle school years are a time of cognitive awakening, realignment of social influences, intense physiological change, and more often than not, emotional turbulence. It is well established that a young adolescent's transition from elementary school to middle school can be considered a time of normal life crisis (Johnson, 1980). The crisis is created by the wide variety of complex personal and environmental changes occurring during this time. This inherently complex and unstable situation demands active adaptation and coping on the part of the child. As Jonathan Cohen mentions in Chapter 1 of the current work, and as discussed in a variety of other research (Blyth, Simmons, & Carlton-Ford, 1983; Lipsitz, 1980; Rutter, 1980), grades five through eight (students 10–13 years old) have come to be recognized as a critical "fall out period" during which many children develop academic and interpersonal difficulties and feelings of alienation that result in significant disturbances in their psychosocial functioning. In addition, there is ample evidence to suggest that this disturbance is too often not transitory but rather creates a greater vulnerability to future negative life outcomes (Blyth et al., 1983; Toepfer & Marani, 1980). Even when serious derailment does not persist, the middle school years represent a developmental period with a high level of risk for disengagement with the learning process (Carnegie Council on Adolescent Development, 1989).

Middle school, therefore, is a critical period for strong support and fortifying actions on the parts of parents and educators. An understanding of the social-developmental needs of children during this time can help make these efforts successful.

ENDURING CHALLENGES OF CHILD AND ADOLESCENT DEVELOPMENT

There is a set of developmental assumptions underlying our approach to working with students to improve their social and emotional functioning and prevent problem behaviors such as substance abuse and violence. To simplify, we view children and adolescents as seeking answers to the following fundamental questions.

How do I view myself and my future? Where do I fit into things? What will I become?

How can I nurture and build positive relationships with peers and adults?

How can I handle life's challenges, problems, decisions, and choices?

How can I develop as a moral, ethical, active, committed human being?

How can I get involved in the world of work? My school? My neighborhood?

How can I develop a positive answer to the question, "Who am I?"

Children's ability to address these questions changes as they grow more mature and sophisticated, but they always feel the kinds of concerns these questions imply. They turn to negative life pathways because they do not see alternative paths. Their sense of identity is narrow, and they often feel hopeless. If they turn to substance abuse or violence or other problem behavior, we must understand this as an attempt to find identity or to soothe the pain of memory of early abuse or neglect, of circumstances that kept them from having positive, nurturing relationships. They find their way to problems because they have no beliefs to sustain them and they lack the judgment and skills needed for thoughtful, careful decision making. This is summarized in the acronym that follows.

Despair
Revenge/Resentment
Uncertainty   =   D.R.U.G.S.
G–dlessness
Social Skill Deficiencies

When we consider students such as Maura and Raffi, to whom we were introduced at the beginning of this volume, we are left to wonder how students can learn under such burdens. What is their motivation? Where can they develop the skills they need to handle the challenges of everyday life? Our work in social decision making and problem solving (SDM/PS) is directed toward providing children of all backgrounds with tools to enhance their lives.

WHAT IS SDM/PS?

What do we mean when we use the phrase "social decision making and problem solving"? This phrase refers to a research-validated theoretical framework and set of procedures for integrating social development and emotional intelligence into the curricular and instructional structure of schools. Before describing specific elements and procedures, we will describe underlying principles and define concepts.

If you were to look in a dictionary to find definitions for problems and decisions, you would find that an "overlap" refers to times in life when one encounters an "unsettled question." We asked participants attending the workshop we presented at Teachers College in October 1997 to consider the unsettled questions that they encountered at different developmental stages: elementary school, middle school, high school, and adulthood. Elementary school situations were whether or not to tattle, whether or not to kiss Mom in public, feeling chubby and shy, wondering if it is OK to cry, and wondering how to deal with bullies. Middle school situations included things such as dealing with emotional turmoil and hormones; zits; getting your period for the first time; peers that make fun of you for just about anything; how to dress; how to manage schoolwork and time with friends; whether or not to try tobacco, alcohol, drugs; how to act with the opposite sex; and whom to talk to about problems. High school situations included how far to go sexually; whether or not to break rules; whether or not to smoke, drink, take drugs; relating to peers with different values and beliefs; how to not get caught cutting class; coming to grips with the limits of your own talent; what courses to take; whom to go to the prom with; whether or not to go to college, how to get in, and how to decide what college to go to; what to do instead of college; and managing a job on top of academic and social demands.

Then we asked about adulthood—that magic time when we think problems will finally be fewer. Participants generated a list of adult unsettled questions that included when and if to marry; when and if to end a relationship; whether to buy or to rent a home; the problem of finding a place to live in New York City; how to find and what to do with free time (if any!); multitasking; sustaining intimacy with a romantic partner; balancing family, parenting, and work; behavior and/or academic problems/decisions regarding children; dealing with ailing parents; health problems of self or family; whether or not to change jobs; whether or not to move for a new job for one of two working parents; bringing meaning into one's life; deciding what is meaningful in one's life; and coping with aging, stress, and "beating the clock."

After participating in this developmental journey, the adults reflected that problems and decisions are something they have experienced in all phases of their lives. Everyone deals with these situations, every day. When adults looked back at the problems encountered in elementary and middle school, they realized that, although the problems mentioned might sound trivial from an adult point of view, they were very serious at the time. While the adult list appeared to be more varied and complex, as a result of increases in roles and responsibilities, some of the adults stated that their childhood and young adulthood problems seemed more difficult because of overwhelming emotions, confusion, and strain on underdeveloped personal resources.

Almost all of the situations the group described included emotional arousal and other people. Some of the problems involved either an internal conflict or a conflict with another person or persons. Some of the scenarios involved helping someone else solve a problem or mediating a conflict between others. Social decision making and problem solving can therefore be defined as the knowledge, skills, attitudes, and beliefs that an individual needs to regulate emotions, think clearly, and negotiate with other people in an emotionally intelligent and socially competent way across situations and over time.

SOCIAL DECISION MAKING AND PROBLEM SOLVING "FIT" WITH DEVELOPMENTAL TASKS OF THE MIDDLE SCHOOL YEARS

Problems and decisions are one of those threads that weave through everyone's life, at every developmental phase. It is difficult to think of any problem or decision in life that is not tied to emotions and social relationships.

In a review of studies looking at developmental changes, tasks, and needs of young adolescents during the middle school years, Elias (1993) identified seven important features linked to success in academics and social adjustment. These features can help children master tasks needed to move forward developmentally and avoid compounding difficulties that can result from serious derailment.

During this time, children need (1) structure and clear limits, combined with (2) opportunities for self-exploration and (3) diversity in routines, topics, and activities. It is also important that they begin to experience (4) a sense of competence, (5) positive social interaction, and (6) meaningful participation and a sense of belonging. Last, (7) accepting responsibility for personal health is critical and predictive of future health.

To the wonder and dismay of many adults, the middle school years are a major turning point in cognitive development. For the first time, children are able to "think about the way they think." In general, it is only by the end of about third grade (student ages 8–9) that children might begin to move from concrete thinking to abstract thought. By the middle school years, most students are enthusiastically and steadfastly exercising these new mental muscles, whether adults like it or not. In the social development area, the primary focus shifts to the world of peer relationships. These characteristics make a social decision-making approach ideal for this developmental period.

Educators utilizing this approach can capitalize on peer relationships, students' interest in broad and varied experiences, and their emerging cognitive abilities to foster students' sense of being able to handle problems competently. This approach accomplishes this task by providing repeated practice of thinking skills and skills for emotional regulation and group functioning by utilizing frameworks and structures that provide both guidance and limits. With these frameworks and structures, educators can foster the safe exploration of diverse points of view and roles. By repeatedly practicing social decision-making skills with classmates and adults, students develop self-identity in the context of social belonging. This implies, however, that students develop sound social judgment and personal decision making in an educational context that promotes a commitment to health and positive social interaction. The SDM/PS approach has been designed to help schools provide this necessary context.

A FRAMEWORK FOR COMBINING CURRICULUM-BASED INSTRUCTION WITH ONGOING SKILL PRACTICE

The SDM/PS approach targets four research-validated competency areas.

1. Skills linked with emotional literacy and regulation. These skills include self-monitoring and regulation of emotion/impulse control, attending, listening, accurate remembering, taking turns, and establishing and respecting group rules for interaction.
2. Behaviors linked with peer acceptance and the ability to work cooperatively in a group
3. Problem-solving and decision-making skills
4. The ability to apply these skills in response to changing social situations

The goals of this approach are to (a) target essential life skills; (b) provide practice and overlearning of these skills, both of which are essential so that students can internalize the skills sufficiently to be able to access them in stressful and complex situations; (c) provide students with comprehensive instruction and classroom and nonclassroom opportunities to use these skills; and (d) expose students to this approach, with some degree of implementation fidelity, over a multiyear period. Why? Research has found that when students practice these skills over a multiyear period, skill gains are maintained, while only one year of skill training can fade out. Further, these skills are better retained when relevant to various aspects of school life, including homeroom/advisory and the discipline system (Elias et al., 1997).

In *Social Decision Making and Life Skills Development: Guidelines for Middle School Educators* (1993), Elias presents an operative set of skills that are empirically linked with social competence, emotional intelligence, and peer acceptance. Systematic skill-building procedures are used to teach self-control, social awareness, and group participation skills while emphasizing critical thinking. Skills are organized into three domains: readiness for decision making, instruction in a social decision-making process, and application of social decision making. The curriculum includes a wide variety of field-tested models for infusing skill instruction and practice into other educational objectives (cf. Elias, 1993, for a full explanation and sets of activities for use in social and academic contexts, in regular and special education, and with parents).

Prerequisite: Readiness for Decision Making

"Readiness for decision making" refers to a climate that must be established and a set of skills that must be learned as prerequisites to thoughtful decision making. We use a Sharing Circle (or, as some of our urban sites have modified the term, "Team Huddle") to begin class discussions and skill-building activities. Basically, in the Sharing Circle, students are asked to share their names and answer a question or two. Questions may involve such topics as one's favorite restaurant or, after a certain level of trust is established, how one feels about a social issue. The Sharing Circle has a great deal of depth and complexity (cf. Elias & Tobias, 1996). At its essence, it allows children to share with one another, to learn to listen to and care about their classmates, and to get some "air time." The Sharing Circle also serves as a segue from the pressures of home and the pace and action of lunch and recess during the school day. It is a format for reflection on the weekend past, the week ahead, and the weekend to come.

We also find it essential to have a visible, clear rule structure in the classroom. A format for this is the classroom constitution (Elias & Tobias, 1996). This allows parallels to academics by introducing the idea that, just as is true for our nation, our classroom functions with a set of rights and a set of rules. Students are involved in creating this list of rights and rules, and it is displayed in the classroom. Typically, when visitors walk in and view the constitution, they are oriented to the pride that the students take in the values and priorities of the classroom. The constitution should be positively phrased, although some educators maintain that a couple of clear "Thou shall not's" are also worthwhile. When problems such as classroom disruption, lack of effort, or poor group work are observed, the constitution is invoked and an improvement plan is created. Parents are highly supportive of classroom constitutions, as these foster clear home-school communication. It also becomes easier to enlist parents' proactive assistance in participating in improvement plans.

Against the backdrop of a climate that fosters social and emotional learning (SEL), specific readiness skills can be built. This domain targets a repertoire of skill areas that are prerequisites for thoughtful social decision making. The readiness domain includes self-control and social awareness and group participation skills. "Self-control" refers to the personal skills necessary for self-regulation and monitoring of emotions and interactive behavior, whereas the social awareness and group participation skills domain focuses on social skills and knowledge linked with successful participation in a group.

As can be seen in the overview provided in Figure 5.1 of the Social Decision-Making Curriculum, the Self-Control Unit includes initial activities to promote group cohesiveness and establish the structure of group rules or the classroom constitution It also includes skills such as listening, accurate remembering, and taking turns. The heart of this unit focuses on skills for regulating emotional reactions and impulsivity. Students are taught to recognize physical cues and situations that put them at risk of "fight or flight" reactivity, which can result in negative consequences and poor decisions. They practice methods for gaining emotional control and link these with self-monitoring of body language, eye contact, use of language, and tone of voice.

The Social Awareness and Group Participation Skills Unit provides instruction in skills characteristic of adolescents who are accepted by their peers. These abilities include giving and receiving negative feedback, praise, and help; perspective taking; exploring characteristics and behaviors of friendship; and group building. This instruction in the context of a peer group can be particularly helpful to a student such as Raffi who does not understand the consequences of behavior and its impact on other people and who has difficulty interpreting social cues.

The Instructional Phase

This domain targets an eight-step framework for organizing clear thinking.

The objective of the instructional phase is to help students develop a metacognitive understanding of their decision-making process and to provide guided practice in the use of an internalized framework for organizing thinking. This is accomplished through a combination of (1) introducing an overall strategy, while also exploring each element of that strategy as a complex skill area in and of itself, and (2) practicing the strategy in the context of a variety of hypothetical, age-appropriate, and open-ended choice and conflict situations. As each skill is emphasized and practiced, its link to the chain of skills that forms the overall strategy is strengthened. Overall decision-making and problem-solving skills are thus built through continual review and recitation. Our research-validation studies through the Program Effectiveness Panel of the U.S. Department of Education demonstrate repeatedly that these procedures maximize students' retention and use of thinking skills beyond the instructional setting (Bruene-Butler, Hampson, Elias, Clabby, & Schuyler, 1997).

SOCIAL DECISION-MAKING CURRICULUM
Phases of Instruction and Target Skill Areas

READINESS PHASE
Skills training in prerequisite skills

Self-Control   **Social Awareness**

Listening   Group-building exercises
Remembering and following directions   Choosing friends
Roleplay   Giving and receiving praise
Keep calm   Asking for and giving help
B-E-S-T (assertive communication)   Starting and keeping a conversation
Resisting provocations   going
Coping with hassles   Giving and receiving criticism
                                                Joining a group

INSTRUCTIONAL PHASE

a. **Skill-Building Lessons:**   **An Eight-Step Strategy for**
   Students overlearn the thinking   **Thinking Through Problems**
   steps for access under pressure
                                                1. Look for signs of different feelings
b. **Facilitative Questioning:**   2. Tell yourself what the problem is
   Adult questioning to facilitate good   3. Decide on a goal
   thinking in real life situations   4. Stop and think of as many solu-
                                                   tions to the problem as you can
                                                5. For each solution, think of all the
                                                   things that might happen
                                                6. Choose your best solution
                                                7. Plan it and make a final check
                                                8. Try it and re-think it

APPLICATION PHASE
Repeated practice in applying problem solving thinking to a wide variety
of interpersonal and academic situations

FIGURE 5.1. Social decision-making curriculum: phases of instruction and target skill areas. *Source:* Elias, M. & Clabby, J. (1989, 1998). *Social decision making skills: a curriculum guide for the elementary grades.* New Brunswick, NJ: Rutgers University, Graduate School of Applied Professional Psychology.

The skill areas can be summarized by stating that when children and adults are using their social problem-solving skills, they are

1. noticing and labeling signs of feelings in themselves and others;
2. identifying issues or problems;

3. determining and selecting goals;
4. generating alternative solutions;
5. envisioning possible consequences;
6. selecting the solution that best meets their goals;
7. planning and rehearsing the details of carrying out the solution and making a final check for obstacles; and
8. noticing what happened and using the information for future decision making and problem solving.

WHAT IS THE RELATIONSHIP OF SOCIAL DECISION MAKING AND PROBLEM SOLVING TO EMOTIONAL INTELLIGENCE?

This is a good time to address a question of clear concern to educators who are hearing a growing number of terms used to describe this social and emotional domain. Even a cursory look at the eight skill areas listed previously makes clear that one cannot have skill deficits and expect to achieve meaningful academic and social success. Social decision making and problem solving are most directly related to the interpersonal cognitive problem-solving (ICPS—"I Can Problem Solve") approach developed by Spivack and Shure in the early 1970s (see Spivack, Platt, & Shure, 1976). Work in SDM/PS began in the elementary schools in the mid-1970s in Philadelphia and in rural Connecticut (Allen, Chinsky, Larcen, Lochman, & Selinger, 1976). Howard Gardner's multiple intelligences model, which came to educators' attention early in the 1980s, included the elements of intrapersonal and interpersonal intelligence (Gardner, 1983). These refer to abilities related to self-knowledge and skills in dealing with social relationships.

In 1995, Daniel Goleman published his book *Emotional Intelligence*. In it, he summarized years of work done in schools, hospitals, workplaces, and families showing that intellectual abilities alone were not sufficient to account for life success. The skills of emotional intelligence—SEL—are needed for individuals to achieve success as students and as workers, as citizens and as parents (Elias et al., 1997; Elias, Tobias, & Friedlander, 1998). In fact, SDM/PS is one of the projects featured in the appendix of Goleman's book as providing the research and practical base for his findings.

What are the skills of emotional intelligence? Goleman (1995) defines five overlapping areas.

1. Self-awareness: recognition of one's emotions; possession of an adequate emotional vocabulary; comprehension of the reasons for feeling as one does in different situations
2. Self-regulation of emotion: the ability to verbalize and cope positively with anxiety, depression, and anger and to control impulses toward aggressive, self-destructive, antisocial behavior

3. Self-monitoring and performance: short-term and long-term goal setting; the ability to focus on tasks at hand, to mobilize positive motivation, hope, and optimism, and to work toward one's optimal performance states

4. Empathy and perspective taking: possession of listening skills; sensitivity to others' feelings; understanding of others' points of view, feelings, and perspectives

5. Social skills in handling relationships: assertiveness; effective expression of emotions; sensitivity to social cues; skills for working in groups; leadership; social decision-making strategies; constructive response to interpersonal obstacles

It is clear that there is great compatibility between emotional intelligence and SDM/PS. The actual decision-making steps of the instructional phase are part of social skills for handling relationships; the first step, of course, is part of self-awareness. The readiness skills are interspersed throughout all of the aspects of emotional intelligence. What was not present in Goleman's work, including the sections on education, was a detailed discussion of implementation. Elias et al. (1997) provide this missing piece by outlining a variety of programs that have had years of effective operation in schools throughout the United States. One of these programs is SDM/PS.

A particular area in which the SDM/PS approach is distinctive is the way in which the skills are integrated into everyday academic and interpersonal contexts in the schools. A teacher who wants to build students' SDM/PS skills during language arts, health, social studies, civics, science, art, gym, or music will find well-articulated strategies and activities to help this take place. This occurs in what we call the application phase.

The Application Phase

The application phase of instruction provides students with ongoing opportunities to apply and practice skills taught in the readiness and instructional domains in real-life situations and within the context of academic content areas. This is accomplished through a combination of (a) structured practice activities/lessons and (b) facilitative questioning on the part of adults.

STRUCTURED PRACTICE OPPORTUNITIES. The application phase curriculum materials provide educators with a wide variety of example structures and materials for infusing a decision-making approach into the way they teach almost any subject area and as a method for addressing real-life

DECISION MAKING: THE REVOLUTIONARY WAR

Directions: For each historical event, include the following outline in your paper.

1. State your colonist's name, occupation or craft, and whether your character sides with the English or as a Patriot.
2. State the historical event or issue.
3. List the different feelings you think your colonial craftsperson might be experiencing. Why does your person feel this way?
4. Write one or two sentences stating clearly what the problem is, from your craftsperson's point of view.
5. What does your craftsperson want to have happen? What is his or her goal?
6. Include a brainstorm of as many solutions to the problem as you can.
7. Diagram four of the solutions, listing both positive and negative consequences.
8. Which solution do you feel is most likely to enable your colonial craftsperson to reach her or his goal?
9. Develop a plan for implementing this solution. Then consider any possible obstacles. How could these be avoided? What will your colonial character do if his or her plan does not work?
10. Be prepared to share with the class what you predict will happen when the plan is put into action.

Question: Did this activity help you understand why the decision to become a Patriot or a Loyalist was so difficult? Was there a correct decision? Was there a wrong decision? Explain.

FIGURE 5.2. Sample infusion activity. Courtesy of Karen Cole, Berkeley Heights Public Schools, New Jersey.

problems and decisions. These lessons and methods are easily adapted to address specific instructional objectives and are flexible enough to use with a variety of content themes, topics, stories, and situations. For example, work sheets and procedures from lessons for a decision-making approach to social studies or for analyzing literature can be utilized, with minor variations, in a wide variety of specific topics addressed in social studies or history or for a variety of authors and works of literature. See Figure 5.2 for an example of a decision-making work sheet adapted for use in social studies by Karen Cole (1997), a middle school teacher in Berkeley Heights Public Schools, New Jersey. After the class covers extensive historical background and explanations of political issues of the time, each student develops a personal historical character to travel with through the historical events of the Revolutionary War. As events occur, the student thinks through each problem from the character's point of view, considering (a) the character's craft or role (i.e., craftsperson, sailor, plantation owner, or other occupation) and (b) whether or not this character has decided to be a Loyalist or a Patriot.

FACILITATIVE QUESTIONING. A primary focus of our training sessions is teaching adults to coach students to use readiness and thinking skills through the questions that they ask. Using the same eight skills mentioned previously as a framework, we train adults to translate the eight steps into questions that prompt an individual or a group to think through a problem or choice. During training, educators practice a variety of modifications of questioning techniques designed for common situations such as mediating conflict, corrective discipline, or obtaining student motivation and input into plans for reaching a goal established by the adult.

GENERALIZATION BEYOND THE CLASSROOM: SYSTEMATIC SKILL BUILDING

The combination of readiness, instructional, and application phase activities creates a powerful combination of forces. The readiness and instructional phases build students' internal resources. By overlearning processes for responding to stress—the provocations and requirements that are part of working in groups, solving problems, and making decisions—students increase their feelings of self-efficacy and *internal control* in relation to their own thinking, learning, and decisions. The application phase provides *external supports* that foster and help to build and promote the use of the same skills.

What underlies the success of these activities is that they are directed at skill building. If there is any aspect of SEL that we find to be most critical and least appreciated by the general public, it is the understanding of what it takes to build a skill, rather than present a lesson or concept. Gagne (1965) articulated this important distinction in relation to academic skills. Learning objectives must be defined clearly in terms of knowledge acquisition and skill development because the learning curve of the student and the instructional methods used for knowledge and skills differ from one another.

When our objective is for students to learn and store information, facts, and ideas, the learning curve shows that most students can pick up this type of information after several learning trials. Although some students need more exposures to the information before they can give us the "right answer" on a test, this type of learning occurs more quickly than the learning involved in acquiring a skill. The learning curve for a skill is more gradual. Skills do not develop through exposure to information. A skill is developed over time, through practice, with feedback, repeated practice, with more feedback, followed by more practice with feedback, and so on. Further, for application of skills to occur in diverse contexts, they must be practiced in those contexts, with feedback provided. The development of a skill is an active process and cannot be expected to occur through exposure to lecturing, reading, or other relatively passive modes of learning. While skill acquisition may require knowledge and information that guide skill practice, and observation of skill performance is beneficial, the only way an individual can integrate a skill into his or her personal repertoire is through an ongoing series of personal practice and feedback trials.

Think about how you learned the skills that you possess, such as driving a car, sewing, cooking, doing mathematical puzzles, or performing science experiments. Or, consider sports: Do you think Michael Jordan would be a skilled basketball player today if he had relied on reading every book on the subject, listening to other people talk about it, and watching basketball every day on television, rather than playing all the time when he was younger?

Now consider Maura and Raffi. Because of all they are going through as they enter and pass through middle school, it is hard for them to connect with everything they are learning at school. Further, they are acutely sensitive to their own imperfections, and therefore they are not especially eager to learn new "social skills." The application phase is a way of creating a climate in a classroom and school in which social decision-making and problem-solving skills are encouraged by emphasizing their utility in everyday academic and social tasks. Only as the exercise of these skills becomes part of the formative structures of classroom and schools can we hope to see widespread generalization. There are two additional factors to consider with regard to developing social and emotional skills.

1. *It is only when a skill is overlearned that it is accessible under stress.* One needs only to reflect on examples from one's own life to realize the validity of this statement. Just think again for a minute of your personal skills. Can you think back to a time when some of them did not come as easily? You may not have consciously acknowledged it, but at some point these skills developed and then became almost automatic. When a crisis or complication comes along, you now have the experience to work through it in a way that would have thrown you into consternation—or even danger—at an earlier stage of skill mastery. The point is, it takes time and practice before any life skill is so internalized that it becomes almost automatic. It is important to think about what this means for SEL. What does it take for students to learn to think clearly, even under stress?

2. *Unlearning and relearning are often more difficult then initial learning.* By the time students enter middle school, they have already practiced many social and emotional skills for quite a few years. Teaching social and emotional skills is different from teaching in some other areas where the student may have little or no prior experience. For example, when teaching someone how to knit or play the saxophone, it is quite possible to find students with no prior experience. If we are attempting to work in the area of emotional regulation or communication skills or problem solving, this is impossible. Middle school students have already developed habits of living.

In addition, some of these habits, such as those learned in coercive family contexts (Patterson, 1982), promote the use of behaviors not appropriate for school or other relationships and social settings. By the time a student is in middle school, that student's social learning has been shaped by a wide range of environmental, interpersonal, cultural, and economic variables that impact not only on behaviors but also on underlying beliefs, values, attributions, and sense of self-identity, to name a few areas. New skills can be taught and developed, but this requires educators to think carefully about what it really takes for a middle school student to develop new life skills. Under stress, most people regress to old learning. Therefore, social and emotional skills must be clearly taught and then continuously practiced with feedback opportunities consistent with what is needed to rethink ideas, challenge old habits, and learn new skills.

HOW TO BUILD A SKILL

The instructional design utilized in SDM/PS curricula is based upon a combination of methods found to be most effective in teaching and building skills. Examples of a variety of methods for integrating this instruction in a middle school context can be found in Elias (1993). Program planning, implementation, evaluation, and logistical issues are also discussed in Elias and Tobias (1996) and in Elias and Clabby (1992). The purposes of "formal" or structured curriculum-based lessons are to (a) isolate and teach a skill and its components, (b) provide students with child-tested activities for practice with feedback opportunities, and (c) establish prompts and cues that refer to the behavioral components rehearsed in the lesson. The prompts can then be used to elicit students' use—or transfer and generalization—of these skills outside the instructional setting.

In the following section, we outline a typical instructional design for all of our skill-building lessons. We will use the skill of Keep Calm, which we call the essential first step to clear thinking, to illustrate this procedure.

1. *Begin with an opening, orienting activity.* Conduct a Sharing Circle (or Team Huddle) and review of group rules or constitution and skills taught to date. The Sharing Circle question could be an icebreaker/team-building question such as "Did you hear about that woman who won the 20 million dollar lottery? What if that happened to you? What is the first thing that you would do for someone else?" A Sharing Circle question can also be related to the topic of the day, such as "Today, we will continue to learn about skills that can help us think clearly, even in highly stressful or emotional situations. Think about a time when you became upset or nervous and thought you were going to lose your cool. Take a minute to think, so you can describe the situation in one or two sentences. Briefly describe a 'trigger situation' and the feelings this trigger situation brings up for you."

2. *Introduce background concepts/definitions.* For the skill of Keep Calm, students explore two background concepts: trigger situations and "feelings fingerprints." The former refers to those situations that elicit emotions and can lead us to lose our cool and not think clearly. The latter refers to physical signs that our bodies use to let us know when we are under stress. Some people feel stress in their stomachs; others get headaches; others experience back pain, shortness of breathing, clenched fists, flushed cheeks, or any of a number of other signs. Many people have more than one sign of stress. When an individual experiences this feelings fingerprint, it serves as a cue to use the skill of Keep Calm as a way of coping with the stress, rather than a more typical "flight or fight" reaction.

3. *Introduce the skill and establish a rationale/motivation to use the skill.* At this point, students are introduced to a skill that can help them to think clearly when they experience a trigger situation and physical signs of stress. They learn about ways emotions effect the autonomic nervous system and the brain and that, under stress, all human beings are at risk of fight or flight reactivity. Stress also hinders our ability to solve problems. Learning to regulate emotional and physical arousal experienced in trigger situations gives students more control by helping them to hook into the frontal lobe of the brain that Goleman (1995) refers to as the emotional manager.

Students learn that breathing is a higher order behavior. The rate of breath is linked with the ability to attend and think. As human beings, we cannot control many of the physical indices explored when we spoke about feelings fingerprints. We cannot say to our heart, " Slow down!" or "Stop, sweat glands!" We can, however, slow down our rate of breath, which, in turn, can impact various physical indices, most importantly, the neural networks in our brain. People have used this knowledge for many years in areas such as the martial arts, and many performers and athletes use Keep Calm or related methods to focus and think clearly under stress.

Until this point, this lesson resembles a lesson for acquisition of knowledge. Students are given information that motivates them to learn more. The next step moves into skill building.

4. *Describe and model the skill by separating it into concrete behavioral components.* Students are exposed to a Keep Calm procedure and concrete behavioral components of the skill. The steps of Keep Calm are as follows.

Step 1: Tell yourself to stop.
Step 2: Tell yourself on the inside, "Keep calm."
Step 3: Slow down your breathing with two long deep breaths.
Step 4: Praise yourself for keeping control.

Initially, teachers model each of these steps and describe the rationale. This procedure is worded to serve as an internalized guide for self-talk to promote transfer to real-life trigger situations. The goal for Step 1 is to stop and interrupt fight or flight reactivity. The second step serves two purposes: (a) self-prompting the use of Keep Calm and (b) interrupting other thoughts that tend to accompany emotional situations. Strong emotions affect cognition. When someone is frightened or angry, the situation tends to elicit extreme and often irrational thoughts such as "I hate you!" or "Oh NO!" or "Nobody likes me!" or "I'll never be able to learn this!" These thoughts are rarely productive and tend to interact in an escalating way with fight or flight tendencies. People cannot think two thoughts at one time. Telling oneself to keep calm not only begins to prompt the use of the skill, but it also interrupts other thoughts that are often unproductive.

Again, students learn to apply these skills in personally relevant situations. In Maura's case, academically challenging situations trigger strong emotions and self-defeating thoughts, while Raffi may be more likely to respond impulsively and aggressively when he is triggered by a peer's comment. Although the applications can vary, the same skills are an essential first step for clear thinking for all.

Step 3 is the most important. Students learn, first through modeling and then through repeated practice, to take slow and deep breaths that reverse the autonomic nervous system and help the brain focus on higher order thinking. The last step, Step 4, was added during our action research years. After giving students assignments to try to use Keep Calm and report back to us about how it worked, we had many eye-opening experiences. Repeatedly, students would share with the group situations that had occurred when the teacher was there. A student might share, for example, that when another student grabbed a book out of her hands she almost hit him, but she stopped herself by using Keep Calm. We realized then that students must take responsibility for self-reinforcement when they use this skill. It is difficult for an adult to praise a student for a lack of negative behaviors. Students are taught that they need to praise themselves for taking responsibility for and control of their own behavior.

   5. *Establish skill prompt or cue.* A skill prompt, such as Keep Calm, now represents a whole set of skill steps or behavioral components that the lesson has presented, modeled, and practiced. This is a key aspect of training, as this prompt can now be used to call upon the use of a more complex set of behaviors that the lesson has allowed educators to establish. This shared language is a key element for promoting transfer and generalization of the skill to situations outside the lesson.

   6. *Assign or create practice activities with corrective feedback.* Role-play simulations of trigger situations or common stressful situations during the school day, such as tests, recess rowdiness, or bus problems, provide opportunities for an array of practice activities. Students who are not role-playing are assigned different components of the skill to observe and then are asked to give feedback. These activities can be repeated in review lessons until the teacher feels the group has acquired knowledge and can demonstrate behavioral components to criteria established by the teacher in response to a cue.

   7. *Give assignments for skill practice to promote transfer and generalization.* After the skill is taught, plans for promoting transfer and generalization are as important as the lesson. Without this element, research has found that the teaching can fade out. Social decision-making and problem-solving materials provide teachers with a range of suggested strategies for promoting skill transfer and generalization. The most basic is the use of prompt and cues to apply the skill throughout the school day—such as before a test, coming in after free time—when real-life trigger situations occur or prior to mediating a conflict. Teachers are also encouraged to find times to relate the skill of Keep Calm to academic content areas, such as critically assessing decisions of characters in current events, history, or literature; health decisions; sports; performing arts; or giving presentations.

   External prompts such as posters, cue cards, visual cues, and signals can also be established between teacher and student, between parent and child, and/or among peers to interrupt fight or flight behaviors during trigger situations. For example, at Martin Luther King Jr. School in Piscataway, New Jersey, a Keep Calm Force of students volunteers its services for a marking period. On the playground, these students wear bright yellow T-shirts on which "Keep Calm Force" is written in black letters. These students are trained to look for incidents of emotional upset and then to stop other students and cue them to "Stop and Use Keep Calm!" by appearing on the scene in their yellow T-shirts. After the upset students begin to calm down, simple prompts for thinking, such as "Think! We can solve this problem; what can we do?" are provided. At Solomon Schechter School in East Brunswick, New Jersey, all students in each grade rotate through recess, taking turns as "nitzavim," which is a kind of mediator. They hold up Stop signs as a cue and use other visual reminders as well to keep the activity from getting stale. The goal of both efforts is to interrupt potentially disruptive situations and to prompt emotional regulation and problem-solving thinking. Other adults, such as parents, community sports coaches, playground aides, bus drivers, therapists, and other community influences, can also be taught to prompt and reinforce the use of the skill in life situations.

The eventual goal is to build students' ability to self-monitor and regulate their own emotional reactions. Future skill-building lessons continue to build upon the skill of Keep Calm. Once students are taught this self-calming breathing technique, an essential first step to clear thinking, the next skill is to learn to self-monitor and regulate the use of B-E-S-T: Body posture, Eye contact, Speech, or the way one chooses to put messages into words, and Tone of voice. This extension of self-control skills to areas of communication and self-presentation is more accessible after using Keep Calm. Instruction and practice of these two skills, Keep Calm and B-E-S-T, are extended to ongoing self-monitoring through lessons designed to promote the application of these skills in real-life trigger situations. A Getting-In Charge Journal is a tool for helping students learn to reflectively monitor this application. Also, journal entries can be kept in student portfolios to assess the degree to which students are able to transfer these skills to common trigger situations.

CONCLUSION

Curriculum-based lessons provide structured opportunities for skill instruction and practice that can then be combined with students' self-monitoring of their own skill development and ongoing external prompts by adults to promote skill use. Our studies show that these elements result in positive student outcomes and significant behavior change (Bruene-Butler et al., 1997; Elias & Clabby, 1992).

We have made tremendous gains in our knowledge of what skills are predictive of academic and life success, and we also know what it takes to develop these skills. The most pressing challenge and questions in middle schools today are the following. How can we organize our educational efforts around predictive skills, using methods that result in students over-learning these skills? How can educators organize themselves to build upon each other's work? How can we ensure that students are exposed with some degree of fidelity to training that occurs over multiple years, using pro-gramming that is integrated and comprehensive? We have addressed these questions in over two decades of work in implementing SEL in the schools, and we present the evidence of that record, and those of many colleagues, as inspiration to those about to embark on this path—a path that is reward-ing, feasible, and will transform one's role from that of giver of knowledge to that of facilitator of learning, and from teacher of students to preparer of children for an array of social roles as adults (Elias et al., 1997).

REFERENCES

Allen, G. J., Chinsky, J. M., Larcen, S. W., Lochman, J. E., & Selinger, H. V. (1976). *Community psychology and the schools: A behaviorally oriented multi-level pre-ventive approach*. Hillsdale, NJ: Lawrence Erlbaum.

Blyth, D. A., Simmons, R. G., & Carlton-Ford, S. (1983). The adjustment of early adolescents to school transitions. *Journal of Early Adolescence, 3,* 105–113.

Bruene-Butler, L., Hampson, J., Elias, M. J., Clabby, J. F., & Schuyler, T. (1997). The improving social awareness–social problem solving project. In G. Albee & T. Gullotta (Eds.), *Primary prevention works: Issues in children's and families' lives* (Vol. 6, pp. 239–267). Thousand Oaks, CA: Sage.

Carnegie Council on Adolescent Development. (1989). *Turning points: Preparing American youth for the 21st century* (Report of the Task Force on Education of Young Adolescents). New York: Carnegie Corporation.

Cole, K. (1997). *In-house SDM curriculum infusion project*. Berkeley Heights, NJ: Berkeley Heights Public Schools.

Elias, M. J. (Ed.). (1993). *Social decision making and life skills development: Guide-lines for middle school educators*. Gaithersburg, MD: Aspen. (Now available from the author)

Elias, M. J., & Clabby, J. (1992). *Building social problem solving skills: Guidelines from a school-based program*. San Francisco: Jossey-Bass.

Elias, M. J., & Tobias, S. E. (1996). *Social problem solving interventions in the schools*. New York: Guilford.

Elias, M. J., Tobias, S. E., & Friedlander, B. (1998). *Emotionally intelligent parent-ing*. New York: Harmony/Random House.

Elias, M. J., Zins, J. E., Weissberg, R. P., Frey, K. S., Greenberg, M. T., Haynes, N. M., Kessler, R., Schwab-Stone, M. E., & Shriver, T. P. (1997). *Promoting social and emotional learning: Guidelines for educators.* Alexandria, VA: Association for Supervision and Curriculum Development.

Gagne, R. M. (1965). *The conditions of learning.* New York, Holt, Rinehart, and Winston.

Gardner, H. (1983). *Frames of mind.* New York: Basic Books.

Goleman, D. (1995). *Emotional intelligence.* New York: Bantam Books.

Johnson, M. (Ed.). (1980). *Toward adolescence: The middle school years. Seventy-ninth yearbook of the National Society for the Study of Education.* Chicago: University of Chicago Press.

Lipsitz, J. (1980). The age group. In M. Johnson (Ed.), *Toward adolescence: The middle school years. Seventy-ninth yearbook of the National Society for the Study of Education.* Chicago: University of Chicago Press.

Patterson, G. R. (1982). *Coercive family process.* Eugene, OR: Castalia.

Rutter, M. (1980). *Changing youth in a changing society.* Cambridge, MA: Harvard University Press.

Spivack, G., Platt, J. J., & Shure, M. B. (1976). *The problem solving approach to adjustment.* San Francisco: Jossey-Bass.

Toepfer, C., & Marani, J. (1980). School based research. In M. Johnson (Ed.), *Toward adolescence: The middle school years. Seventy-ninth yearbook of the National Society for the Study of Education.* Chicago: University of Chicago Press.

6

The Development of Responsibility in Early Adolescence

Approaches to Social and Emotional Learning in the Middle School

Ruth Charney, Linda Crawford, and Chip Wood

In this chapter we hope to bring alive a key issue in early adolescence: the development of responsibility—a major contributor to positive social and emotional and academic behavior within the school context. Our interest in this subject grows out of our work with teachers around the country who have learned and utilized The Responsive Classroom® approach to teaching.[1]

THE RESPONSIVE CLASSROOM

Six Basic Components

There are six basic components to The Responsive Classroom: classroom organization, the Circle of Power and Respect, rules and logical consequences (including schoolwide discipline approaches), academic choice, guided discovery, and assessment and reporting to parents. These six components provide teachers with simple and workable management structures for everyday classroom use. They provide administrators with clear, sensible, and practical approaches to school reform. The Responsive Classroom accentuates the full integration of social and academic learning in every aspect of the school day. Through the following six components, the important skills of cooperation, assertion, responsibility, empathy, and self-control are modeled by teachers and practiced by students consistently and on a regular basis.

CLASSROOM ORGANIZATION. Adolescents often have concerns involving personal space, furniture, display of student work, time constraints, and the need for physical activity in a classroom environment. Arming middle school teachers with knowledge about adolescent development enables them to have productive discussions concerning these issues with their students during advisory periods and then to make decisions about their learning space in collaboration with the students. Teachers gain valuable insights from these discussions, and students gain experience with democratic decision making.

CIRCLE OF POWER AND RESPECT (CPR). The Circle of Power and Respect provides a structure for middle school students to know and understand each other. It began as an outgrowth of the morning meeting used in the early grades and now includes four components: a greeting between students; an opportunity to share what's happening in one's life; a lively activity; and news and announcements.

This clearly structured routine used in advisory periods teaches students the value and importance of greeting and recognizing each other as members of the same learning community. Sitting facing each other in a trustworthy space at the beginning of the day, students engage in and build effective communication skills, including empathic listening. They also practice cooperation, assertion, and responsibility by having the responsibility of running the circle once the teacher has sufficiently modeled the routine.

RULES AND LOGICAL CONSEQUENCES. This approach to discipline emphasizes building rules and expectations based on the students' own goals, what it is that they hope to accomplish in school. The rules proactively help them achieve their goals. Students learn how to take responsibility for behavior by creating, practicing, role-playing, and living the rules.

Logical consequences teach students that they will be held accountable for their behavior but that they can stop inappropriate behavior with honor, fix things when they go wrong, and build self-control. Rules that have been generated in a democratic way with substantial student input and that are based on the students' own hopes and dreams for the year have special meaning for adolescents. By imposing logical consequences wherever possible for infractions of these rules, our use of discipline retains that meaning.

ACADEMIC CHOICE. Academic choice refers to formal structures that teachers use to increase student initiative in learning and in developing academic skills. Through a process that involves student decisions in planning, working, and sharing their work, students learn to take initiative within assignments during a single period as well as over the life of an extended research project.

GUIDED DISCOVERY. Middle school students who are taken through exploratory introductions to materials and ideas perform at a higher level than those who are given rote instruction. Guided discovery of new and old classroom supplies and center areas teaches responsibility without any preconceived assumptions about what students do or do not know about taking care of the environment. In academic subjects it provides a way to introduce students to new activities through a familiar structure. Guided discovery helps build a supportive, intellectually challenging environment.

ASSESSMENT AND REPORTING TO PARENTS. By engaging parents in goal setting and dialogue at the beginning of the school year, The Responsive Classroom helps create meaningful relationships between parents, students, and teachers around mutually understood goals. Then information transmitted about academic achievement, standardized tests, and behavior exists in the context of caring.

The Development of Responsibility

It is clear that the development of responsibility is a primary task of adolescence and is the responsibility of both the teacher and the student; that is, it requires interaction. We argue that the development of responsibility requires an iterative continuum of

$$\text{relationship} \rightarrow \text{practical activity} \rightarrow \text{reflection}$$

and that this continuum needs to be consciously established in the daily practice of middle schools so that it becomes an honored ingredient in scheduling decisions, advisory programs, community service, and academic instruction. We believe that the gap remains wide between what young adolescents need in their school day and what they usually experience as daily fare in most U.S. middle schools. We would contend that both Maura and Raffi, the young adolescents journeying through the chapters of this book, could benefit immensely from different structures and approaches in their schools. Our reading of their school experience does not suggest that any part of it has been central in a positive way to their development. School, in fact, seems quite tangential. We suggest it need not be so.

Recent research by Wentzel (1997) found that perceived caring from teachers was predictive of "motivational outcomes" for students. In her study, a teacher who cared was described by students as a teacher who "makes a special effort, teaches in a special way, makes class interesting, talks to you, pays attention, listens, asks what's wrong, talks to me about my problems, asks if I need help, tells you when you do a good job," among other positive descriptors. Results from her longitudinal research "suggest that perceptions of caring teachers are related to students' academic efforts and to their pursuits of *prosocial and social responsibility goals* [emphasis added]" (p. 415). In other words, relationships with caring adults in the school setting are requisite experiences for positive academic and social action. This research is supportive of a dynamic, interactive psychological approach to the construction of identity in adolescence (Gilligan, 1982; Haviland & Kahlbaugh, 1993; Miller, 1986) and to the general concept of caring (Arnold, 1997; Noddings, 1992; Wood, 1991).

Our work as practicing teachers and teacher educators in schools for the past 25 years has convinced us that *relationship precedes socially responsible action.* In the school setting, relationships between teachers and students and between students are heavily dependent on the purposeful structures the teacher creates in the classroom environment to foster positive interaction. In other words, relationships don't just happen. They are facilitated by the "practical activity" generated by the teacher in the lesson plans used to deliver instructional content. They emerge from the ways in which the teacher uses homeroom time. They evolve for good or ill dependent on the teacher's skillful use of his or her knowledge of key developmental issues for young adolescents. This is what we call the social curriculum.

In The Responsive Classroom, we have formulated an array of practical activities appropriate to the developmental needs of children at different ages. We work with children and teachers from kindergarten through eighth grade. At each grade level we match important developmental milestones to specific tasks that will stretch students in their social and emotional growth, just as we introduce new academic challenges to stretch cognitive growth.

Maura and Raffi seem not to be engaged in school in tasks that help them reflect regularly with their peers with the help of adult leadership. In the middle school years, knowing that peer relationships are of paramount importance in the development of identity, we help teachers structure their schedules, classroom environments, and academic time in ways that foster respectful relationships within safe boundaries for all students and teachers, the well liked and the marginal. The practical activities that we suggest for these grades include specific approaches to the use of homeroom time, or advisory periods, where we also try to build the concept of "home" into this "room." Specific activities that teach and strengthen communication skills for students including debate, discussion, verbal games, and humor are given a safe daily structure. Practical activity that provides practice in responsibility is built into the school day through service to the school, work with younger children, classroom jobs, and care for others. Responsibility is carefully packaged with limits that protect the students from falling off a cliff but that still allow them to climb the moral mountain of adolescence.

Young adolescents crave freedom *and* responsibility. It is our job to provide clear expectations and reachable goals so that they can develop a moral compass to guide them through the discovery that freedom is not attainable without responsibility.

The Importance of Reflection

The key to making responsibility a living reality for young adolescent students is to provide them with the opportunity to reflect on their learning and behavior throughout the school day. Reflection is not something that happens automatically. Time for reflection needs to be provided, and teachers need their own strong social skills to utilize this time well. Without reflection, social and emotional learning (SEL) remains fragmented and temporary at best. As Likona (1991) has argued, "Of all the processes of moral education, moral reflection is aimed most directly at developing the cognitive, rational aspects of moral personality. At the same time, however, this more self-consciously rational aspect of moral education should be carried out in such a way as to foster union of cognition and affect—so that children come to feel deeply about what they think and value" (p. 151). From our point of view, this coming to feel deeply about what they think and value is essential. It is a primary goal of the continuum of "relationship → practical activity → reflection" in the identity formation and development of responsibility in young adolescents. It is coming to care about caring—metacognition and metaemotion.

In the most concrete terms, we believe this sequence can be best supported through carefully facilitated interactions that foster connectedness in the classroom and school. The Responsive Classroom can help provide these experiences for teachers and students. We will now turn to an examination of the implementation of this approach in the practical reality of everyday middle school life. What does it take to move students toward more responsible action? What focus do teachers need to deepen their teaching in this direction? Linda Crawford addresses these issues as she examines her work as a consulting teacher for Northeast Foundation for Children (NEFC).

IMPLEMENTATION OF THE RESPONSIVE CLASSROOM: ST. CHARLES MIDDLE SCHOOLS— LINDA CRAWFORD'S STORY

In the spring of 1996, 24 educators (referred to as the "turn-around trainers") from four middle schools in St. Charles Parish, Louisiana, began work with me to collaborate in building strong learning communities in their classrooms. The plan was for them to learn the strategies of The Responsive Classroom, implement them in their classrooms, and then introduce them to their colleagues. St. Charles Parish is a large, 10,000 student suburban system located near New Orleans. Students come primarily from lower and middle class homes. Teachers and administrators wanted schools in which young adolescents could thrive socially and academically, where they could cross the threshold from adult-directed to self-directed responsible living. What approaches could they use that would empower adolescents to be more responsible for themselves and for others?

In our sessions on the first day we developed ways to do this by brainstorming 50 activities that teach responsibility. The list included common activities such as silent reading and journal writing, in which students could show their ability to concentrate and to control the impulse to talk and fool around. It included partnered activities such as board games and group activities such as service projects in and outside of school, fund-raisers, competitive and cooperative games, project displays, student councils, assisting the teachers, and student-led activities and meetings. These activities could provide interesting, lively ways for young people to enjoy themselves and each other while learning to be more responsible. They could also provide opportunities for students to reflect on the effectiveness of their efforts to be more responsible.

The teachers knew that to make the strategies work, students needed to be able to manage themselves. To manage themselves, they first needed to feel connected: Relationship precedes responsibility. These educators could see that such connections weren't happening automatically. More and more students were coming to school with poor social skills. Many did not seem to know how to work things out or to assert themselves without being rude or overly aggressive. They did not regularly show empathy for each other, nor did they support or encourage each other. Although St. Charles Middle

Schools have good safety records, students often acted as if school were a dangerous place, not a place where they felt safe or where they belonged. Many, like Maura, spent their social time hanging out exclusively with cliques of friends; others were loners, like Raffi. Some worked hard just to stay out of trouble; others acted out, often as a way to get people to pay attention to them. Rudeness, sarcasm, and put-downs were common fare.

In such an atmosphere, it was unlikely that students would rise to the challenges of responsibility. They needed to know how to trust, enjoy, and cooperate with one another before they could consistently hold up their side of agreements and work assignments. They needed to learn how to assert themselves, participate fully in activities, feel safe enough to put themselves forward, and develop some autonomy. They needed to experience feelings of empathy in order to care for themselves and each other, especially when there was stress or pressure. They needed to be able to monitor themselves, to know when they were slipping, to self-correct, and to respond positively to adult correction, so that they could restore themselves when they were off center and return to their commitments. They needed to be able to use the power of reflection to guide their lives.

A consistent, effective structure was needed to teach social skills and to create the relational context and opportunities for reflection in which students could be launched toward responsible independence. I began teaching the components of The Responsive Classroom to provide such a structure. Teachers learned the specific social skills upon which they would concentrate: cooperation, assertion, responsibility, empathy, and self-control (CARES). They would use these five fundamental skills (Gresham & Elliott, 1990) as the touchstone of their work in the classroom. These basic social skills are the core of the social curriculum in The Responsive Classroom (cf. Elliott, 1997).

We discussed how each skill is entwined with every other skill. The teachers saw that it would be difficult to teach self-control if a student lacked empathy or to teach cooperation if a student rarely behaved assertively. And the development of responsibility, the quality the teachers were especially targeting, seemed to depend upon the other four skills of relationship.

I set about helping the teachers create the specific structures necessary for the development of the social skills. This was done not by addressing the skills separately in "values" lessons but by incorporating them into the daily routines and subject-area lessons of the classrooms and school as a whole, through modeling, practicing, and role-playing. Teachers used the six components of The Responsive Classroom as their framework, looking at how each component could fit into the specific traditions, schedules, and student/staff populations of each of their four schools. These are not new methods but rather a combining, articulation, and presentation of good practices in simple, direct language. Teachers could see the strategies modeled, think about how they would try them out with their students, make adjustments where necessary, and then pass them on to their colleagues.

Choosing a Focus: Circle of Power and Respect, Academic Choice, and Rules and Logical Consequences

The turnaround trainers from St. Charles were seeking a way to maximize the powerful learning that can occur within a social context, especially for young teenagers, for whom socializing is so compelling. They decided to focus initially on three components of The Responsive Classroom: the Circle of Power and Respect (CPR), academic choice, and rules and logical consequences.

CIRCLE OF POWER AND RESPECT. They began by discussing CPR and the role it can play during the advisory period in building strong relationships and in preparing students for the academic day. Two components of CPR seemed particularly relevant to the concerns of the teacher-trainers—the greeting and the opportunity to share. During the greeting, every member of the group is greeted, and every member greets someone else. The greeting may occur in many forms, but it always includes calling every person by name as he or she is greeted. Sharing offers a structured venue for sharing important personal events. The students have plenty of opportunities in their lives to chat with each other, but the encounter in the circle is not ordinary chatting. It takes place under the watchful eye of a caring adult who makes sure everyone is included, all comments are respectful, and each person who shares feels a sense of significance and belonging.

The turnaround trainers suspected that the students' opportunity to share what was going on in their lives would eventually become the most powerful component of CPR for their students. This would not be easy to teach, but it was clearly worth the effort. The trainers knew the sharing component would be the most challenging one, because of the sarcasm, put-downs, and one-upmanship that are so prevalent among adolescents in middle schools.

They discussed how to provide CPR during a 15-minute advisory period, as well as how to conduct it over a longer period when time might allow a more extensive conversation. They also talked about how it could be used both to calm and to enliven participants through friendly and respectful exchanges about social and academic topics within a group context. The trainers expressed excitement about bringing the model of CPR back to their teachers and their advisory periods.

ACADEMIC CHOICE. On the second day, the turn-around trainers worked on facilitating academic choice during advisory periods and in academic subjects. They discussed formal teacher structures that would encourage students to take more initiative in making decisions about their academic work, and they practiced providing constructive choices for students' 50-minute academic periods.

RULES AND LOGICAL CONSEQUENCES. On the third and last day of the workshop, the trainers addressed the sticky issue of behavior management in the middle school. They began by setting up a forum in which students would be able to express their authentic hopes for the year. Then they moved into how these hopes and dreams could be fulfilled by creating rules that would allow students and teachers to work together harmoniously during the year. This rule-making process was democratic and participatory, with the final rules being made and agreed upon by everyone. Next, the trainers worked on ways the rules could be practiced and modeled in an active way, rather than just talked about or listed. They also focused on logical consequences to be used to respond to individuals who break the rules and discussed structures for schoolwide discipline policies. Trainers from each of the four schools then met in teams to create their own behavior-management strategies and schoolwide discipline plans.

The turnaround trainers left their first Responsive Classroom workshop ready to begin implementing the Circle of Power and Respect, academic choice, and rules and logical consequences in their own classrooms. As the school year began, the challenge was to integrate the new strategies with previous practices in advisory periods, using the new CPR structure at least a couple of times per week. The turnaround trainers described their experiences enthustiastically when they met again a few months into the next school year. One teacher described her success: "I use a signal for keeping on task, and I use it consistently and for small things. I have each group generate their hopes and dreams for their library class, and the rules. I make sure we live up to those rules by not talking unless there is complete attention. Now the students can be working all over the library, and I can always pull them together again."

At the November meeting, the group prepared for a January workshop in which the turnaround trainers from each of the four schools would introduce CPR and academic choice to the rest of the staffs in their schools with the help of an activity and training notebook that they had assembled. The workshops were a success. Their colleagues felt that they had learned a great deal that would be useful to them in facilitating good advisory periods; they had fun doing it, and they bonded more, as staffs, than they had in a long time.

After implementing the circle and academic choice for about a month in their own classrooms, teachers expressed as much enthusiasm for the new methods as their teacher-trainers had previously expressed. One teacher noted, "Cliques are not sitting together now. Students developed a bond through sharing with different peers, a bond they would normally share only within their groups or cliques."

Introducing Rules and Logical Consequences to Their Schools

The teachers were beginning to see an increase in student self-control, confidence, and our most important goal—responsibility. When teachers were critical or discouraged, it was almost always because students were being disrespectful. The trainers knew it would be important to introduce the rules and logical consequences section of The Responsive Classroom. We decided that I would speak to each of the faculties as a whole, rather than leaving it up to the turnaround trainers to introduce this approach to establishing and maintaining rules in the classroom. Many teachers in the district had been using various forms of more external discipline up until then. Their techniques included checklists and "three strikes and you're out" approaches, with steps of consequences that eventually ended in suspension for the worst repeat offenders.

During the presentations of The Responsive Classroom rules and logical consequences to each of the four schools, school staffs gathered in a circle and began with a mini-CPR. Then they moved into an in-depth discussion about how to help middle school students become responsible, self-controlled, cooperative participants in a caring community. The majority of the faculties were sympathetic, but in every group there were those who were skeptical or even cynical toward The Responsive Classroom's assertion that without rewards or punishments, it would be possible to manage students who had not shown themselves to be very responsible to date.

The aftermath of the workshop was a flurry of conversation about what really works to help children become responsible adults. One of the four schools began a formal consideration of the question in a staff meeting before the end of the school year. There, they wrangled over some of the fundamental differences between behavior modification, punishments, and rewards, on the one hand, and participatory, democratic, and intrinsically motivated growth in behavior, on the other. Other staffs discussed the issues informally for the next month or so, until school ended, planning to directly address the issues during the August faculty meetings before the opening of school.

The story of this dedicated group of teachers is not a unique phenomenon. Some of the same issues come up over and over again as junior highs and middle schools try to create the kind of caring community that can support young learners during adolescence. But change is occurring. "I've changed my whole teaching style!" noted one teacher. "I'm disappointed with myself now when I lose my calm and patience. My students laughed when I enforced a consequence. I asked why, and they said, 'You don't seem mad when you give out consequences—you keep being nice, and keep on teaching!'" I think that's the wisdom we need to make our middle schools truly successful—be nice, and keep on teaching as if the future depended upon it . . . because it does.

The Change Process

The hard work of these turnaround trainers and classroom teachers is an important example of the kind of professional development effort that is required to help middle schools consider the SEL variables that will produce change in student behavior and performance in early adolescence. In the St. Charles Parish school district, all of the ingredients seem to be in place to continue to produce positive outcomes as the work continues. Let's review these ingredients.

1. The district evidenced a commitment to SEL in its philosophy that was aligned with the National Middle School Association tenets and the Carnegie Report on Middle Schools.
2. The district was simultaneously implementing The Responsive Classroom at the elementary level, building continuity of approaches to SEL.
3. Protecting professional development time was deemed essential in the district. Release days, in-service workshops, classroom coaching experiences were not compromised.
4. Homeroom schedules were designed to provide meaningful time for advisory periods at the beginning of the school day.
5. Teachers grew in their caring behavior (as described by Wentzel, 1997) in a way that was critical to student motivation and effort. They came to personally value the time and attention given to relationships in teaching and learning both socially and academically.
6. The degree to which teachers knew their students deepened as evidenced by their comments, indicating the formation of significant relationships between teachers and students as well as between students.
7. Student behavior improved as a result of The Responsive Classroom strategies, which included the provision of more responsibility in advisory periods and, for a few teachers, in regular classes. The change in behavior and motivation noted by teachers was clear evidence of more responsible action by students.

8. Finally, some teachers provided opportunities in advisory periods and regular classes for students to reflect on the changes in teacher approaches and in their attitudes toward school.

RESPONSIBILITY AND FREEDOM: RUTH CHARNEY'S STORY

At NEFC's laboratory school—the Greenfield Center School—cofounder Ruth Charney has spent the last decade immersed in the lives of hundreds of young adolescents and has had the opportunity to reflect on the strategies required to provide meaningful school experiences that build responsibility. We end this chapter with her story of possibilities.

* * * * *

For the last 10 years, I have been teaching in a mixed-age (students range in age from 12 to 15 years) seventh and eighth grade self-contained program. In our K–8 school, becoming what we call an "Upper" is an important rite of passage. When asked, the students explain that to be an Upper means more homework and freedom. By freedom, they largely mean they don't have to line up to go outside—they just go. The perceptions are mostly true. The program involves more homework, more freedom, and, therefore, more responsibilities. It is a common thrust of our program to continue to provide and teach more responsibility. Our strong contention is that it must be taught, can be taught, and is a disaster if not taught. By teaching, I mean opportunities to learn and opportunities to make mistakes with the ongoing guidance of concerned and attentive adults. I also mean a sequence of tasks appropriate to young adolescent development that takes students from where they are to where they must stretch and go to next.

I recall a time when I was in junior high and decided to make my family a celebratory dinner—by myself! I had grand illusions. My cooking repertoire at that point did not usually include *alone* or *fancy*, so I was pushing it! I gathered my ingredients, cut out my recipes (coq au vin—whatever that was), and was very cocky until I started to cook. How do you sauté? What is minced garlic? What is a double boiler? In no time, the entire family was in the kitchen cooking away with some cheer and probably relief. This, of course, became a family story oft repeated with affectionate chuckles intended to reveal my *reach* rather than my *grasp*. Responsibility requires some of both, which is the crux of the teaching dynamic.

Every year our Uppers also do some cooking. They provide all the meals necessary for three days of camp that are part of our autumn curriculum.

Divided into meal groups, they plan a menu, write out a detailed shopping list, and make sure that the list is within budget. My dinner groups tend to do spaghetti or spaghetti or spaghetti! It is simple and doable, with edible results. One year the dessert contingent went off to make their brownies only to discover that the recipe called for butter, which they hadn't put on any shopping list. Someone had the idea to substitute oil. A cup of oil added to the brownie mix produced one of the more revolting concoctions and one of the few productions that no one even tried. But the story passed on into legend, and now more care goes into making up the shopping lists. We learn with safety. In the end, meals are made, served, eaten, and cleaned up with tremendous pride of accomplishment. *Reach* and *grasp*.

It is easy to overlook some of the most basic elements of what it means to gain and manifest responsibility in adolescence. Often, we are so caught up in the day-to-day activities that we do not see the things that are working and have come to fruition. This struck me when I left our Uppers class for a number of days to help out with a younger class. One of our teachers had resigned abruptly. There would be a three-day hiatus between one teacher leaving and the next arriving. I agreed to be part of a team that would help with the transition. A teacher's leaving is a severe disruption for any class, and certainly it was for this one. Feelings of sadness, resentment, and confusion were surfacing among the students, acted out largely on one another.

The first morning was edgy and testy. It was fortunate that the teaching team knew the routines and schedule, because we had our work cut out for us in getting the students to work. After 30 minutes of a morning meeting (the primary school counterpart to the Circle of Power and Respect), I had not been able to move along to other subjects such as the math activity, language arts skills, or even sharing. I was dealing with "hands to yourself," "sit up," "no faces," and I was also redirecting inappropriate comments. Days later, when I was back in the Uppers class, we went through a poetry lesson, a Circle of Power and Respect, and a lively debate about a movie, and I suddenly realized that we had not stopped once for a disruptive act. I was impressed and moved.

I present this not as two extremes—the younger class will improve and the older students will have their off days—but as an illustration that in the developing person so much is learned, unlearned, and learned again. The Upper students were sitting in close contact (all 40 of them) and listening, working, responding, and thinking. They could demonstrate a host of social skills as well as intellectual ones. They waited turns, acknowledged different ideas, kept their bodies still and alert, and yet they were not passive. There were laughter, controversy, and conversation. From 8:15 until 9:30, when many would leave for their "crew jobs" and others would go to different classes, they were a focused and thoughtful group, taking care with themselves and others, being responsible for themselves and others.

Our eighth graders have crew jobs. They work one hour, four days a week, for the school—some in the office, some in the library, and most in the classrooms of younger students. They run reading or math groups, help with writing, teach art or drama, soccer or games. For the younger students, the Uppers provide a lap to sit on in all school gatherings and an older person to hug. Uppers are role models, helpmates, and teachers. "What do you need to be doing now?" I hear Fred saying to one of his eight-year-old charges, as he redirects her firmly but with humor back to her writing. And even when it gets "boring" or there are better options or there is an urge to slack off, the eighth graders take their jobs seriously. The crew members are punctual, reliable, and on task. There is a deserved sense of importance, of being needed and loved that comes, in part, from the drudge, the wear and tear of keeping up with the job over time. It is a rite of passage as well, the culmination of other years when these students were perhaps the ones tutored.

Grasp and reach. The doors close on the algebra class at 8:15. You have to be there. Literature assignments are given out on Tuesdays and due the following week. You have to be there; do it. Expectations are clear and emphatic. At the same time we observe and note when someone waffles or slips. We may be ready to step in or modify, to give more structure, to break down the week's assignment into smaller chunks. "Show me that you have done questions 1–3 by Thursday." Long-term assignments and independent work times involve work habits the children have been gaining for years now. Independence and responsibility are learned under the watchful eyes of the teacher. "Show me," the teacher says, "that you can complete the next problem set on your own." And they do. Seventh and eighth graders exercise skills they have learned under academic choice during work periods we call "work/choice." They practice decisions: decisions about what work to do in school on a day where there is plenty of help or about how much in-school time they want to use for their assignments or for other things like tutoring, working on a craft, or reading quietly. Some, distracted by their friends or overstepping their reach, leave too much to do at home and don't get their work done. Logical consequences the next day might include the loss of the privilege of working on a choice that day. A logical consequence might mean sitting alone to work on an assignment missed rather than working with friends at a busy table. Opportunities are provided to learn personal needs, structures, self-discipline, and responsibility.

Contradictions are common in early adolescence. Cruelty exists side by side with compassion. Generosity may be followed by a callous act. Compliments given artfully and freely follow sharp insults. And how often I note that the conceptual grasp exceeds gestures and actions. Standards held up for others are waived for oneself. The faultless logic brought to bear in one instant may easily become the illogical faultfinding of another moment. The mantra for freedom exists side by side with the less admissible cry for order, safety, and limits. The perspective is both grand and egocentric. My students admire the courage to be different even as they worry constantly about what others will think. "Social cool," one seventh grader says, "is not about wearing the right logo, but about not copying someone else's logo." So how do you conform and also be yourself? The social obstacle course is impossible, and who among us does not recall the unnerving vigilance it took to survive the pitfalls of adolescence?

Recently, the students were asked to create a vision of the classroom they wished to have. I was struck that all their visions concerned the social curriculum. They talked about acceptance, about boys and girls being friends, about the seventh–eighth grade mix, about not being afraid of criticism, about being able to be who they really were. They wrote their vision statements in their notebooks. They shared these sentiments in small groups. They compiled and posted a list of "hopes and dreams."

On Friday an angry buzz was circulating about a weekend event that included some but not all of the class. A few, who were not invited and wanted to be, were making resentful remarks and generally acting up. Days later, during a Circle of Power and Respect class meeting that started with no agenda and stony silence, it finally came up. One side was voiced: "We say that we have these visions about acceptance and then some of us are left out." Other sides were voiced: "This is about our out-of-school life. Aren't we entitled?" It was not an easy dilemma. It took some time before either side would acknowledge the other's validity. Finally, the party giver made a brave remark: "I gave the party because last year I was never ever invited." William, who was not invited, acknowledged that he would have done the same thing.

Hurt is often the impetus for change. How often, when the instigator of cliques becomes the shunned one, will there be a new level of understanding? And yet the desires to fit in, to be invited, to be in the know, will not always go well with the desires for justice.

These young adolescents were trying to wrestle with complex social realities. Some came away from this particular encounter relieved. Some came away even more upset. As the teacher, I too came away perplexed, knowing there are often no easy right answers and that fairness can sometimes be relative; perhaps it was sufficient that a hard situation could be discussed with consideration and respect, that the discussion could include certainty as well as uncertainty, and that a student could say, "I'm sorry. I acted badly."

Accountability is at the very heart of a responsible act. We want our children to accept their mistakes and their accomplishments and the rocky road that often requires both. We know, from our practice, that responsibility teaches responsibility. And we know equally well that we don't always use what we know. Too often we hoard the responsibility, or we give it up but withdraw it suddenly when evidence of failure results. Responsibility needs to be taught with the same care and appropriate tools as reading or art. *Reach* and *grasp*.

CONCLUSION

Underlying the extensive opportunity these middle school students have to experience responsibility is the foundation of powerful relationships. It is clear that the students Ruth Charney shows us are known by her and her colleagues and that they know each other well. It is also evident that together they spend significant time reflecting on their interactions, on their academic and social studies. How has this happened? At the Greenfield Center School the practices of The Responsive Classroom are consistently in place from year to year. During the first six weeks of school we devote significant attention to establishing rules with students based on their hopes and dreams. We attend to setting expectations but also to modeling and practicing them. The beginning of the year is full of relationship-building activity. Teachers work side by side with students to organize classrooms. A student editor creates a weekly page of news written by classroom reporters for the family newsletter. All school activities and yearly rituals build relationships schoolwide. The continuum of relationship → practical activity → reflection effectively contributes to the students' growing ability to make accountable use of extensive responsibility within safe limits and to grow to a place of ownership of behavior as peers, tutors of younger children, independent scholars, and cooks. The use of this responsibility continuum can be an effective teaching approach in the middle school and can have a significant impact on the SEL of early adolescents like Maura and Raffi and on their teachers.

NOTE

1. The Responsive Classroom has been the major professional development effort of the Northeast Foundation for Children for the past 10 years of its 17-year history. Begun by practicing public school teachers and administrators in 1981, NEFC now works with over 200 schools annually. In Greenfield, Massachusetts,

NEFC operates a small, independent, K–8 lab school with 180 students. The foundation also produces books, tapes, and articles through an active publishing house.

REFERENCES

Arnold, J. C. (1997). *A little child shall lead them*. Farmington, PA: Plough.

Elliott, S. N. (1997). *The responsive classroom approach: Its effectiveness and acceptability in promoting social and academic competence*. Madison, WI: University of Wisconsin.

Gilligan, C. (1982). *In a different voice*. Cambridge, MA: Harvard University Press.

Gresham, F. M., & Elliott, S. N. (1990). *The social skills rating system*. Circle Pines, MN: American Guidance Service.

Haviland, J. M., & Kahlbaugh, P. (1993). Emotion and identity. In M. Lewis & J. M. Haviland (Eds.), *Handbook of emotions*. New York: Guilford Press.

Likona, T. (1991). Moral development in the elementary school classroom. In W. M. Kurtines & J. L. Gewirtz (Eds.), *Handbook of moral behavior and development: Vol. 3. Application*. Hillsdale, NJ: Lawrence Erlbaum.

Miller, J. B. (1986). *What do we mean by relationships?* Wellesley, MA: Stone Center.

Noddings, N. (1992). *The challenge to care in schools: An alternative approach to education*. New York: Teachers College Press.

Wentzel, K. R. (1997). Student motivation in middle school: The role of perceived pedagogical caring. *Journal of Educational Psychology, 89,* 411–419.

Wood, C. (1991, Summer) Maternal teaching. *Holistic Education Review,* 3–10.

7

Social and Emotional Learning

A Psychoanalytically Informed Perspective

Steven Marans and Jonathan Cohen

Anna Freud was first a teacher and then the founder of child psychoanalysis. Freud and subsequent generations of child psychoanalysts and analytically informed clinicians and educators have always been attuned to how psychological ("emotional"), social, and biological forces interactively develop; what facilitates, blocks, or "derails" development; and what we can do to promote health, responsibility, and the capacity to learn (Freud, 1930/1974). Child psychoanalysis and progressive education are two of the original and major social movements that contributed to and shaped what is now called social and emotional learning (SEL) (see Chapter 1). Whereas early progressive educators focused on the "whole child" in the classroom and pedagogy to promote traditional academic learning and SEL, child analysts focused on the essential nature of children's social and emotional lives. Child analysts are particularly attuned to how unrecognized feelings and thoughts shape children's mental and behavioral lives and what we can do—as educators, parents, and health-care professionals—to facilitate healthy development. From the inception of child psychoanalysis, its practitioners have worked collaboratively with educators and parents to study, understand, empathize with, support, and help children over time.

Child analysts recognize that the school is an important source of structure, guidance, and containment through most of the course of a child's development. The structure exists in a variety of forms, ranging from the physical plant, to schedules and routines, to clearly delineated rules and expectations. Typically, there are a high level of adult supervision and a range of consequences—rewarding and punitive—that can be used to encourage good behavior and discourage or constrain misbehavior. For example, a child can expect ongoing encouragement, praise for prosocial and academically successful behavior, and occasional awards, honors, or other recognition. For poor performance or misbehavior the child may face the teacher's disapproval, the threat of poor scores and academic failure, or more restrictive sanctions such as time out, detention, restitution, suspension, and expulsion.

School ideally and potentially offers a variety of healthy, phase-specific avenues for impulse expression and gratification of impulses. Consistent with their primary mission, schools promote learning, self-challenge, and the satisfaction of acquired competencies through academics. Extracurricular activities such as sports, art, music, theater, journalism, debating, creative writing, and similar endeavors supplement strictly academic avenues for sublimation of the sexual and aggressive urges that are part of normal development. In addition to providing opportunities for personal gratification, reward, and community recognition, each of these activities also provides a much needed forum for the development of group affiliations and shared prosocial values. These competencies are in turn supported by the structure imposed through adult supervision, teaching, and personal engagement and through the rules, demands, and schedules of daily school life. Sadly, such opportunities have all but disappeared in many or most of our urban schools (Erikson, 1959).

A PSYCHOANALYTICALLY INFORMED PERSPECTIVE ABOUT SEL

As discussed in Chapter 1, there is a range of SEL programs and perspectives. Some are very detailed, prescriptive, curriculum-based programs that can be used to teach a class, just as we teach English or history (see Chapter 3). Some present a sequential program that is aimed at a particular problem, such as violence prevention (see Chapter 8). Some SEL programs present a point of view about social and emotional development accompanied by a set of activities that educators can integrate into whatever academic or nonacademic school activity they are involved with (see Chapter 6). And some present a perspective about development and social and emotional functioning that can inform all that we do in school.

Most importantly, a psychoanalytically informed perspective about SEL represents a framework that educators may utilize to further understand and to generate questions about how we can teach and learn with children as well as with colleagues. In addition, there are some SEL programs that emerge from a psychoanalytically informed perspective. Many of these focus on the formative years when the foundation for social and emotional functioning is established. Some analytically informed SEL programs focus on how we enhance social and emotional competencies for all children (Shure, 1994; Spivack, Plat, & Shure, 1976); others focus on particular groups of at risk students (Kusche, Garfield, & Greenberg, 1983; Kusche & Greenberg, 1994) and/or on particular problems (Twemlow & Sacco, 1996; Twemlow, Sacco, Geis, Hess, & Osbourn 1996). In this chapter, we will consider an analytically informed perspective about children's lives over time and how it may enhance our capacity to empathize and work with students and colleagues.

Psychoanalytic theories of child development and observations of children focus on how the interplay of emotion, thoughts, modes of communication, physical activity, and play is reflected in moment-to-moment and day-to-day functioning. One of the hallmarks of a psychoanalytically informed perspective is attunement to how *unrecognized* thoughts and feelings color and potentially shape behavior and development. We are all vulnerable to being influenced by feelings and thoughts that we do not fully recognize in the moment—unrecognized or "unconscious" (literally unknown) thoughts and feelings. An analytically informed perspective about SEL suggests that unrecognized experience (memories, thoughts, feelings, sensations, wishes, defenses, and expectations) will affect our interests, motivation, and capacity to learn.

A psychoanalytic perspective on child development is also always invested in integratively and collaboratively learning about the following seven dimensions: (1) the status of the child's biological equipment and intellectual endowment and how these may shape developmental experience; (2) areas of the child's strengths and preferred modes of adaptation; (3) specific developmental tasks that the child is now experiencing and the various ways in which they have been and are currently negotiated; (4) areas of vulnerability and implications for progressive development; (5) the impact of various life events on the course of development; (6) the nature and status of unconscious conflict; and (7) the defensive activities associated with the child's attempts at conflict resolution. In the following discussion about thinking developmentally and about SEL programs for all children, for at risk students, and for faculty, we will show how considering these dimensions raises useful questions and ideas.

ACROSS DEVELOPMENTAL PERSPECTIVES

Effective teaching rests on our capacity to empathize with the student. And, it is well known that we need to understand where the child is "living" developmentally to empathically understand the child's experience. A psychoanalytically informed perspective about development always includes an appreciation of how past conscious and unrecognized experiences color and shape current experience as well as how future developmental challenges "bump up against" the present. As children's lives develop over time, it is always useful to ask the following questions: How has the past affected the present? What meanings is the child (family and peers) attributing to these changes? and How are upcoming developmental challenges shaping present experience? Throughout the child's development into adolescence, the world of challenges, expectations, experimentation, affiliations, and achievements grows. The influence of family relationships is never completely left behind. However, with the introduction of school and the broader community of the neighborhood, the child's sphere of important relationships expands beyond the family to include teachers, peers, and other admired figures. These new relationships and settings bring with them additional sources of structure, expectations, achievements, satisfactions, and disappointments.

Through the course of development—cognitive advances and bodily changes, increased academic and extracurricular challenges, and the expanded capacity for introspection and self-awareness—children experience continual pressure to reevaluate the self and their identity, adequacy, and competence. Accordingly, there is a push to fend off, counter, or react against feelings of inadequacy. These efforts may include aspirations and achievements in the classroom, on the playing field, or in the hierarchy of the peer group. Pride in one's body and abilities may be complemented by or, where other achievements are limited or unobtainable, supplemented by external or superficial embellishments to the self (Laufer, 1985). By adolescence and often much earlier, this latter characteristic is evident in the markedly increased attention to physical attributes (e.g., hair, complexion, and figure or build) and material accompaniments (e.g., clothing, cars, trucks, and jewelry) or the assertion of one's identity via the rejection of family and socially sanctioned values. With increased opportunities for social comparison and competition there is an equally powerful threat of failure—an ever-present danger of feeling small, inadequate, awkward, incompetent, or different.

On another level, there exist a newly awakened arousal and excitation associated with sexual maturation. The adolescent is confronted with sexually provocative relationships and fantasies in the media and with numerous real-life opportunities for seduction or for frustration with the lack thereof (Freud, 1958). Finally, for both adolescent males and females, there is the experience of excitement associated with power, control, and intimidation as a means to ascend the pecking order of social groups and, for some, the aggression-based hierarchy of organized gangs.

The Internal and the External Worlds

Although many children succeed in negotiating both internal and external demands, using the order, stimulation, and opportunities provided by families, schools, and the community, too many children fail in their endeavors. In many instances, the reasons are neither simple nor readily perceived. For some, academic failure may be a function of modest intelligence or of a specific linguistic, attentional, and/or nonverbal disability that, without appropriate instructional supports, may lead to inordinate frustration and a variety of outcomes including anger, depression, self-criticism, hostility, apathy, indifference, defiance, or a full-press rebellion. In other cases, a child may consistently fail to meet deadlines or complete assignments, do work hastily or haphazardly, or come to class late or not at all, revealing limited intrinsic motivation, ambition, self-discipline, or pleasure in mastery; a competing need for immediate gratification; and/or limited encouragement, structure, or guidance from the family and broader social milieu. Alternative gratifications may come from intimidating others, involvement in the drug trade, exploitation, violence, vandalism, or other antisocial behavior. These outcomes are not simply school-bound failures but rather reflect a complex interaction between social, cognitive, emotional, constitutional, biological, and familial factors. Therefore, it is often invaluable for parents, educators, and mental health professionals to assess the whole child in order to engage in coordinated planning.

Life is fundamentally relational. We need others to survive. How children become connected with others provides the foundation for so much in life. An overlapping and equally critical dimension of life is how children feel about themselves and others—their conscious and unrecognized narratives or images of self and others. Outside of the family, teachers often represent the most important connection a child has with an adult. However, the ways in which the child relates to the teacher will be determined, in large part, by the child's past and current relationships. Therefore, although the teacher may have much to offer in the form of a new relationship, he or she is often confronted with behavior and learning styles that reflect well-established patterns of relating and a set of responses to inner turmoil.

The first step toward developing interventions is to recognize and understand the various pathways for children's developmental difficulties and the specific areas of functioning that may be impaired along the way. There is often a complex interplay of factors that can lead to poor concentration and inattentiveness in class; underachievement and academic failure; provocative, clowning, and/or oppositional behavior that can result in isolation from the peer group; learning difficulties; low self-confidence; the decision to drop out of school; and criminal behavior.

Maura and Raffi

How did Maura's and Raffi's past experience with teachers, peers, and family members and with their own strengths and weaknesses affect their current experience as middle school children? Maura and Raffi, like all children, are encountering the preadolescent/early adolescent developmental challenges that Solodow (Chapter 2) details.

Maura clearly feels able and good about herself in many ways. Yet, curiously and importantly she also "carries" the narrative that she is "dumb." Maura seems to feel that this narrative is too dangerous to be heeded. What are the conscious and unconscious meanings that she ascribes to "dumb"? Is Maura signaling something that she feels anxious and/or guilty about? Is she trying to tell herself and others about a conflict—something that she desperately wants or needs but is simultaneously afraid to reveal directly? When she calls herself "dumb" she is in a way "shutting down" or putting a lid on learning. Is this one of the ways that Maura protects (or defends) herself?

We do not know the answers to these questions. However, it is clear that Maura needs an opportunity to discover more about herself. Discovering what feels dangerous to her and what "dumb" means may allow her to meet preadolescent and adolescent developmental challenges in productive and healthy ways. Otherwise, she is in danger of continuing to avoid, to run away from, herself. We predict that Maura's developmental potential and capacity to learn will be inhibited and undermined by her continued feelings that she is not intelligent (and related narratives) and by her avoidant behavior.

Raffi clearly feels the universal human desire to connect with others. However, when he has difficulties and/or becomes concerned about not getting what he wants, he often complains about physical aches and pains and/or teases and taunts others. This is a problem. Not only do these attempts at problem solving fail, but also they alienate others and cause new problems! Raffi now shows relatively serious social and emotional problems, and he is at risk for developing even more severe difficulties. What can we do to help? What are the underlying medical, psychological, social, economic, and/or societal problems that shape Raffi's current difficulties? Will a curriculum-based SEL program help Raffi in substantive ways? Would it be helpful for Raffi to develop an ongoing relationship with a "big brother" or a member of the clergy? Does he and/or his family need additional help from mental health professionals?

Psychoanalytic-Educational Collaborations

From the beginning of child analysis to the present, practitioners have worked with educators to understand and promote the social and emotional development of children (Biber, 1961; Edgcumbe, 1975; Furman, 1987; Freud, 1963; Twemlow et al., 1996). Often what this means on a practical level is simply talking together about what we know (and don't know!) as parents, educators, and mental health professionals. These discussions often reveal that we know much more than we thought we did as they clarify the patterns of a child's strengths and weaknesses. Ideally, this creative problem-solving process results in concrete plans that involve the child as an active participant.

For their part, many child analysts have invested in collaborative approaches to applying what has been learned in the clinical situation to settings outside of the therapeutic consulting room: in pediatric wards, institutional care facilities, the courts, child welfare agencies, and work with police officers. Although child analysis focuses on the inner, emotional life of the child, there has also been a long tradition within the field of examining the relationship between the inner lives of children and the social and academic worlds in which they develop (Cohen, 1997; Marans et al., 1995).

Changes in policies and practices that truly advance the best interests of children—whether in pediatric wards, institutional care, foster placements, or custody disputes—occur only when child psychoanalysts and their nonanalytic colleagues engage each other in the process of exploring their different vantage points. It is in this context that psychoanalytic principles of development have been integrated and applied to the observations and experiences of other professionals involved with children. When a common language is developed to express the observations, concerns, and approaches of separate professionals, our attempts to understand and respond to the children at greatest risk for limited potentials and/or developmental psychopathology can be expanded and explored.

PROMOTING SOCIAL AND EMOTIONAL COMPETENCIES

Our capacity to be effective educators and school specialists is based on understanding who our students are developmentally, academically, psychologically, and socially. The more we connect with our students, the more effective we are as educators in general and at promoting social and emotional competencies in particular. Thinking psychoanalytically raises many questions that may further our capacity to empathize and connect with students. Here are a few examples: (1) What is a particular student feeling worried or unhappy about? (2) When students become anxious, are they handling a difficulty in a manner that provides opportunities for learning, or are they protecting themselves in ways that inadvertently insure that they will not be able to solve the problem (like Raffi)? (3) How are students consciously and unconsciously feeling about themselves, and is there a discrepancy between what they say and their behavior? (4) What feelings and thoughts might a student be having that he or she does not recognize or understand?

In this volume, a range of programs and perspectives is presented to aid our capacity to promote social and emotional competencies within our students. A psychoanalytically informed perspective can be usefully integrated into any and all of these. An analytically informed perspective reminds us to ask, What are we *not* seeing now: what is unrecognized? An analytically and developmentally informed perspective suggests that we all experience weaknesses and worries—students and teachers alike— and the important questions are, What is our worry (or weakness) now? How mild or severe is it? How are we (helpfully or not) managing (defending) this? and How is it affecting our capacity to learn, relate, and develop?

These are complex questions that do not yield simple answers. Educators who are invested in promoting social and emotional competencies know that even when we use helpful, research-validated SEL curricula this is just one part of the teaching and learning process. Ultimately, we want and need to connect with individual students and classrooms of students. The analytically informed dimensions that we have begun to delineate here can further our ability to understand not only our students but also our colleagues and ourselves.

WORK WITH AT RISK CHILDREN

For many of our nation's children development occurs in environments that can neither provide consistent structure nor the basic sense of safety that is so crucial to mastery and achievement. As a result, from early in these children's lives, their experiences impede the buildup of the internal psychological structures that are necessary for achieving an increasing sense of autonomy, competence, and pride in academic, social, and personal endeavors. When children are deprived of the optimal intrafamilial sources of support, extrafamilial institutions may offer the last opportunity to introduce structure.

However, the service providers in these institutions—educators, mental health professionals, medical providers, protective service workers, and law enforcement officers—tend to operate in isolation in their attempts to address the multiple needs of these children and families caught in the cycle of adversity, violence, and despair. As a result—like the individual, the family, and the broader community—they too may find themselves overwhelmed and immobilized. Alternatively, if these desperate service providers are able to share areas of expertise and a detailed understanding of children's developmental needs and capacities, they will be in a stronger position to devise effective strategies.

As described in Chapter 1, many children in our classrooms are at risk for becoming "stuck" academically, socially, and/or emotionally. In fact, many if not most classrooms today include students who are stuck. There are many SEL programs designed specifically for at risk children. For example, much of the violence-prevention and conflict-resolutions work was initially directed at inner-city youth, many of whom grew up in single-parent homes or in families and/or neighborhoods marred by violence. These programs have made a difference for some children (Aber, Jones, Brown, Chaudry, & Samples, 1998).

From the psychoanalytically informed perspective there are a number of programmatic and curriculum-based SEL efforts that have been applied to work with learning disabled children (Shure, 1994; Spivack et al., 1976); with deaf children (Kusche et al., 1983; Kusche & Greenberg, 1994); and with bullies and "school yard" victims (Twemlow & Sacco, 1996; Twemlow et al., 1996). Psychoanalytic thinking has also centrally shaped the Zero to Three/National Center for Clinical Infant Programs and a variety of extraordinarily important primary and secondary prevention efforts with infants and their parents.

There are many factors that contribute to a child being at risk and/or developmentally derailed (see Chapter 1). A psychoanalytically informed perspective does not result in any simple prescriptions. In addition to the principles described previously, an psychoeducational-analytic attitude includes two overlapping ideas: an appreciative attitude and an integrative perspective. An appreciative attitude refers to the belief that all individuals do the best they can. We all have problems and conflicts. An appreciative attitude advances communication and the establishment of healthy, responsive, and respectful relationships in and outside of the classroom. If we empathically understand why children do what they do, it is much easier to adopt this kind of appreciative attitude.

It is relatively easy to tell ourselves to be empathic and appreciative but not always so simple to practice. Sometimes (if not often), this is due to not understanding another person's experience. Sometimes a student's behavior "pushes a button" within us. For example, many learning disabled children sometimes act in "lazy," avoidant, and/or oppositional ways. There are certainly many factors that contribute to this kind of behavior. To the extent that we do not understand what is driving this behavior, we will naturally feel impatient, if not irked. We have discovered that this kind of "lazy" behavior is sometimes importantly related to the intermittent nature of mild to moderately severe learning disabilities. Severe disabilities tend to be chronic in nature: they occur all the time or virtually all the time (e.g., blindness). However, mild to moderately severe learning disabilities appear intermittently. For example, sometimes a child can sound out or spell a word correctly and sometimes not. As a result, the child (and grownups too!) cannot predict when the disability will complicate learning and performance.

Naturally, this gives rise to a sense of helplessness in the face of anticipated—but unpredictable—difficulty (Cohen, 1987). We all fear helplessness. Avoidant behavior is one common means that many children (learning disabled and "able" alike) use to protect themselves from something feared. A psychoanalytically informed perspective also always asks, What does this behavior (e.g., avoidance) mean? Why now? What conscious and unrecognized meanings is the child attributing to this experience? and What am I feeling (e.g., irritation), and what can I learn from these reactions that will aid my empathic and educative efforts? These are powerful, appreciative questions that can help teachers and students build a platform for communication and connection. Without this platform, there can be little substantive learning and teaching.

A psychoanalytically informed perspective is integrative. How can we begin to understand how the students' strengths, weaknesses, wishes, and characteristic ways of coping or defending themselves relate to how they are learning and developing? These are usually substantive questions for teachers and learners to wonder about. We suggest that they are essential questions when we work with at risk students. There is usually not one single source of a child's difficulties: economic, societal, psychological, social, or biological. Integratively understanding the nature of the child's problems helps us to empathize and genuinely appreciate that the child is doing the best he or she can.

Many educators know that these empathic and appreciative qualities provide the foundation for effective, nurturing relations with children. Since the inception of progressive education almost a hundred years ago, there has been a growing appreciation and acceptance that we need to understand the whole child. What this has meant and to what extent it is practiced (as opposed to existing as an ideal) has varied greatly. Child psychoanalytically informed work has sought to further educators', mental health professionals', parents', and children's senses of how various facets of the inner and outer worlds interact. There is never a simple program or prescription for discovering the array of developmental, social, economic, psychological, and biological factors that results in who a given child is now.

SOCIAL AND EMOTIONAL LEARNING FOR EDUCATORS

Social and emotional learning for educators seeks to enhance self-reflective capacities in ways that promote our ability to empathize and effectively teach. We believe that SEL learning in schools can and needs to focus on educators and school specialists as well as on "regular" and "special" education students.

To enhance our capacity to become more helpfully self-reflective, it is useful to think about a series of specific questions that will shed light on how and why we teach and learn. What helps us to learn? What gets in the way of our being effective and creative learners? How do we learn to know what we need to know about ourselves as teachers/learners? How do we form the inner monologue that allows us to have a productive running educational-social-emotional discourse with ourselves? These questions may lead to our discovering more about what it means for us to be learners.

And then, how does our learning process compare and contrast with those of our students? In other words, which of our students are similar to and/or different from us in the ways that they learn? What helps us to teach? Why? What gets in the way of being an effective and empathic educator? What helps us to work collaboratively? Why do we teach the way we do, and how is this related to our past mentors and models? What helps us to use (integrate) what we are learning? These are complex questions with few simple answers. Over the past decades, many educators have discovered that SEL about these and related topics powerfully enhances our capacity to more effectively empathize, teach, and learn.

A psychoanalytically informed perspective about educators' lives over time adds several important dimensions to the questions described previously: To what extent do we feel that unrecognized thoughts and feelings color our experiences and the answers to these kinds of questions? How can we engage in a process of discovery (within ourselves, colleagues, and/or others) that will further helpful self-reflection? We all normally become more or less anxious during the course of our work. What makes us anxious? How do we manage our anxiety or defend against it? To what extent do these modes of managing our anxiety help and/or hinder our capacity to empathize, teach, and learn? How has our past experience (e.g., as students) affected our current experience (e.g., as educators)? For example, when a child like Raffi is obnoxious with peers and/or teachers when does this "get to us" and how do we manage this? All of us have particular kinds of situations and students that we particularly enjoy and others that we dislike (if not hate). Our learning about these kinds of moments represents one type of SEL that can support us and enhance our ability to teach and learn.

Ongoing SEL for educators is as important as SEL for our students. In fact, SEL for educators provides the foundation for all that we do to further the social, emotional, and academic capacities of our students. Being a reflective educator is an important part of the progressive educational tradition. Dewey, Montessori, and Anna Freud (when she was a teacher) all in their own ways underscored this notion. In recent years, there has been a resurgence of interest in how we can and need to promote educators' capacity to be reflective and involved with "teacher-centered" learning (see Chapter 9).

To engage in this form of learning, we need to feel safe. This is true for both adults and children in general and with regard to substantive SEL in particular. Often there is little time in our daily schedules to take a step back and reflect upon the internal and interpersonal pressures that may subtly or dramatically color our experience as a teacher or school specialist. As difficult as it is to find the time and place to engage in this form of learning, we believe that it essentially supports our continued SEL as well as our students'. It is a challenge—for teachers and administrators—to find the times and places to support SEL for educators.

CONCLUSIONS

Social and emotional learning programs today range from a point of view about children and social and emotional competencies to very detailed, prescriptive, curriculum-based programmatic efforts. And there are many programs that include a point of view about children with an accompanying menu of activities that educators may integrate into whatever they are doing. The psychoanalytically informed perspective about SEL that we describe here provides a framework for understanding children's lives over time. There is a great need for programs that can be studied and, if useful, replicated across many sites. However, all educational efforts (be they programmatic curriculum-based programs or not) rest on the teacher-student(s) relationship. Our ability and/or inability to understand where the child is "living" and to empathize with and recognize the student's experience and our own determines how successful any programmatic effort can and will be.

Psychoanalytically informed thinking can enhance our own capacity to recognize where children, the group, and we are "living" psychologically and socially. This process of discovery is often furthered when we have an opportunity to collaboratively discuss our work with analytically informed educators and school-based mental health professionals (Manning, Rubin, Gunther, Gonzales, & Schindler, 1996). A psychoanalytic perspective invites us to ask complex questions about what is clear as well as what is unrecognized, about how the past as well as upcoming developmental challenges may be coloring the present, and about how students' and educators' ways of managing internal and interpersonal experience shape our capacity to learn and teach.

REFERENCES

Aber, L. J., Jones, S. M., Brown, J. L., Chaudry, N., & Samples, F. (1998). *Resolving conflict creatively: Evaluating the developmental effects of a school-based violence prevention program in neighborhood and classroom context*. Manuscript submitted for publication.

Biber, B. (1961). Integration of mental health principles in the school setting. *Prevention of mental disorders in children* (pp. 323–352). New York: Basic Books.

Cohen, J. (1987). Learning disabilities and psychological development in childhood and adolescence. *Annals of Dyslexia, 36,* 287–300.

Cohen, J. (1997). Child and adolescent psychoanalysis: Research, practice and theory. *International Journal of Psychoanalysis, 78*(3), 499–520.

Edgcumbe, R. (1975). The border between therapy and education. *Psychoanalytic study of the child* (No. 5). New Haven, CT: Yale University Press.

Erikson, E. (1959). *Identity and the life cycle.* New York: International University Press.

Freud, A. (1974). 1922—1935 Lectures on psychoanalysis for teachers and parents. In *The writings of Anna Freud* (Vol. 1, pp. 73–136). New York: International University Press. (Original work published 1930)

Freud, A. (1958). Adolescence. *Psychoanalytic Study of the Child, 13,* 255–278.

Freud, A. (1963). The concept of developmental lines. *Psychoanalytic Study of the Child, 19,* 245–265.

Furman, E. (1987). *The teacher's guide to helping young children grow: The teacher's manual.* Madison, CT: International University Press.

Kusche, C. A., Garfield, T. S., & Greenberg, M. T. (1983). The understanding of emotional and social attribution in deaf adolescents. *Journal of Clinical Child Psychology, 12,* 153–160.

Kusche, C. A., & Greenberg, M. T. (1994). *The PATHS Curriculum.* Seattle, WA: Developmental Research and Programs.

Laufer, M. (1985). Adolescence and psychosis. *International Journal of Psychoanalysis, 67,* 627–639.

Manning, D., Rubin, S. E., Gunther, P., Gonzales, R. G., & Schindler, P. (1996, July). A "worry doctor" for preschool directors and teachers: A collaborative model. *Young Children,* 68–73.

Marans, S., Adnopoz, J., Berkman, M., Esserman, D., MacDonald, D., Nagler, S., Randall, R., Schaefer, M., & Wearing, M. (1995). *The police–mental health partnership.* New Haven, CT: Yale University Press.

Shure, M. (1994). *I can problem solve (ICPS): An interpersonal cognitive problem-solving program for children.* Champaign, IL: Research Press.

Spivack, G., Platt, J. J., Jr., & Shure, M. (1976). *The problem solving approach to adjustment.* San Francisco: Jossey-Bass.

Twemlow, S. W., & Sacco, F. C. (1996). Peacekeeping and peacemaking: The conceptual foundations of a plan to reduce violence and improve the quality of life in a midsized community in Jamaica. *Psychiatry, 59,* 156–174.

Twemlow, S. W., Sacco, F. C., Geis, M. L., Hess, D., & Osbourn, J. (1996). *Creating a peaceful school learning environment: Findings from a controlled study of an elementary school prevention focused, antiviolence intervention.* Paper presented at a seminar entitled Adolescent Violence, the Menninger Clinic, December 13–14. Manuscript submitted for publication.

8

Waging Peace in Our Schools

Social and Emotional Learning through Conflict Resolution

Janet Patti and Linda Lantieri

Today we face one of the greatest challenges educators and other concerned adults will ever have to grapple with—how to reclaim our schools as caring, peaceable communities of learning. For many years, educators have realized the need to comprehensively address the social, emotional, and ethical development of young people along with the teaching of academic skills and content. Efforts to educate the heart along with the mind in the school context have come under a variety of banners such as affective education, cooperative learning, character education, and child-centered learning. Yet now, more than ever, schools need to adapt a broadly conceived and well-coordinated strategy to cultivate early adolescents' social, emotional, and ethical development.

To participate as contributing citizens in today's and tomorrow's world, young people need to learn about the diversity of its people and cultures; they need to develop their thinking about how to approach conflict, handle emotions, and solve problems. Across our nation, teachers, school officials, and parents are looking to schools to provide students with the skills and competencies that will protect them from becoming victims or perpetrators of violence. Young people need guidance and skills that can prevent them from making potentially harmful decisions that could hurt themselves and others. Schools are seeking out programs that will help middle school youth develop social and emotional skills that will foster resiliency and promote the development of caring, socially responsible young adults.

THE RESOLVING CONFLICT CREATIVELY PROGRAM

This chapter examines the work of the Resolving Conflict Creatively Program (RCCP), one of the largest and longest running models of social and emotional learning (SEL) in the United States. It demonstrates strategies for incorporating a comprehensive and systematic approach for integrating SEL through the lens of conflict resolution and intergroup relations into the daily life of middle school classrooms and schools across the United States.

Vision and Goals

RCCP began in 1985 as a joint initiative of Educators for Social Responsibility Metropolitan Area (ESR Metro) and the New York City Board of Education. The program started in three schools in Brooklyn, New York, expanded to many more schools within New York City by 1988, and still continues in New York under the auspices of the New York City Board of Education and ESR Metro. The RCCP National Center, an initiative of the national office of ESR, serves to disseminate the program throughout the country, operating in over 350 schools nationwide in 10 school districts in eight states. Daniel Goleman, author of *Emotional Intelligence* (1995), lauded RCCP, saying, "The Resolving Conflict Creatively Program is a model of emotional intelligence, a sane prescription for what ails our children, our schools, and our communities" (Lantieri & Patti, 1996).

When Tom Roderick, executive director of ESR Metro, and Linda Lantieri began the program in New York City schools some 13 years ago, their vision was guided by a shared commitment to educating children in the ways of peace. Ghandi's words "If we are to reach real peace in this world and if we are to carry on a real war against war, we shall have to begin with the children" were very real to them. They asked the following questions: What would help young people handle their emotions better and think differently about conflict and diversity? How could we best assure that young people would learn fundamental social and emotional skills along with their academic skills?

While the national global perspectives surrounding peace were paramount, Roderick and Lantieri agreed that to attain peace in the world it would be essential to address young people's SEL by teaching conflict resolution and intergroup relation skills at the interpersonal level. And so, the work of RCCP is rooted in teaching concepts and skills that build classrooms and school communities that model democratic principles. The young adults in these schools recognize the role they play in becoming socially responsible citizens of a pluralistic, participatory society.

RCCP's primary strategy is designed to reach young people through the adults who relate to them on a daily basis at home, in school, and in their communities. The goal is to foster young people's social and emotional development by focusing on emotional literacy, conflict-resolution skills, and intercultural understanding.

Vital to RCCP's mission is a vision of schools themselves as communities. One of its central goals is to transform the culture of participating schools. Through understanding, empathy, and respect for one another, a cooperative school spirit can be established.

Model of Implementation

RCCP's "peaceable schools" model reflects the experiences and practices developed by educators in schools and communities over many years. The essential components for effective implementation follow.

CURRICULUM COMPONENT. The K–12 classroom curriculum needs to focus on key skills: active listening, assertiveness (as opposed to aggressiveness or passivity), the expression of feeling in appropriate ways, empathy and perspective-taking, cooperation, negotiation, the appreciation of diversity, and methods for countering bias. RCCP lessons involve role-playing, interviewing, group discussion, brainstorming, "teachable moments," and other experiential and affective learning strategies.

PROFESSIONAL TRAINING. Professional training and ongoing support for teachers provides 24 hours of introductory training on the RCCP curriculum as well as training in communication, conflict resolution, and "infusion" strategies for integrating these concepts and skills into social studies, language arts, and other academic subjects. Each teacher is assigned a staff developer who visits the school between 6 and 10 times during the year to help with preparation, observe classes, give demonstration lessons, discuss concerns, and otherwise help sustain that teacher's efforts in the classroom.

PEER MEDIATION. A student-led mediation program provides a strong peer model for nonviolence and the appreciation of diversity and reinforces students' emerging skills in working out their own problems. While peer mediation makes a large contribution to a more peaceful school climate, it is not a substitute for an effective disciplinary policy; if strictly enforced sanctions against fighting are not in place, students are unlikely to turn to mediators for help.

PARENT TRAINING. Parent training enables RCCP to reach beyond the school yard, to increase family support for children's efforts, and to give parents the opportunity to learn more about intergroup relations, family communication, and conflict resolution. RCCP offers a series of four 3-hour workshops called Peace in the Family. At the workshops, parents can think about how they act as parents—what works and what they would like to do differently. RCCP provides concrete skills in various aspects of communication such as active listening for receiving messages and I-messages, for asserting one's feelings and needs in a nonjudgmental, nonattacking manner.

ADMINISTRATOR TRAINING. Administrator training introduces RCCP concepts and shows school administrators how they can use their leadership to encourage everyone within the school community to embrace and model humane, democratic, and creative approaches to dealing with conflict and diversity.

The RCCP model has been successfully implemented in urban, suburban, and rural communities across the United States. Each school district has adapted the model according to its own personal characteristics and needs.

THE MIDDLE SCHOOL CURRICULUM: TECHNIQUES AND PRACTICAL STRATEGIES FOR TEACHING SEL

The middle school years provide the perfect opportunity to address the psychosocial needs of students and to offer them skill building to help them cope with the internal and external conflicts they face. At a time when many middle school youngsters ruminate about themselves, their negative self-perceptions often convince them that they are not smart, not liked, or not attractive. A responsive classroom curriculum provides these young people with opportunities to express and explore their concerns. In this way, more students, like Maura, can develop the social and emotional strength that allows them to hear how certain behaviors alienate them from others and to strive to change these behaviors. The daily life of the classroom becomes a safe community in which adolescent issues can be shared among peers and in which students can be guided by a caring adult.

RCCP classrooms incorporate six themes into the curriculum: cooperation, caring communication, expression of feelings, appreciation of diversity, responsible decision making, and conflict resolution. Classroom teachers teach direct skill-based lessons in each of these areas. They also design lessons that infuse the newly acquired skills and strategies into their academic teachings. "The goal of the classroom teacher is to establish a 'peaceable' classroom, one in which these themes are apparent. Peace is regarded as a dynamic process that everyone works toward and believes in" (Kreidler, 1994).

COOPERATION. One of the first skills developed is cooperation. At the beginning of the year, language arts teachers might have students complete group stories. Math teachers might ask students to design and solve word problems together. Through a variety of cooperative activities, middle school youngsters learn to value cooperation and working with their peers. When teachers foster this learning, young people learn how to work together on tasks as well as how to reflect upon and modify their own behaviors. The key is encouraging the students to evaluate their own behaviors as well as those of the group. Teachers make the commitment to stress the importance of social skills while teaching academic tasks.

CARING COMMUNICATION. Like cooperation skills, the theme of caring communication is also developed. Real discussion and dialogue depend on honest, open communication. Middle school students learn to speak their feelings and actively listen to others. Through role plays and simulations, students experience the different effects that good and poor listening have on the speaker's willingness to openly and nondefensively communicate. They learn how to paraphrase and reflect the speaker's words, to ask clarifying questions, and to summarize at the end of conversations to assure that the parties clearly understand each other.

EXPRESSION OF FEELINGS. We encourage students to express their positive and negative feelings. Put-downs such as "you're ugly," "you're dumb," and other painful comments are common at this age, but they don't have to be. Through role plays and group exercises, the students learn that these negative, hurtful words are unacceptable. The newly acquired I-message becomes a powerful tool for the students: for instance, I feel *angry* when you *call me a name* because *it hurts my feelings*. Young adolescents don't always use the formalized sentence patterns. Instead, they adapt their own versions of I-messages and use their words creatively to respond to hurtful criticisms.

Role plays and group simulations help young people identify their feelings and practice expressing them. Journal writing also provides a positive vehicle for expressing and identifying emotions. Students share their writing with a trusted peer for a few minutes. This special time in which someone lends them a listening ear can free them to focus on the lessons of the day.

The better middle school students become at expressing their feelings, the easier it is for them to voice their hurt, disappointment, or anger toward another in a constructive and nonviolent manner. They learn that anger is a normal, healthy feeling that needs to be conveyed in productive ways. Young people need help to explore the reasons behind their anger, to release their anxieties, and to express their self-doubts. If anger is suppressed, it only erupts at a later time. Many early adolescents, similar to Raffi in his earlier years, keep these fears and doubts inside. Anger without a vehicle of expression can result in self-destructive behaviors such as drug and alcohol abuse, or it can extend its reach to others in some form of violence.

APPRECIATION OF DIVERSITY. Middle school youth are overly concerned about appearance and being accepted by their peers. They struggle to find their own identity in a media-concentrated culture that promotes images of sexual prowess and physical beauty as the norm. Exploring the theme of appreciating differences, so essential to a generation who are inheriting a pluralistic, interdependent world, helps them to honor our human differences not limited to race, ethnicity, gender, intelligence, appearance, abilities, and religious beliefs. Teachers help young people recognize and appreciate diversity and different perspectives.

Every facet of the peaceable classroom guides students to discover their own cultural frames of reference and those of their peers. Differences are honored and spoken about. Discussions about prejudice and discrimination aren't taboo. Young people explore their own stereotypes and unlearn the misinformation they have acquired about groups who differ from them. They learn to see past their own tinted lenses and to suspend judgment about others.

Sixth, seventh, and eighth graders learn how to identify, intervene in, and interrupt prejudice. Understanding the impact of discrimination on individuals and groups is a crucial component of the curriculum that is in need of exploration. Middle school youth look beyond their school and community and analyze how society creates social biases, how discrimination becomes institutionalized, and how certain groups have more privileges than others. Classroom and schoolwide policies reflect these new learnings.

RESPONSIBLE DECISION MAKING. Making responsible decisions is a hard task for us and even harder for the young adolescent who feels torn in a million directions. Learning how to make decisions in conflict situations is even more difficult. Middle school teachers in peaceable classrooms take the time to assist students to chisel away at the old destructive patterns they often use to make decisions and to empower them with new tools to make informed, responsible choices. Although there are many decision-making models available, here is one we teach middle school students.

- Tell what the problem is.
- Find as many different solutions as possible.
- Decide which solutions are "good."
- Choose one solution and act.

CONFLICT RESOLUTION. In the middle school curriculum, students explore the negative and positive consequences of different ways of handling conflict: aggression, collaboration, compromise, giving in, avoiding, delaying, appealing to authority. Young people become involved in decision-making processes through regularly scheduled class meetings in which they problem solve about class issues. In class meetings, they have a chance to use all the skills they have previously learned to say what they feel in nonattacking ways, to listen actively, and to be open to different points of view. Teachers and students together establish certain ground rules for the group, including not using put-downs and listening to each other without interrupting. Central to this practice is that young people learn that they can resolve problems themselves. The teacher facilitates the meeting so that ideas come from the students; it is not the role of the teacher to solve any of the problems that are brought to the group.

Finally, middle school students are ripe for using their conflict-resolution skills to help themselves and others. With a firm understanding of the concepts of conflict resolution and the wealth of skills they develop throughout the year, middle school students can successfully negotiate with their peers. Peer-mediation programs are implemented as supports to everything the students are already doing in the classroom. Trust is established, and conflict situations that once appeared bleak become manageable.

If we provide our young people with the skills they need, the opportunities to use them, and recognition for their accomplishment, resilient youngsters will emerge who are ready to help build school communities we can all be proud of. In this kind of classroom environment, young people achieve their very best—supported by each other and the adults who teach them.

WHAT IS THE IMPACT OF RCCP?

An early independent evaluation of the RCCP–New York City site, released in May 1990 by Metis Associates, found that more than 87% of the teachers said that RCCP was having a positive impact on their students.

Teachers and administrators reported the following changes among the students: less violence in the classroom; increased spontaneous use of conflict-resolution skills among children; increased self-esteem and sense of empowerment; increased awareness of feelings and verbalizing of those feelings; more caring behavior; and more acceptance of differences.

RCCP was highlighted in a National Institute of Justice report (De Jong, 1994). The U.S. General Accounting Office also lauded RCCP's work in its report *School Safety* (1995), which found that RCCP is "widely regarded as one of the most promising violence-prevention programs among public health experts."

The RCCP Research Program has begun assessing the effectiveness of the RCCP in New York City during the 1994–1995 and 1995–1996 school years (Roderick, 1998). The study, funded by the federal Centers for Disease Control and private foundations, has three components: a short-term longitudinal process and outcome study of the impact of the RCCP on 9,000 children in 15 elementary schools; a management information system tracking the implementation of the program; and in-depth interviews with teachers in a subset of participating schools.[1]

With such a large sample, the child impact component of the study could not be based on direct observation of children. Accordingly, the researchers put together a set of age-appropriate surveys that could be administered to children in their classrooms. These included measures of problem-solving strategies, aggressive fantasies, and hostile attributional biases. Previous research has shown that children's scores on these measures are correlated with their actual behavior. Initial findings of the study, based on year one data, consistent with previous studies of child development, confirmed that youngsters grow more aggressive over time. Children in this study, irrespective of their participation in the RCCP, increase their aggressive tendencies with age. Younger children can often generate more solutions to problems than adolescents who see fewer options available can.

The study also indicated that in classrooms where teachers taught lots of RCCP lessons, there was a significant positive impact on children's development over the first year of the study. In these classrooms children's hostile attributional bias was significantly lower compared with children in classes where teachers taught few or no RCCP lessons. Additionally, their choice of aggressive strategies for interpersonal negotiation was significantly lower. They did not show a decrease over time in their use of competent interpersonal negotiation strategies.

During the 1996–1997 school year, Metis Associates conducted an evaluation of the impact of RCCP in the Atlanta Public Schools in three elementary schools, one middle school, and one high school after two years of implementation. Findings include the following.

64% of teachers reported less physical violence in the classroom.
75% of teachers reported an increase in willingness to cooperate in
the classroom.
92% of students felt better about themselves.
Over 90% of parents reported an increase in their own communication and problem-solving skills.
The in-and-out-of-school suspension rates at the RCCP middle school
decreased significantly while non-RCCP middle school rates
increased during the same period.
The dropout rate at the RCCP high school decreased significantly
while non-RCCP high school rates increased during the same period.

LESSONS FROM THE FIELD

Reflecting on our work over the past decade we have identified seven factors that have contributed to RCCP's success.

1. RCCP asks for a long-term commitment (of at least five years) from
   any school system that wishes to do this work. RCCP starts with a
   commitment at the school district level—because the monetary
   resources and other supports often reside at the school district level.
   These resources are necessary to sustain this work over time. This
   is helpful for any agency to think about when working with schools.
2. Whenever possible, the work is undertaken in partnership with a non-
   profit, community-based organization devoted to furthering this type of
   work and a school system needing the work. This collaboration creates
   a certain leverage, which ensures the program's quality and sustainabil-
   ity. It also helps bring in the extra funding needed through grants.
3. The work is viewed as a basic part of children's education, not as
   an add-on. No long-lasting change is going to happen unless the
   RCCP principles become part of the entire school's as well as the district's culture. These skills and concepts, once integrated into the curriculum framework of a district, will become institutionalized.
4. RCCP is as much about issues of diversity as about prosocial skills
   and conflict resolution. These three areas are often on separate tracks
   in the educational community, causing efforts to become fragmented
   in schools; it is best to view them as part of the same pie.
5. RCCP components and curricula were developed over the course
   of many years with input from the people RCCP serves. It is important for the work to be based on sound pedagogy and child development theory.

6. RCCP staff members are educators, practitioners with long-term experience in schools. They are familiar with the culture of public schooling. It is helpful to know the place in which you want to try to effect a change—schools have their own distinct cultures.

7. The RCCP model involves all levels of the school community, providing training and support to students, teachers, administrators, support staff, parents, custodians, and secretaries. RCCP is not just about youngsters learning conflict resolution. All the adults in the school community learn to be more socially conscious and ethical. It is common to hear young people and adults in RCCP-participating schools speak a common language that guides the decision-making process and the resolution of conflicts.

Finally, it is important to evaluate the work constantly. Ongoing formative evaluation, as well as more outcome-based evaluation, is essential to effect wonderful, transformative changes in teachers' and students' senses of themselves and their world.

CONCLUSION

It becomes clear that the skills and concepts that are taught in a program such as RCCP are the competencies needed to bring us into the 21st century. And as we take part in preparing young people to play a role in our future, we need to reorder our priorities. Currently, we spend $30 million an hour on national security—enough money to implement a comprehensive school-based program that would teach young people these skills in 600 schools for an entire year. These 600,000 youngsters would then actively engage in the process of changing our schools, communities, and larger society.

Which way will we go? How will future generations judge us? How will we be remembered? Several Nobel Peace Prize laureates are urging the United Nations to declare the year 2000 the "Year of Nonviolence." This is exciting news for all of us who are committed to finding nonviolent solutions to society's most urgent problems. We will need young people who are emotionally intelligent to carry this task forth.

NOTE

1.   The principal investigator for the child impact study is Dr. J. Lawrence Aber, director of the National Center for Children in Poverty. The teacher interviews were conducted and analyzed by researchers from the Center for Children and Tech-

nology (now also the New York City Office of the Education Development Center) under the supervision of Dr. Jan Hawkins, director.

REFERENCES

De Jong, W. (1994). Building the peace: The Resolving Conflict Creatively Program. *The National Institute of Justice Report*. Rockville, MD: National Institute of Justice.

Goleman, D. (1995). *Emotional intelligence*. New York: Bantam Books.

Kreidler, W. (1994). *Conflict resolution in the middle school*. Cambridge, MA: Educators for Social Responsibility.

Lantieri, L., & Patti, J. (1996). *Waging peace in our schools*. Boston: Beacon Press.

Metis Associates, Inc. (1990). *The Resolving Conflict Creatively Program, 1988–89: A summary of significant findings. Evaluative report*. New York: Author.

Roderick, T. (1998). Evaluating the Resolving Conflict Creatively Program. *The fourth R*. Washington, DC: National Institute for Dispute Resolution.

U.S. General Accounting Office. (1995). *School safety: Promising initiatives for addressing school violence* (GAO/HEHS-95-106). Washington, DC: Author.

9

Social, Emotional, and Political Learning

Peggy McIntosh and Emily Style

We ourselves have never experienced any school learning that is not social and emotional in its implications and consequences. The process of being schooled delivers social and emotional messages to a student in everything from the route of a school bus through end-of-the-day glimpses of school custodians cleaning up the building. Classroom decorations, student behavior in corridors, homework assignments, textbooks, and the minute-by-minute body language of teachers and students carry embedded and various social and emotional messages. Practices of tracking, grading, and counseling make visible and audible the socializing judgments of elders about the comparative standing of young people. How could students not pick up social and emotional lessons from the charged atmospheres of assemblies and athletic programs? The fact that many students do not relish much about school has social and emotional causes and explanations. Parents' and communities' relation to and demands on schools also have contexts and dynamics that are social and emotional.

If there is no such thing as education that does not have social and emotional dimensions, why isn't this more commonly understood? We think it is a curious and political matter that education generally is not seen, and does not present itself, as doing social and emotional teaching, when in fact it does so. Social relations between people and emotions within and between individuals exist within matrices of power relations. Teachers, even sociopolitically trained ones, and political scientists themselves have trouble seeing and teaching about the bearing of power relations on the daily ways we live our lives. Close-to-home power relations are a taboo subject in K–12 schooling and in the majority culture of the United States. Power relations are therefore little understood systemically. Students, however, learn about power by watching, by imitating, by avoidance of what they fear. Their

experience of the school bus, the custodian-servants, the tracking and grading systems socializes them to suppress most emotional responses to the
stratified political and psychological structures within which their socialization takes place.

Teachers have trouble teaching about power intentionally or, as Peggy
McIntosh says, *advertently.* Teachers have absorbed social, emotional, and
political learning as part of their own schooling in which matters of power
were, for the most part, evaded. At times, teachers teach about power when
a blowup occurs on the playground, in the cafeteria, or in a classroom and
a school crisis occurs. At such a time, some social, emotional, and political
learning may take place within special forums, though they often have a mut-
ing, rather than clarifying, effect: for example, acts of routine violence may
be renamed as "isolated incidents," rape may be called "assault" or "sexual harassment," and killings through drunken driving by out-of-control
teens may be designated simply as "tragedies."

For the most part, our inadvertent teaching about power, social relations, and emotions in school delivers a message that these matters really
cannot and should not be handled in school: they are beyond the pale of
education. This message relates to power. Most schools will leave children
no better off, no more knowledgeable about power systems, than they were
when they entered. While offering a socially desired commodity called education, schools deliver the message that any attempt to fathom students'
social, emotional, and political locations within power systems must be left
outside, at the schoolhouse door, and that the school cannot help students
to understand themselves or others in certain ways that powerfully affect
their daily well-being, security, and chance for development.

The authors of this chapter are involved in helping teachers to do more
effective and *advertent* emotional and social education. To do so requires
that teachers pay attention to their own past (political) schooling, within
power structures that socialized each to be this, not that; to do this, not that;
to see this, not that; to act like this, not that; to believe this, not that; to feel
this, not that. We cannot foster teachers' capacity to do better and more self-
aware social and emotional education within a political vacuum. We see traditional and most current schooling as restraining both teachers and students
within existing power structures through (unacknowledged) social and emotional denial that power structures exist in the society and the psyche.

To talk with teachers about social and emotional learning (SEL) without addressing their own experience of the political dimensions seems to us
to be both sentimental and disempowering. To learn why one feels like an
outsider or an insider, or why groups can't get along, or why bullying and
teasing and sexual harassment exist and are often overlooked by adults in
a school, or how often teenage violence is fostered by schools requires teach-

ers to look at themselves. It requires that we look at what was done to us in school and how we lived then and live now politically, in institutions, families, and in our own self-appraisals. It also requires that we look at the powers we have in our hands to see if we want to use them to change education so that it promotes the growth and development of all, including ourselves.

THE SEED PROJECT

Here we describe our work in the National SEED Project on Inclusive Curriculum (Seeking Educational Equity and Diversity). Its model for adult development of K–12 teachers involves them in local building-based, year-long seminars led by teachers for teachers who are their own colleagues. The aim of the seminars is to help teachers make school climates, curricula, and teaching methods more gender fair and multiculturally balanced. SEED seminars invite teachers' conscious attention to social, emotional, and political education. We feel that unless teachers can do for themselves what was not done for them in the way of breaking silence and isolation around social, emotional, and political learning, they will continue in the patterns of denial they have grown accustomed to living within and (inadvertently) enforcing.

For the last 12 summers, we have prepared 40 teachers to lead year-long SEED seminar groups in their schools. In the process we have developed many exercises that help us see and reflect on the social, emotional, and political educations we received through inadvertent instruction on taboo subjects of power, especially with regard to gender, ethnicity, sexuality, class, race, group dynamics, community relations, commonalties, differences, jobs, roles, authority, and intragroup relations. The aim of these exercises is to foster *advertent* growth and development in social, emotional, and political learning in all who are touched by the SEED Project, whether they are the 40 seminar leaders each year,* the hundreds of teachers in their seminars, or the thousands of students whom those teachers teach.

We describe here just 7 out of some 50 interactivities (our term for activities in which everyone participates, with no one simply functioning as an observer) that we use in working with new SEED leaders and in our work consulting with and speaking to educators in many other contexts. We invite readers of this volume to imagine how the students Maura and Raffi described at the beginning of this book might participate in each of the

---

*The Minnesota SEED Project also trains over 30 seminar leaders each summer as does New Jersey-based SEED. As branches of the National SEED Project, Minnesota is in its seventh year of operation and New Jersey is in its fifth.

following exercises if these exercises were offered in their middle school classrooms. In addition, we invite readers to imagine their own participation in any of these engagement activities.

Background of the SEED Model

Faculty development seminars about new scholarship on women were sponsored from 1977–1985 at the Wellesley College Center for Research on Women. These Mellon seminars for college and university faculty and the concurrent Mellon Fellowship Program rested on the assumption that new scholarship on women does not simply add new information but calls into question both old information and underlying assumptions about what constitutes knowledge in the academy and in life in general. The seminars sparked new understanding of self and others within socially constructed bodies of knowledge and behavior.

Information about Mellon seminars' processes of inquiry and their intellectual excitement led to requests for similar seminars for K–12 teachers. Peggy McIntosh, who had been coordinating the Mellon seminars as part of a regional and then national program, obtained four yearlong grants from several foundations to coordinate regional Dodge seminars on how new work on women and understudied aspects of men's lives might potentially alter the K–12 school curriculum. Emily Style participated in the second-year Dodge seminar in 1984–1985 and co-led the fourth-year Dodge seminar in 1986–1987, widening attention to affective and autobiographical aspects of teacher development. Style also introduced her conceptualization of "curriculum as window and mirror" and the idea of "making textbooks of our lives" that she had written about in an earlier Teacher Corps work, *Multicultural Education and Me: The Philosophy and the Process, Putting Product in Its Place* (1982). These conceptual frames joined with McIntosh's "Interactive Phases of Curricular and Personal Re-Vision: A Feminist Perspective" (1983) as examples of theory that is poetic, evocative, and personalized through metaphors, analogies, vignettes, anecdotes, and narratives of experience. Teachers were invited both to fill these frameworks with their own experience and to devise alternative frameworks that might serve them better.

For seminar discussion of books and teaching methods, we increasingly turned to a format of what we now call "serial testimony," in which all participants around a table have a chance to speak in turn, without necessarily responding to each other. Participants also suggested topics to go into or brought in readings, co-creating the curriculum. We found that such openness led seminar members to take an interest in and trust each other more than usual. McIntosh noticed that two power-related phenomena seemed to occur once the group had bonded in a relationship of mutual

respect. Once all felt *heard,* the social relations, emotions, and politics res-
onated differently, even amid discussion of charged material; at that point
it seemed that anyone could "lead" (facilitate) the group. Moreover, members of the group seemed to accept leadership, that is, trust the process of
being "led" and their own authority related to the material more than
before.

It seemed that if teachers could learn to lead seminars in a way that distributed power and respect, then seminars did not need a leader from "outside" or "above." Teachers could facilitate school-based seminars on their
own anywhere. The project could, and did, become national and for the last
12 years has prepared teachers to lead seminars in their own school sites,
public and private, in over 30 U.S. states and in 10 other countries.

New seminar leaders are prepared for the seminar task during a week-
long residential workshop in the summer. During the New Leaders' Week
we try to provide a balance of content and interactivities with an emphasis
on teachers' taking themselves seriously, "making textbooks of their lives,"
and coming to greater consciousness about their own social, emotional, and
political schooling so that they can do more intentional education of others. The interactivities tap into what Peggy McIntosh named as the Evaded
Curriculum for Susan Bailey's (1992) *How Schools Shortchange Girls.* The
Evaded Curriculum includes "the functioning of bodies, the expression and
valuing of feelings, and the dynamics of power." As that report stated,
"power differentials ... are perhaps the most evaded of all topics in our
schools. . . . If we do not begin to discuss more openly the ways in which
ascribed power, whether on the basis of race, sex, class, sexual orientation,
or religion, affects individual lives, we will not be truly preparing our students for citizenship in a democracy" (pp. 81–82).

Training Exercises

The SEED New Leaders' Week models over 50 experiential activities that
help to unpack the Evaded Curriculum. These activities help SEED seminar
participants to experience as part of their adult and organizational development *advertent* social, emotional, and political learning. Each of the following exercises rests on a key SEED Project idea.

Principle: Make "textbooks" of the lives in the room.
Activity: Write and read/Girl/Boy pieces using the discipline of the circle

Before the summer workshop, we send the 40 teachers who are preparing to lead seminars Jamaica Kincaid's (1985) short autobiographical piece
called "Girl." We ask participants to write their own version of voices in
their heads from early childhood telling them how to be a boy or a girl.

We tell them that at the opening meeting of the workshop they may read all or part or none of their piece.

For the opening circle on the first afternoon of the residential week, no one wears a name tag. It is not clear to new leaders which of the 60 people in the room are staff members and which are new leaders like themselves. There is no formal welcome. Sitting in a circle, we read, or occasionally say, the words we have brought in response to the Kincaid assignment. McIntosh repeats the statement that participants may read all or none or part of what they have brought. They may choose to listen rather than read. The point, she says, is to hear each other around the circle. She reads part or all of her own "Girl" piece and turns to the person on her left. Reading around the circle usually takes two hours.

For many people, this activity draws up deeply buried, influential teachings from childhood. The listening circle enables all 60 participants to respond (mostly in silence, sometimes with empathic sounds or laughter) to what others call up, to hear commonalities and differences, to sort and sift and connect. This assignment, including what Style has come to call "the discipline of the circle," is a *political* arrangement that invites and rewards intense listening to others' stories and forecloses the possibility of issues-oriented discourse on gender in the abstract. Hearing of personal (and political) teachings given to others deepens one's awareness of one's own early teachings as well.

Many participants' voices and body language show the impact of the training received with regard to gender and also (often) race, class, sexuality, fear, avoidance, self-censorship, self-doubt, self-denial, and silence. Themes surface and recede. Messages that have worn well take on stark contrast beside the many that have not. There is laughter at familiar prescriptions and at particularly pungent formulations. Kincaid's piece is written in the imperative voice, and most of the speakers therefore use the imperative voice in their pieces. The effect is that adults become mediums of transmission for decades-old messages coming directly through us all over again and offered to a circle of listeners in the here and now.

"Becoming" a boy or a girl for most people in the circle required a lot of training and repetition and warning. One was not automatically, easily, or naturally a boy or girl but needed to have one's gender socially constructed, artificially channeled, so as not to encroach on the territory of the other, sometimes called "opposite," sex. Those who escaped such conditioning within their families and cultures stand out by contrast with those who remember emphatic teaching about shaping themselves to fit a gender norm. Leaving the circle, most if not all have a heart and head full of cultural constraints, obligations, and coping strategies in relation to those they themselves received.

The Girl exercise works to "make textbooks of our lives," in the words of Emily Style. It also answers her call for a balance of attention to both "scholarship on the shelves and scholarship in the selves." Kincaid's piece is the (published) scholarship on the shelf to which we respond. The Girl activity is orchestrated to include everyone in the circle as the authority on his or her own experience, invited to speak on personal terms and not to comment on others' words, except by muted responsive exclamations and facial expressions in the course of the serial testimony process. All individuals are included.

This exercise, which Peggy McIntosh devised in 1985, teaches about "gender" differently than an abstract discussion on gender, by tapping into everyone's own deep internal development in a gendered world. We find that abstract discussions of gender (or any other complex matter with systemic dimensions) invite familiar conflicts and impasses. They result in an issues-oriented, familiar-refrain, group-melee, often polarizing, unsatisfactory pattern. This pattern operates in classes with students as well as in faculty meetings and does not advance awareness; abstract discussion usually keeps most faculty or students ("stuck") in familiar locations, most being silent observers of others and all but a few wishing to be elsewhere.

Principle: Use curriculum "as window and mirror."
Activity: Responses to Garza pictures in timed, paired conversation

Emily Style devised this exercise. She spreads on tables, desks, or the floor photographs of paintings by Carmen Lomas Garza that are found in the collection published by the New Press entitled *A Piece of My Heart/ Pedacito de mi Corazon* (1991). She asks each participant to choose a picture and to pair up with any other person to discuss their chosen pictures. She restates her idea that at its best, curriculum can serve as both window and mirror. She imagines the curriculum as an architectural structure that schools build around students. Ideally, for each student, this structure will provide windows out, into the experiences of others as well as mirrors of the student's own reality and validity. Style points out that the Garza pictures may seem to serve some people as windows only, as one did for her when she first saw it, a man with a flaming cone of paper stuck in his ear. However, upon reading that the title of the picture was *The Earache*, she came to remember the hot salt bag used for earaches in her family that she had forgotten years ago. Suddenly, the picture became a mirror as well.

Style asks participants to study a Garza picture in order to identify some window and mirror elements relative to their own experiences. This examination of the picture is done in silence. Then she asks each participant to talk to his or her partner for three minutes about how the painting serves as both personal window and mirror or perhaps not, as the case may be.

The second partner is invited to speak as though the first has not spoken. The task is not to respond but to start fresh. If a partner runs out of words in the allotted time, both discussants are asked to remain silent because silence itself holds many elements.

In a debriefing, Style asks, "How was this activity for you?" The responses palpably refute the charge that multicultural curriculum is "divisive." All participants find some self-mirroring elements in the pictures they have chosen. In other words, they find common ground in their identification with the scenes and people of the pictures. Most *also* find elements strange to them. Many find differences in areas that they do not know (but did not necessarily know that they did not know). The illustrations carry a lot of cultural specificity about daily life, behavior, customs, dress, food, families, celebrations, and living arrangements. In each picture, it is clear that something is going on, though the nature of the event may be quite opaque to some observers.

By way of teaching about acculturated social behavior, Style asks for a show of hands from those who had trouble filling their three minutes, then from those who found it hard not to interrupt the speech or the silence of those who did not fill all of their three minutes. She invites all to ponder what these responses show them about themselves. The ripple of response in the room indicates that these questions in themselves open up significant windows and mirrors about speaking and listening behavior. It has been our experience that the three-minute time frame invites people to get into a second and even third layer of rumination about a picture and to be heard out, while they embark on wording thoughts about a picture about which they may have thought they had little to say.

The Garza illustrations are colorful, detailed scenes of rural or village life in Texas in the 1950s. Most feature at least four people engaged in activity that one could describe to a curious five-year-old child, allowing a strong sense of common ground in the midst of cultural specificities. Often Latin participants upon finding some culturally familiar and intimate details have a very strong positive reaction to this activity. Their pleasure in it points up how few mirrors have existed in curricula and staff development projects for this population of teachers and students and, likewise, how few curriculum materials serve as "windows" for non-Spanish-speaking teachers and students.

Principle: Note the "Evaded Curriculum."
Activity: "Passing Notes" in response to the Harvey/McIntosh dialogue

Ken Harvey, a SEED seminar leader, and Peggy McIntosh co-wrote a four-page dialogue about sexuality in the spring of 1997. In this activity, we distribute copies and allow a few minutes for reading it before asking participants to do what we call "Passing Notes." The Passing Notes activity like the other activities described in this chapter may be used in classroom contexts as well. All are what we call "interactivities," and all are inclusive in the sense that everyone participates; no one is simply an observer, though continuing to listen rather than speaking is permitted.

McIntosh and Harvey's dialogue posits that many adolescents who are said to be confused about their sexuality may, in fact, be quite clear about their homosexuality. However, the dominant society is equally clear, saying that they are not welcome. They get this message and, in some cases, see no way that their lives can go on. Therefore they commit suicide, whereupon they are called "confused." McIntosh and Harvey discuss this rhetorical strategy as part of the denial of the existence of homosexuality. Adults try to get students to delay their self-identification and deny their self-knowledge in the hope that "normal" heterosexuality will prevail. The Evaded Curriculum entails silence on gender in general, on sexuality in general, and on homosexuality in particular. The silences are part of the colossal inadvertent social, emotional, and political teaching in which adults, including teachers, often collude consciously or unconsciously.

Using the Passing Notes activity on subjects such as homosexuality and teen suicide that are fraught with social, emotional, and political overtones allows teachers to express many different thoughts and make several different responses to others' thoughts. The structure of the activity itself invites complex conversation and multiple conversations. On a piece of paper, participants write their names and a brief comment in response to their reading of the Harvey/McIntosh dialogue. Then participants pass their comment to the next person. In an auditorium, those at the ends of rows pass (or receive) papers to (or from) those above (or below) them, and a runner is needed to carry notes from the last person in the back row to the first person in the front row. Each new recipient reads what is on the sheet, makes a response, and at the signal passes it on again. The time per response needs to be lengthened as the exercise goes on, as the paper fills with a train of thoughts: for the first response, perhaps one minute; then one and a half minutes, then two, and three, and so on. At the stopping time, each paper is returned to the original writer whose name appears at the top. Now each person who launched a thought can see where others took it.

Passing Notes can be especially useful for subjects about which many people are conflicted. It ensures that many points of view are expressed and complexified. In this version, each person in effect "speaks" four times, once to launch a comment in response to the Harvey/McIntosh dialogue and then three times to respond to comments of others. There is no public reading of any opinions. The facilitators may not learn any of what has been said in Passing Notes, an activity that expressly encourages a practice not officially allowed in school which evades the scrutiny of authorities.

On matters in which a traditional liberal arts' diversity of opinion is desirable, this technique of getting many ideas on the table is familiar. Yet the exercise differs significantly from a liberal arts *discussion* because it offers no public chance to state a thesis, make a case, assert an opinion, or take on another person in front of a group. It invites a high degree of informality, brevity, and affect. A note is usually a quick jotting to a nearby person, with nothing much riding on it in the way of expected responses, appraisal, or judgment. In the case of this exercise, however, the writers of the original notes know that their words will be seen and responded to by several others, however briefly.

The structure of this silent, plural conversation recognizes and honors the vulnerability of most teachers in that it deals in writing with the matter of homosexuality in a way that will be seen by a few others, one at a time. It offers a protected space in which to respond thoughtfully to a nearly universally taboo subject of the Evaded Curriculum, and in the case of the Harvey/McIntosh dialogue, a matter so serious it is a life-and-death matter for significant numbers of young people.

Passing Notes therefore unlocks public silence about sexuality without asking teachers to go public with their views or the private experiences of their own embodied lives. From the variety of reactions and responses received through Passing Notes, any participant can realize that there is much complex body-life as yet unaddressed in most diversity work. The participants discover that there are tangled emotions in teachers about how or whether all students and teachers feel safe in school with regard to their sexuality; about whether homosexuality is natural or learned; and about whether talk about sexuality is appropriate in schools, or possible for them personally, at this point in their own adult development. Passing Notes requires no final words; it can help to open any topic previously closed to public discourse in school or, for that matter, in professional development programs for teachers.

This exercise could be expanded to fill much more time, so that it becomes serial testimony in written form. Magda Lewis's words on storytelling capture some of the politics we find in the Passing Notes exercise and in the longer exercises that we suggest might grow out of it: "What makes storytelling political—and, therefore, potentially transformative—is the fact that other stories may also be told" [read *other notes* may also be written] (1993, p. 17).

The reality of homosexuality is problematic and evaded in many schools, by many teachers, parents, and students, given the sensibilities of most societies of the United States and around the world. Passing Notes provides a way into a controversial topic and a way of seeing whether and how others are willing to deal with it.

Principle: Learn from "a tradition that has no name"/many names.
Activity: Respond to Lanker photos in timed, paired discussion

Barbara Omolade, an educator and activist leader, has called Black women's leadership oriented to development "a tradition that has no name," stating that she was well trained in this tradition as an apprentice to Ella Baker (1994). Three feminist scholars—Belenky, Bond, and Weinstock— used Omolade's phrase as the title for their 1997 book, *A Tradition That Has No Name: Nurturing the Development of People, Families, and Communities.* And we, in turn, use the phrase to pay tribute to understudied developmental (often maternal) ways of being and the many named—and unnamed—people, past and present, who have engaged in community caretaking of various kinds.

For this interactivity, we make use of the striking portraits of "75 Black Women Who Changed America" as profiled by photographer Brian Lanker. We think that we first experienced a version of this exercise led by Molly Murphy McGregor of the National Women's History Project a number of years ago when she consulted to the National SEED Project. Subsequently, both Cathy Nelson, codirector of Minnesota SEED, and Emily Style have developed ways of having faces in the room meet faces bound in a book. Actually, to set up this activity requires physically taking apart one or more copies of *I Dream a World* (Lanker, 1989), a relatively expensive and visually stunning book. However, once the portraits are removed and rubber cemented back-to-back with the transcribed words of the woman pictured, the set of photos can be used many times. Sometimes we invite participants to take the photos with them at the close of a session. Whether or not we do that, often a few portraits "walk away" when participants cannot bear to part with a likeness of someone they've become attached to.

We prepare one and a half times as many portraits as there are people in the group. We lay the pictures out on surfaces or post them on walls. We ask participants to choose a portrait that attracts them, to spend time looking at it and reading on the back the words of the woman it portrays. This takes 10–12 minutes. Then we ask participants to find a partner with whom they have not spent much time. Cathy Nelson's words on what to do next came from her long experience (as a public high school history teacher) with students who hate history and have gone through the motions of learning it without ever being engaged by traditionally taught versions. When she uses the exercise in Minnesota SEED, she instructs participants to introduce their partner to the woman who is the subject of the portrait they have chosen, saying, "I would like to introduce you to ..." before explaining what it is about this particular picture that attracted them so that they selected it.

Then, the participants are to tell their partners *one* thing that *interests them* about this woman, from her own words and information on the back of the portrait. Nelson has strong words for stock school reports on historical figures in which bored students list exact dates of birth and death that are meaningless to everyone in the room. She insists that we *not* pass on any information just for the sake of providing information. We must tell something about this woman's life or thought that *interests us*.

This exercise in taking Black women's history seriously starts with choosing a person whose name the participants may or may not know and then learning from her own words what she wished to say about herself at the time when Brian Lanker interviewed her and took her picture in a place of her own choosing. Her face and body speak first; her words next. All of the (10" × 10") portraits, moreover, take up equal space regardless of the women's public fame.

The narratives of these women reveal diverse ways of living, negotiating, coping, creating, and committing themselves to communities, cultural survival, and social justice. No one form, model, or archetype of "the Black woman" is created or even suggested. Seventy-five diverse Black women are introduced to participants and then by participants to each other. These women have existed and in many cases still are living, but their singular and plural histories are hardly taught in schools, except perhaps during Black History Month. Cathy Nelson times participants as they go through the steps of this exercise. She exemplifies the teacher-as-student in explaining (echoing Audre Lorde) how she came to make curriculum out of this book: "I teach what I need to learn."

But such learning, we note, goes beyond simple facts *about* women. The point is for each person to make a connection in which one learns *from* a chosen companion-woman speaking on her own terms from her own ground. In this exercise, one starts into history through human identification with a face and body, then hears the words of the embodied person and can absorb as much or as little of the biographical information given in a small sidebar as one desires. The activity opens up an antiabstract, autobiographical approach to history, social studies, psychology, sociology, economics, Black studies, women's studies, and American studies. It posits that a social and emotional connection can be made between the person choosing the picture and the woman in the picture. While Lanker has, in a sense, framed each woman, individually and collectively, the portraits testify to a truth that White writer Eudora Welty (1984) heralded in *One Writer's Beginning*:

> The frame through which I viewed the world changed too, with time. Greater than scene, I came to see, is situation. Greater than situation is implication.

Greater than all of these is a single, entire human being, who will never be confined in any frame.

The Lanker exercise enters the territory of "issues" through human actors' stories, unlike many history and social studies classes that deal with "social issues" in the abstract. A school unit on race, for example, may focus on the civil rights movement; a unit on gender on the women's movement; a unit on labor on labor movements of the early 20th century. The Lanker narratives and pictures hold experiences of race, gender, and class, but the individual's identities and stories cannot be subsumed under "issues." Their worlds have both commonality and diversity and help readers to see both systemically and empathetically. The lineup of photos includes a number of very famous Black women such as Rosa Parks, Toni Morrison, and Maya Angelou, whose status as racial exceptions in U.S. society is offset by the fact that their narratives are as human as any of the other testimonies, implying that there are a lot more Black women where these 75 came from. As Alice Walker (1971) puts it:

> To acknowledge our ancestors means we are aware that we did not make ourselves, that the line stretches all the way back, perhaps, to God, or to gods. We remember them because it is an easy thing to forget: that we are not the first to suffer, rebel, fight, love and die. The grace with which we embrace life, in spite of the pain, the sorrows, is always a measure of what has gone before. (p. 1)

One thread that runs through the words that many of these 75 women use to tell about themselves is that they do not see themselves as solo achievers but as *members of communities* that helped to advance them and that they in turn help to advance. Many of the women have been involved their whole lives in "making and mending the fabric of society," as McIntosh puts it, or "finding one's development through the development of others," in the words of Jean Baker Miller (1976). This is the tradition explored in *A Tradition That Has No Name: Nurturing the Development of People, Families, and Communities* by Belenky, Bond, and Weinstock (1977). One important part of inclusive curriculum is to learn from what has not been articulated about the development and maintenance of matrices, holding environments, for human existence. The words of the Black women in Lanker's, as in many other books, amply testify to the continued existence of vibrant traditions that hold groups together—socially, emotionally, and politically.

Most U.S. history texts poorly support curricular attention to making and sustaining of family and community ties. *I Dream a World* richly supports the discussion of such ties with the testimony of women who have made this their business, their calling, and their road to survival. The exercise casts Black women as prime teachers, thinkers, sustainers, historically and spiritually, in making family, community, and personal connections. All students can learn about the sustaining tradition these women represent, a tradition that in fact bears many names—including those of the parents and grandparents of the students in any given classroom. The exercise does not reduce any Black woman to a person defined by the "issues" she has experienced, nor portray any Black woman as merely an unlucky inheritor of racial disadvantage. The pictures carry honor and convey dignity. And the participants in this exercise study women whom, in many cases, they were taught to overlook, fear, cheat, neglect, or patronize. This is strong emotional, social, and political education for White teachers and students in particular. And for teachers and students of color in other ways.

Principle: Pay attention.
Activity: Study lemons with a partner

Teacher talk about students in faculty lounges sometimes carries a school-weary theme: "seen one, seen 'em all." The lemon activity implies "seen one, seen one." We ask pairs of people to choose lemons from a basket and to become acquainted with their own lemon by discussing it with their partner. Some see lemons as objects, some as characters; some will attribute life histories to their lemons. After two minutes, all return their lemons to the basket. When Emily Style does the exercise, she sometimes says that she will ask participants to find their lemons again, mentioning that when she did the exercise at Harvard Graduate School of Education a few years back ALL students found their lemon. So, she is wondering (casually, of course) whether this group will "reach the Harvard standard." She then pours all the lemons out onto the floor, and a free-for-all ensues.

If the exercise is introduced very casually and is done by individuals and not pairs, it takes people by surprise and the success rate in reconnecting with one's lemon is not very high. When people are told ahead of time what will be asked of them and/or they work in pairs, the success rate is high. The lessons that can be learned are several; in either case, the main lesson is "pay attention." But to lemons?

Not all lemons are alike, any more than people seen in one social grouping are all alike. Not all participants have, or use, equal powers of observation. Some people's partners have to find their lemon for them or tell them they've brought back someone else's lemon. The exercise shows that details matter. Little things carry history. Lemons bear large and small marks of heredity and environment. The exercise gives a chance for description of kinds other than analysis: metaphor, narrative, projection, and play of various sorts. The exercise shows that collaborating with a partner can provide a reality check and improve the chance of accurate observation and identification.

It is unusual to see a piece of fruit as a subject for leaders to be concerned with. The activity itself may seem trivial. It, however, teaches by analogy that "seen one, seen 'em all," which doesn't even apply to lemons, certainly can't apply to neighborhood, race, income, test scores, credentials, sexuality, or physical ability. Pay better/deeper/more attention, the exercise instructs. See the differential details of what you are looking at. Increase knowledge of your and others' capacity to observe. Think back. When was the capacity to observe educated in you? Rewarded in you? By whom, where? Are you as a teacher increasing and rewarding students' capacities to observe? To observe what? When? Where? Would the Lemons Activity be useful for your students? Are you teaching them respect for many different ways of *reading* the world?

Planning for this activity requires, preferably, finding lemons that do not have brand names stamped on them. We have found that some participants will name their lemons. Some will wish to take them home. Some will experience the exercise as too old (it has been around for a number of years) and/or too trivial. Others will find it refreshing because it involves something usually associated with the kitchen in an academic setting. Certainly one lesson the Lemon Activity can hold for educators is that a child who has not been seen as distinctive, as having detail, may be easily lost in the crowd. Teachers and schools have the power to lose students; the choice of whether to do so is a deeply political matter of educational structure, policy, and attentiveness.

Principle: Acknowledge that the multicultural world is also interior.
Activity: Individually fill out "Circles of Our Multicultural Selves" sheets and discuss with others in pairs, threes, or fours.

Simplistic multicultural work can imply that each of us has a unitary identity, a single self. Relational theory implies that the self exists in and is composed of its relations to other beings and forces in the world. We believe that it is not necessary to go into relational theory in order to help teachers see many aspects of their interior lives as co-existing. We also believe that multiple group memberships held by anyone bear on how we see and experience life and that projections onto us by others and ourselves because of our group memberships can bring social and emotional comfort and distress at different times. An exercise we use to complexify the sense of multiculturalism is called Circles of Our Multicultural Selves. It implies that diversity is not just "out there;" it is also "in here."

We ask each participant to write his or her name in a circle in the center of a sheet of paper and then to draw a number of circles around the central circle and to put into each circle the name of a group with which the participant identifies. Many participants write in aspects of their identity without prompting. For those who wish, Style will list some aspects of group identity that the participants may wish to consider. These can include religion, race, profession, workplace role, physical appearance, gender, age, hobbies/pastimes, ethnic group/country of origin, family role, friendship ties, sexual orientation, college affiliation, political belief/ideology identification, regional location, home neighborhood, language(s) spoken, and state of health.

During the SEED New Leaders' Week we ask participants in small groups of 12 (10 participants and 2 co-leaders) to go around the 12-person circle (timed or untimed) and to explain what they put in the written circles as aspects of their identity. If done quickly, this exercise may make little impression on some participants. The experience of it deepens when participants are invited to add more and when further discussion is called for by such prompts as: Think about a time when you felt proud to be a member of a certain group; think about a time when it felt painful to you to be a member of a certain group; or, what is one thing you wish people would never say about a group to which you belong?

This exercise can take anywhere from 15 minutes (3 for writing, 12 for reading around the circle) to an hour, as the narratives deepen. The whole exercise encourages insight into the following questions: Who am I? How do I experience myself? How do others see me? What do their perceptions do to me? These are social, emotional, and political questions. Teachers and students are rarely asked to reflect on their social, emotional, and political locations relative to others and to talk about these to each other. What can seem at the start like a minor exercise about group association or status can turn into a major self-examination.

The exercise can also move in the direction of self-knowledge about how little sense of *interior diversity* the society has encouraged and how even in multicultural work there is a push toward objectifying "the other" as exterior rather than as a facet of one's self, projected outward. The Circles activity implies that we have ties to many groups but also no ties to some groups. What if we were to see ourselves as potentially involved in all groups? McIntosh wrote about this in her 1990 Interactive Phase Theory paper on race:

> The multicultural worlds are in us as well as around us; the multicultural globe is interior as well as exterior. Early cultural conditioning trained many of us as children to shut off connection with certain groups, voices, abilities, and inclinations, including the inclination to be with many kinds of children. Continents we might have known were closed off or subordinated

within us. The domains of personality that remain can fill the conceptual space like colonizing powers. But a potential for more plural understanding remains in us; the moves toward reflective consciousness come in part from almost-silenced continents within ourselves. (p. 13)

We have used two alternative discussion formats beyond the 12-person circle for this exercise. First, we use talking in pairs, as described for the Garza pictures exercise, which may be timed or not; it may also involve a debrief on self-discovery through questions about speaking and silences, or it may not. We have also used groups of three or four (sometimes called microlabs), going around the circle, with serial testimony followed only at the end by open discussion, or "cross-talk."

The exercise focuses on both outer identification and the inner complexity of the self, which can change over time in its many relations within varied circumstances. It works against the idea that we need to find out what *one* thing we are and be that. It illuminates the multiplicity of our connections to many people and groups as a fundamental part of our humanity, not as a sign of a fragmented personality. It permits the sense of identity to be more plural and fluid in teachers, so that teachers in turn may encourage their students to see themselves as complex characters with capacities for speaking in many idioms (linguists call this capacity code-switching), for seeing many points of view (educators call this a sign of a liberal education), and for respecting and living civilly with many kinds of people (political scientists call this citizenship in a democracy).

Principle: Realize your and others' "politics of location."
Activity: Tell autobiographical vignettes about "Race and Me" around the circle

This exercise derives from one devised by Joan Countryman, a long-time consultant to the National SEED Project who is currently serving as the head of Lincoln School in Providence, Rhode Island. As a math teacher, she elicited what she calls students' "math autobiographies." She asked students to imagine a vivid moment involving them and math and then to answer four questions about it: Where are you? Who else is there? What is happening? How do you feel about it?

Countryman then asked students to write a second vignette. Students were told that if the first scene was chiefly negative, the second should be positive. She found that the first one was usually negative and that many students had trouble coming up with a positive one. Discussion followed, on whatever terms Countryman specified.

McIntosh has taken to asking the same four questions to bring forth vignettes under the themes of Race and Me, Class and Me, or School and

Me. For example, she asks participants to conjure up a vivid moment involving themselves and race and to think about it (30 seconds) or to write brief notes about it (2 minutes) so that they can then answer the four questions. Using the discipline of the circle, the participants tell vignettes in the present tense, starting with the phrase "I am . . ." in response to the first question.

We have found that several types of avoidance, inexperience, and fear can interfere with the telling of vignettes in the present tense or the reconstructing in the present of a remembered event from the past. Some participants think they must provide background; some tell of a generalized situation; some never locate themselves within the frame of the picture they draw. Some locate themselves in the picture but go into great detail about things that do not have to do with race in any clear way. Some give a vignette but do not say how they feel about what they have described. Many, however, tell a story, revealing a capacity to talk about "race" without a lot of self-censorship and to offer their thoughts to others in context of this activity.

One problem of racism and all the other "-isms" has been that some people speak for (or guess about) others. This exercise aims to locate speakers in their *own* experiences, *not* speaking for or about others. Locating oneself autobiographically in a story and conversely locating the story in oneself allows for reflection on how and where one was located in the vignette, in the picture it makes. Since the overwhelming majority of vignettes about race involve power, they italicize power relations as well as social relations.

The question, Where am I? brings up place; Who else is there? usually brings in other people; What is happening? reveals things done, witnessed, said, and thought. How do you feel about it? often brings up what is hardest to discuss: mixed, hurt, or anguished feelings; anger, sadness, shock, grief, remorse, awakening, understanding coming too late. Using the discipline of the circle, the vignettes are read or told. Each person's own words join with the words of others as the serial testimony unfolds, revealing (some of) the complexities of "race" as experienced by actual people present in the room.

It is possible to invite some cross-talk on what has been heard and/or then to repeat the process with a second vignette for each person, positive in outcome if the first one was negative and vice versa. Not surprisingly, many participants have difficulty in coming up with a positive vignette under the heading of Race and Me. Significantly, some repeat the first "negative" vignette, now seen as positive for the effect it had on the raising of their awareness or changing their capacity to see and act in racially constructive ways.

The exercise promotes sensitivity to what Adrienne Rich calls one's "politics of location" (1984). Keeping to the present tense and telling of a particular moment in the past allows recovery of a specifically *located* experience. It gives help in seeing one's specific location in different *systems* of hierarchy and makes it easier to understand that *everyone* is located in multiple "places." Nobody is simply a victim or victimizer, an oppressed person or oppressor. Each person holds some power at some times in some respects in some places. Our intricate "politics of location" produce mixes of emotional feelings and tangles in social relationships, which traditional schooling usually does not help us to recognize or untangle. Use of Countryman's vignette exercise indicates that Race and Me is a very-present scenario in contemporary lives, even in "all-White" places in the United States.

Vignettes told in this exercise may date from yesterday, today, last week, or years ago. Hearing them disperses the idea that democracy is fully working and that the playing field is level. But no abstract use of data or argumentation is needed; the exercise, which in Style's phrasing "makes textbooks of our lives," also affirms an insight often stated in A. K. Rice Group Relation conferences, as we have both experienced them: the data is in the room. We do not need to go to the polls or other texts to get a sense of how race relations are being expressed in the United States. They are carried by/in/with us. The social, emotional, and political learning challenge is how to work with a group's own data in a developmental way.

CONCLUSION

The activities we sketch out here can be effectively used with students at a number of different grade levels. At one school, the students said that whenever they got something *really* interesting to do in class it turned out that the teacher got it from a SEED seminar. So they wanted their own SEED class. They got it, and 17 juniors enrolled in a semester-long course of SEED readings, videos, and interactivities. This was not enough for them. In their senior year, these students presented SEED work to the rest of the senior class, who determined that their graduation gift to the school would be a SEED day, offered to all teachers and students in grades 9 through 12. The day was led by seniors and involved SEED interactivities, readings, and videos. We view this as a gift to the school from students who realized their need and hunger for social, emotional, and political education that would open up the Evaded Curriculum. Two features of the day were an open dialogue by seniors on Ebonics and a panel of alumni (adults) who were lesbian but had not been able to say so during their student years at the school.

We believe that schools' silences surrounding the emotional feelings and social relationships of people of all ages are a political phenomenon serving to keep power where it now is. Students are taught about strife in history classes. This is strife as military and public, distanced from their lives and "managed" by powerful people in public life. The implication is that strife is the domain of certain powers that be. Meanwhile, teasing, bullying, harassment, and other types of strife in schools themselves go unaddressed in the curriculum.

It is no accident that close-to-home SEL occurs inadvertently rather than intentionally. If students and teachers could say more of how they feel and why, and how they relate or don't relate to each other and why, they might critique an economic or educational ideology that sets them up to be lonely, scared, isolated, and at odds with each other. Teachers in the SEED New Leaders' Week often find themselves overpowered with relief at finding a place where they themselves can be in more authentic relation to other teachers than their schools (as workplaces for adults) usually allow.

Creating communities that work is a highly charged political act. The silence surrounding social and emotional education is a politically conservative silence, saying in effect, "You and we cannot do anything except in our individual lives; our stories do not exist in history. Be quiet and answer the test questions on other people's thinking and actions, or on math where there are no people, or on science which is about things beyond your control. Your silence, your capacity for doing what the teacher asks, and your willingness to ignore teachers' incoherence, school-based strife, and the arbitrariness of grading and assessment practices will safeguard you. In this way, you will survive school, and that will be your reward." Many, however, do not believe in this reward and drop out mentally, if not physically. Those who do believe in it can become passive, nonvoting citizens of the United States.

Schools cannot do social and emotional education unless educators examine why we have not been doing it before. Educators John Dewey and Maria Montessori each in their own way advocated it in earlier eras; however, with the erosion and loss of progressive and practical traditions has come a loss of experiential and meaningful components in schooling. Is it possible that most adults wish schooling to fail students and students to fail school lest students call us as adults on our own agendas and methods of fending off their embarrassing questions about the violent and inequitable state of the world? We believe that all adults and young people can gain if students and teachers develop healthy balances of affect, political feeling, social courage, intellectual depth, and physical health. The damper on the balanced development of children comes from adult evasions that cost the whole society heavily, economically and in every other way.

We feel that schools need to exemplify, embrace, and teach what educational philosopher Jane Martin (1985) names as the "3 C's" of education: care, concern, and connection. Education without these will continue to incapacitate most youth with regard to social, emotional, and political learning. Educational practice today rarely connects training of the *mind,* seen individualistically, with the *emotions* and with the *power* relations attending both. We believe that unless the political reasons for having excluded *advertent* social and emotional language are recognized, current attempts to promote SEL will be apolitical, ahistorical, and sentimental, despite good faith, preventing students and teachers from obtaining balanced self-knowledge, social fairness, and intellectual tenacity and depth.

REFERENCES

Bailey, S., et al. (1992). *How schools shortchange girls: A study of major findings on girls and education.* Wellesley College Center for Research on Women/AAUW Report.

Belenky, Bond & Weinstock. (1997). *A tradition that has no name: Nurturing the development of people, families, and communities.* Basic Books.

Garza, C. (1991). *A piece of my heart/pedacito de mi corazón.* New Press.

Kinkaid, J. (1985). Girl. In: *At the bottom of the river.* Vintage Books.

Lanker, B. (1989). *I dream a world: Portraits of black women who changed America.* Steward, Tabori & Chang.

Lewis, M. (1993). *Without a word: Teaching beyond women's silence.* Routledge.

Martin, J. (1992). *The schoolhome: Rethinking schools for changing families.*

McIntosh, P. (1983). *Interactive phases of curriculum and personal re-vision: A feminist perspective.* (Working Paper No. 124.) Wellesley: Wellesley College Center for Research on Women.

McIntosh, P. (1990). *Interactive phases of curriculum and personal re-vision with regard to race.* (Working Paper No. 219). Wellesley: Wellesley College Center for Research on Women.

Miller, J. (1976). *Toward a new psychology of women.* Beacon Press.

Omolade, B. (1994). *The rising song of African-American women.* Routledge.

Rich, A., (1985). Notes toward a politics of location. In: *Blood, bread, and poetry: Selected prose 1979–1985.* W. W. Norton & Company.

Style, E. J. (1982). *Multicultural education & me: The philosophy and the process, putting product in its place.* Teachers Corps.

Walker, A. (1971). *Revolutionary petunias & other poems.* New York: Harcourt, Brace, Javanovitch.

Welty, E. (1984). *One writer's beginning.* Cambridge: Harvard University Press.

10

The Cognitive, Emotional, and Behavioral (CEB) Framework for Promoting Acceptance of Diversity

Norris M. Haynes and Steven Marans

From their earliest years through adolescence, children are increasingly likely to meet and interact with others whose race, ethnicity, and backgrounds differ from their own. Between 1980 and 1990, there was a 34.5% increase in the Hispanic population in the United States and a 15.8% increase in the Black population. This compares to a 7.7% increase in the White population. It is estimated that between 1990 and 2000, the Hispanic population will increase by 26.8% and the Black population by 12.8%. These increases compare to a 5.2% growth in the White population. There are also large percentage increases in the Asian-American populations across the United States. These trends are predicted to continue well into the 21st century (Ponterotto & Casas, 1991).

In addition to race and ethnicity, other differences, for example, gender, social class, physical characteristics, and sexual orientation, may serve as focal points for intolerance and conflict among adolescents. In this chapter, we discuss a framework that may be useful in promoting tolerance for differences among adolescents in schools. The cognitive, emotional and behavioral framework (CEB) draws on psychodynamic principles of development and what has been learned from their application in a variety of contexts, as part of the Comer School Development Program (Comer, Haynes, Joyner, & Ben-Avie, 1996).

In these contexts, the framework described in this chapter attempts to promote tolerance for differences by understanding the developmental contributions to attitudes toward others who are different and by examining the cognitive, emotional, and behavioral ways in which these attitudes are expressed.

The cognitive component of the CEB framework refers to knowledge, expectations, and beliefs about others; the emotional component refers to children's accompanying feelings and affective reactions; and the behavioral component consists of the observable actions toward others who are different.

CONTEXT

In the search for greater autonomy the adolescent's attitudes and values may undergo significant change as the locus of influence begins to shift from family to peers. However, adolescents' earlier experiences greatly influence their current views of the world. Lessons and attitudes that were already internalized are easily shifted from one situation to another over time when these perceptions and attitudes become an integrated part of the adolescents' internal schema for perceiving and responding to events and people in their world (Comer, 1988; Vontress, 1995). In adolescence there is a crucial confluence of attitudes derived from the past and those shaped in the present. We see this clearly in the cases of Raffi and Maura as they deal with changing and conflicting emotions and become their own persons in search of their identities. Context includes several key dimensions: (1) adult modeling; (2) culture and expectations; (3) school and classroom climate; (4)planned interactions; and (5) curriculum, instruction, and assessment.

Adult Modeling

Within the school context, the adults' roles and attitudes contribute to adolescent identification with these significant adults. These identities play an important role in helping to shape or influence development from sources independent of family and peers. Children are more likely to internalize principles they are taught when the teachers with whom they identify actually demonstrate the attitudes and behaviors that they teach. Adults must be aware that the language they use, the attitudes they display, and the behaviors they engage in can help to promote a message of respect for differences or a message of intolerance. If what we teach in a formal way conflicts with the informal messages we send, we not only contribute to children's confusion and struggle, but we also endanger our own credibility as reliable persons of authority and as admired figures of identification whose behavior is worthy of modeling.

Culture and Expectations

A culture of mutual respect, caring, and sensitivity is one that helps to promote prosocial attitudes and behaviors, including acceptance of and respect for differences. The tacit and explicit norms and rules that govern behavior in the school setting help to define what is acceptable and unacceptable treatment of individuals. The tone that is set in the school establishes expectations for standards of interpersonal relationships among the students beyond school walls as well. Formal presentations and discussions of tolerance must be connected to a larger culture of understanding and empathy in individual classrooms and within the entire school community.

Dr. James Comer's program of school reform and improvement emphasizes the importance of the ecology of the school in promoting holistic child development. In over 700 schools across the country, the Comer School Development Program is being implemented to help schools provide the kind of supportive environments that children need in order to grow and develop well and to learn well and think well. Teaching children empathy and respect for differences is best done in a broader institutional context that supports a sense of order, respect, and community. Therefore consideration of the specifics of how we teach tolerance and respect for differences needs to encompass the goal of achieving such an environment so that the lessons and principles that are promoted may take root.

School and Classroom Climate

As an important aspect of the research agenda for the Comer School Development Program, the first author designed school climate questionnaires for students, teachers, and parents, which examine various dimensions of school climate. For example, one questionnaire examines the nature of the interpersonal relationships (student-student and student-teacher) that exist in the school; how involved parents are in the daily activities and decision-making processes in the school; and what kinds of relationships exist between parents and staff. One of several studies assessing school climate was conducted in an elementary school in a major northeastern urban school district. This school was selected because it was part of a group of schools nationwide being considered for special implementation of the Comer School Development Program in combination with other school improvement strategies. The results of the questionnaire indicated that students felt that there were very poor relationships among students and that the relationships between staff and students were also not very good. The teachers felt that the relationships they had with the children were very good, but they saw the interpersonal relationships among the students as being problematic.

Given these different perceptions about student-teacher relationships as well as the existing poor relationships among students, we developed focus groups involving staff and students. The focus groups revealed that many of these perceptions and problematic relationships had to do with students' perceptions of intolerance. The students, for example, felt that their teachers and fellow classmates displayed insensitive and intolerant attitudes. While teachers agreed that there was a significant amount of tension in the school, they were not able to identify some of these contributing issues such as insensitive remarks about students, bias in applying discipline, perceived prejudicial attitudes in the academic labeling and classification of students, tracking, and a general lack of cultural awareness.

The focus groups helped the entire school to develop a better understanding of what the climate was like in the school and how it was impacting on children's behavior. There was a growing recognition of the connection between the general climate and high rates of absenteeism and low levels of academic achievement. It became clear that issues that were of interest to the educators and psychologists, such as students' achievement, behavior, and attitude toward school, were all connected to students' perceptions of being isolated, disregarded, and treated disrespectfully by their peers and their teachers.

As a result of the review findings, members of the school's planning and management team developed a respect campaign that involved some of the following: (1) they increased multicultural activities; (2) they placed posters in strategic places identifying the school as a place of respect and caring; (3) they promoted basic courtesies in student-student and staff-student interactions; (4) they requested greater involvement of parents in school life; and (5) they implemented various discussion and focus groups to address critical issues in the school. At the end of the year we went back and reexamined the climate. As we looked at the data we saw a tremendous improvement in the climate, and also we saw a very great improvement in such behaviors as absenteeism, school attendance, and some of those issues we all care about (Haynes & Perkins, 1997).

Planned Interactions

Children of different socioeconomic and ethnic backgrounds often live in different communities and seldom interact with one another outside of the school setting. Cross-cultural interactions in schools help to promote mutual respect and acceptance and should not be left to chance. Schools can plan activities that allow students of different backgrounds to interact in growth-promoting ways. At different developmental levels these activities may take various forms ranging from organized play and group activities that provide opportunities for basic socialization in preschool to more formal discussion groups and dramatizations about differences, tolerance, and respect in middle and high school.

It is important to provide structured opportunities for these interactions to occur outside of school in the form of extracurricular activities. These opportunities reinforce and strengthen the connections and affiliations that are promoted and develop during school hours. Some schools in the Comer School Development Program national network, for example, sponsor an annual international day during which the cultural diversity of the school is celebrated and the various cultural groups share aspects of their cultures with the school community. This sense of community is reinforced through after school programs and activities, which are mainly run by parents. By participating in these culturally rich activities and programs, children deepen their awareness and understanding of different cultures and increase their respect for others.

Curriculum, Instruction, and Assessment

The context for promoting respect for differences includes exposure to culturally sensitive content information and the use of instructional strategies and assessment methods that respond to the learning styles and learning needs of children from different backgrounds. For example, the data on cooperative learning (an instructional method that organizes students in collaborative problem-solving groups) indicate benefits for all children. However, the data also suggest that the cooperative learning method is particularly effective for enhancing the academic and social development of minority group children because their cultural backgrounds value cooperation and sharing of resources over individualistic and competitive interactions (Haynes & Gebreyesus, 1993). There is also strong evidence in support of using culturally sensitive assessment instruments and methods to determine the achievement potential and performance of children and adolescents from different backgrounds. According to Armour-Thomas and Gopaul-McNichol (in press), students from minority groups and different cultures who were earlier classified as special education eligible and learning disabled have been reclassified to regular and high achieving groups when retested with instruments and in ways that are culturally sensitive.

DEVELOPMENTAL CONSIDERATIONS

Anxiety and Need to Be in Control

Many times negative reactions to people who are different stem from lack of self-awareness, self-understanding, and self-acceptance. There may also be latent unresolved internal conflicts related to one's early developmental experiences or perceived negative experiences with others who are different. However, the tendency to locate sources of discomfort outside of oneself may also play a major role in an individual's sense of intolerance and of self being externalized and translated into intolerance of others. Providing opportunities for self-reflection, self-analysis, self-awareness, and self-growth can often help to change the very basis for the prejudicial attitudes and behaviors that individuals display. This is especially important among adolescents who may be experiencing emotional conflicts around identity, change and transition, and sexuality and independence (Marans & Cohen, 1996; Freud, 1972). In fact, acts of intolerance may give the struggling adolescent a feeling of control and reduce feelings of anxiety by locating an enemy who can be excluded, attacked, or controlled. This kind of "mastery" may serve as a poor and destructive substitute for mastery of impulses and anxieties that feel out of the individual's control.

Affiliation Needs

The need to belong is a powerful human motivator. During adolescence this need to affiliate and identify with the norms and values of the peer group is particularly strong. There is a shift from one's sense of affiliation and belonging and dependence on parents, guardians, and adults to a different kind of affiliation and dependence on the peer group. For young adolescents this group identity helps to define how they interact when they are together. There is the in-group–out-group phenomenon in which those who are different may be treated with suspicion or even disdain. The individual feels safe and secure in sameness with group members on salient group characteristics. In fact, individuals may express both loyalty and identification with the group by distancing themselves from those who are different.

SOCIAL LEARNING

In many cases intolerance and prejudice toward individuals and groups who are different are learned or reinforced through social learning and modeling and can be unlearned (Bandura, 1986). Many children learn to be intolerant from negative stereotypes of and messages about certain racial and ethnic groups in the society. These stereotypes and messages are often internalized and become part of the cognitive and emotional schema that children use to respond to others.

Stereotypes, prejudices, and intolerant attitudes come from a variety of sources including the family and the school. Many of the negative prejudicial attitudes we see among adolescents stem from identification with the values in the family or peer group, which may or may not be reinforced at school. This point raises a much broader issue of what educators can do to counter some of the other influences to which children are exposed. The school as a whole should stand for certain values that are in direct contradiction to prejudice and intolerance in any form. Educators must also draw upon the insights gained from child development and psychology to help frame interventions that best prepare adolescents to respond humanistically to differences. The CEB framework is based on knowledge and understanding of child development and cognitive, humanistic, and behavioral psychological perspectives.

COGNITION (KNOWLEDGE, UNDERSTANDING, THOUGHTS, BELIEFS, EXPECTATIONS)

We need to help adolescents do the following.

- gain new knowledge and understanding
- adjust thinking
- change beliefs and expectations

In an attempt to increase knowledge and understanding about specific differences, we may pose the following questions: Do adolescents need to have knowledge about others who are physically challenged or about people who are different from them in some germane way? How do adolescents begin to inform their thinking about individuals who are different? How do we, as adult educators and mental health professionals, begin to change or adjust the beliefs and expectations that adolescents have of others? As we work with adolescents in our schools, it is important to help them to understand and process their own cognitions about other individuals and groups; to help them explore and analyze their beliefs about and expectations of others who are different. This may require that adolescents acquire new kinds of information that may change their beliefs about others. Effective interventions may include the following: (1) developing curricula focusing on the achievements of individuals and groups; (2) sharing information about the struggles and challenges faced by individuals and groups; (3) providing opportunities for interactions with others who are different.

EMOTION (FEELINGS AND PHYSIOLOGICAL REACTIONS)

We need to help adolescents to accomplish the following tasks.

- become more aware of feelings
- identify and name feelings
- associate specific feelings with specific beliefs and attitudes
- monitor changes in feelings, beliefs, and attitudes

It is not enough just for adolescents to talk about what they think or believe. They also have to think about how they feel about others who are different. Adolescents' being in touch with their emotions is consistent with Howard Gardner's (1995) notion of "intra-personal intelligence" and is a necessary component in expanding the range of tolerance. As educators help students become aware of feelings associated with perceptions of differences and intolerance, it may be helpful to identify specific physiological changes that occur as a result of emotions. For example, if someone directs a bigoted remark at an adolescent, the adolescent can relax more completely if he or she is aware of physiological body changes, including changes in pulse rate, breathing, muscle tenseness, and other indexes. These reflect the intense physical changes that often precipitate direct conflict. As adolescents become more conscious of specific, discrete affects such as fear, anger, dislike, and disgust and of how these emotions affect them physically, they may be better able to monitor and control their emotional responses in situations where differences and intolerance have previously triggered powerful negative social interactions.

Adolescents may achieve emotional awareness and control in several ways: (1) in small group counseling and discussions; (2) in one-on-one counseling and guidance sessions; (3) through dramatization and role plays; or (4) through poetry and other creative forms of expression.

BEHAVIOR (OBSERVABLE ACTIONS THAT HAVE DIRECT OR INDIRECT EFFECTS)

We need to help adolescents to do the following.

- become more aware of actions
- identify and describe actions

- associate specific actions with specific feelings and cognitions
- think of the consequences of each action
- think of positive action alternatives and consequences
- implement positive action alternatives

The behavioral component of the CEB framework has to do with actually acting out and expressing in very observable and palpable terms what adolescents think and feel. The cognitions become translated into emotional feelings, which have physiological components, and the feelings in turn are expressed in real, observable behaviors, which are most often the visible, demonstrable expressions of intolerance. Emotional reactions are often below the surface, and behavior is a very important manifestation or symptom of a deeper underlying problem. For example, when students in a classroom make fun of or avoid and ostracize another student who has a physical handicap, there are underlying emotional responses such as fear and anxiety.

Approaching tolerance from this more holistic perspective conforms with the goal of educating children: you can begin to talk to children at different developmental levels about how their minds work and how behavior and feelings are connected.

A helpful strategy to assist individuals to change their attitudes and behaviors in a variety of contexts is to provide opportunities for them to reflect on their experiences and how these experiences may have shaped and influenced their attitudes and behaviors. In helping adolescents to change intolerant attitudes and behaviors, the use of reflection questions as an integral aspect of the CEB framework may be effective.

CEB REFLECTION QUESTIONS

Adolescents should be encouraged to use the CEB Reflection Questions to guide them in monitoring, assessing, and adjusting their cognitions, feelings, and behaviors in their interactions with others who are different.

Cognition Questions
- What and how much do I know about X individual or group?
- What do I think and believe about X?
- Why do I think and believe this way?
- What do I expect of X?
- Why do I have these expectations?
- How may I increase my knowledge and understanding of X and the associated culture?

- How may I change my thoughts about, beliefs about, and expectations of X?

Emotion Questions
- What feelings do I have about X? (identify and name feelings)
- Why do I feel this way? (relate feelings to cognitions)
- Is this feeling rational, fair, and healthy?
- How can I change the way I feel?
- What new positive feelings can I have?

Behavior Questions
- How do I act toward X? (identify and describe specific actions)
- Why do I act this way? (relate specific actions to specific feelings and cognitions)
- What effects do my actions have on X and on me?
- Are my actions rational, fair, and constructive?
- How can I change my actions?
- What new actions can I implement?

A CASE STUDY

The following hypothetical case study and analysis are included to stimulate discussion and to generate additional ideas about the possible application of the CEB framework.

Martha

Martha Cox is a 12-year-old 7th grader. She recently transferred to Aspiration Middle School. When Martha was 5 years old, she was involved in a tragic car accident that claimed the lives of her younger brother and father. She and her mother survived the accident. Martha's mother miraculously escaped serious injury while Martha suffered major injury to her head, back, and legs. As a result of her injuries, Martha is now confined to a wheelchair.

Life for Martha has not been easy. She has endured many surgeries, and it is still often painful for her to perform simple tasks requiring gross motor movements. She also experiences tremors in her hands and legs. Yet, Martha and her mother have always been determined that Martha should receive a normal education in a mainstream class situation.

What has been worse than the physical pain for Martha is the psychological and emotional stress that she suffers from the often unkind stares, insensitive remarks, and exclusion from peer-group friendships. One day last week the class was planning a hiking trip. Everyone was excited about the trip, and the students were engaged in a very lively discussion about the various trails and things to see. During the discussion Martha felt isolated and alone because she could not go and could not feel the excitement of planning for this trip.

The week before that, while Martha was going through the line to get her lunch in the school's cafeteria, a girl named Marge came up to her and said, "May I help you get your lunch? I have been noticing how hard it is for you to manage going through the line and how mad some of the children get with you for holding them up. I feel so badly for you. I'd like to help." Martha politely declined the girl's offer. She cried inside during lunch and wept openly later when she told her mother about her lunchtime experience. She explained to her mother that she feels that she is seen as a helpless, useless person who deserves pity. She does not feel that she is treated as an equal in this school, as the capable, intelligent person that she is. She said to her mother that she knew that this would never have happened to her at her old school. She wishes that she was back there and longs for her old friends.

Analysis

Martha's classmates at Aspiration Middle School exhibit behaviors of intolerance by isolating her, excluding her from decisions, and at times seeming to patronize her. Marge's offer of help to Martha in going through the lunch line appears to be admirable and well meaning, yet she framed her offer in words that expressed pity and concern that Marge was causing other students inconvenience by holding up the line.

Encouraging and helping Martha's classmates to reflect on their behavior would be valuable but would not be sufficient. It would be important to engage them in a process of reflecting on the feelings that Martha's disability evokes in them and then guiding them through understanding those feelings. It is possible that some of Martha's classmates are afraid that associating with Martha may in some way cause them to become similarly disabled. It is also possible that Martha's classmates avoid her because they are anxious about saying the wrong thing to her (as Marge did) or because they feel uncomfortable and sorry for her. Martha is physically different in a significant way from her classmates, and this sets her apart in their minds and may justify their social distance from her. They stare at her and make unkind remarks among themselves because they do not understand the nature of her physical condition. They may feel frightened by her damaged body and physical limitations.

As Martha's classmates are helped to examine the basis for their feelings, they would begin to consider their knowledge of persons with disabilities and would begin to adjust and change those cognitions. It is likely that Martha's classmates believe that she cannot participate in physically challenging activities or does not want to do so. They may view Martha's physical disability as a limiting and debilitating condition. Unfortunately, by avoiding her, they do not get to know and understand her well enough as a person to appreciate her strengths. Her condition comes to define in her classmates' minds who she is and who she is not.

Martha feels rejected, hurt, and isolated. No one except her mother knows how she feels because there is no process available to her, in her class, to express her feelings. It would be helpful to Martha and her classmates if the teacher provided opportunities to discuss the issue of differences in a way that did not single out Martha but that addressed the need for empathy and understanding of differences. The classroom context should be one that makes it possible for Martha's classmates to address their cognitions and feelings about Martha's disability so that they could behave more appropriately and treat her more humanely and fairly.

CONCLUSION

The CEB approach to teaching tolerance is holistic, systemic, and responsive to children's developmental needs. It is holistic in the sense that it takes into account the multiple dimensions of intolerance. The approach is also developmentally sensitive in that it considers the physical, cognitive, and emotional changes that adolescents experience and the struggles that they face in forging an identity that defines who they are vis-à-vis the world around them.

In seeking to promote understanding and respect for differences, it is important to consider the values that schools and classrooms promote among students. The climate in schools and classrooms reflects the collective values and standards of interpersonal relationships and interactions that prevail. The climate is a measure of the essential nature of how individuals are regarded and treated. It is an imperative that educators help students develop a set of values and standards that would eliminate insensitive and intolerant behavior in the classroom and beyond. A climate of mutual respect and regard for all, regardless of group and individual differences, is just as important as the specific processes and strategies for teaching tolerance and respect for differences in schools and classrooms.

REFERENCES

Armour-Thomas, E., & Gopaul-McNicol, S. (in press). *Assessing intelligence: Applying a bio-cultural model*. Thousand Oaks, CA: Sage.

Bandura, A. (1986). *Social foundations of thought and action: A social-cognitive theory*. Englewood Cliffs: Prentice-Hall.

Comer, J. P. (1988). Educating poor minority children. *Scientific American 259*(5), 42–48.

Comer, J. P., Haynes, N. M., Joyner, E., & Ben-Avie, M. (1996). *Rallying the whole village: The Comer process for reforming education*. New York: Teachers College Press.

Gardner, H. (1995). *How are kids smart? Multiple intelligences in the classroom*. (Videotape). Port Chester, NY: National Professional Resources.

Haynes, N. M. & Gebreyesus, S. (1993). Cooperative learning: A case for African-American students. *School Psychology Review 21*(4), 577–585.

Haynes, N. M., & Perkins, B. (1997). *Changes in school climate perceptions: An intervention study*. New Haven, CT: Yale University Child Study Center.

Marans, S., & Cohen, D. (1996). Child psychoanalytic theories of development. In M. Lewis (Ed.), *Child and adolescent psychiatry* (pp. 156–170). Baltimore, MD: Williams & Wilkins.

Ponterotto, J. G., & Casas, J. M. (1991). *Handbook of racial/ethnic minority counseling research*. Springfield, MA: Charles Thomas.

Vontress, C. E. (1995). The breakdown of authority: Implications for counseling African-American males. In J. G. Ponterotto, J. M. Casas, L. A. Suzuki, & C. M. Alexandern (Eds.), *Handbook of multicultural counseling*. Thousand Oaks, CA: Sage.

Implementation and Future Directions

Part III presents reflections on where we are today and what directions we might consider as we seek to create, institute, and improve programs and perspectives to promote SEL within our middle schools. In Chapter 11 Ron Brandt describes some of the lessons he has learned about educational movements from his perspective as a major contributor to educational reform. There is no reason why those of us who are committed to integrating SEL into our schools need to repeat old mistakes. Learning about and applying Brandt's recommendations will enhance the likelihood that the SEL programs and perspectives described in this volume will become integral, useful facets of school life rather than the latest in a series of educational fads.

When we work with students, we want to promote learning; how do we know whether our work is effective? Placing our efforts within an overarching framework can help us to proceed in a thoughtful way. In Chapter 12, I describe the five basic dimensions that influence the nature of any intervention—whether in the classroom or in psychotherapy—and how these dimensions relate to current SEL programs and perspectives.

11

Successful Implementation of SEL Programs

Lessons from the Thinking Skills Movement

Ronald S. Brandt

Social and emotional learning (SEL) is both a new and a very old idea. In all cultures and in every generation, educators and parents have been concerned with children's sense of well-being and ability to get along with others. Certainly in today's social environment, teachers have no choice but to attend to their students' personal and social development, even when their first priorities are academic knowledge and skills. What is new, to some degree, is the array of carefully planned programs, including those described in this book, that are designed to teach desirable attitudes and behaviors. Using these tested resources, teachers can prevent problems rather than reacting spontaneously as problems arise.

The current interest in the concept of SEL was spurred by publication of Daniel Goleman's (1995) influential book, *Emotional Intelligence,* and reinforced two years later with *Promoting Social and Emotional Learning* (Elias et al., 1997). The idea of planned SEL programs, however, originated somewhat earlier. Just as many of the reform studies of the 1980s were well under way when *A Nation at Risk* (National Commission, 1983) emerged on the national consciousness, most of the 23 programs listed in the appendix of *Promoting Social and Emotional Learning* had been operating for years when *Emotional Intelligence* captured educators' attention. Still, it was Goleman's work that brought them to prominence and launched the current movement.

A MOVEMENT?

But, one might reasonably ask, is SEL really a movement? And do we want it to be? Many people, including teachers, are troubled by the tendency of educational leaders to chase one topic after another, dropping last year's emphasis for "this year's new thing." Informed observers point to a sorry record of innovations given much fanfare and lip service but not followed up. Members of the general public, concerned about apparent low standards and fuzzy thinking, feel the same way. Polling organizations like Public Agenda (Johnson & Immerwahr, 1994) report that people don't understand why educators seem so infatuated with questionable fads rather than putting "first things first."

Mindful of the difficulty of keeping schools focused on a theme long enough to ensure institutionalization, advocates, including the Social Emotional Learning Project at Teachers College, Columbia University, and members of the group known as Collaborative for the Advancement of Social and Emotional Learning (CASEL), are cautious. They welcome the surge of interest in their field and the opportunity to disseminate their work, but they recognize that SEL will probably soon yield center stage to the next "hot topic" that comes along.

Under the circumstances, it may be useful to consider why education seems so vulnerable to trendiness, whether SEL is another movement, and if so, what can be done to ensure that it has lasting impact.

EDUCATION'S TRENDS

For as long as I can remember, but especially in recent decades, public schools have been subject to what some call "fads" and others "trends." Although this tendency is frequently criticized, educators and the organizations that serve them continue to search eagerly for the latest hot topics. As editor of publications for a large professional association for many years, I helped promote numerous such themes, including cooperative learning, interdisciplinary curriculum, performance assessment, and multiple intelligences.

Although I am embarrassed by the apparent superficiality of our profession's attentions, I believe it can be explained in part by educators' honest desire to make schools better places for children. Most such movements reflect an optimistic (some would say idealistic) view of the learning process and the aspiration to avoid the rigid, stultifying practices associated with formal education. Although the various movements focus on different aspects of education, each is defensible. From a progressive standpoint (although perhaps not from other legitimate points of view), the question is not whether cooperative learning or interdisciplinary curriculum is more important, or whether to teach thinking skills rather than SEL. These are all different facets of what we consider good practice. Educators must be concerned with curriculum *and* instruction *and* discipline *and* parent relationships. They must teach reading *and* mathematics *and* music *and* health. They are not so much fickle as constantly turning from one important element of their work to another.

Also contributing to the situation are the dearth of sound, convincing research and lack of agreement among authorities that make practitioners doubtful about any claims of scientific validity. Educators sometimes declare that whatever they are doing is "based on research," but in practice they seldom rely primarily on research findings when making decisions. Because the professional knowledge base is so diffuse, and because practitioners sometimes lack confidence in even the findings they know about, they tend to be swayed by other influences.

The various movements that have attracted educator interest in recent years differed from one another in many ways but had some elements in common. Most were closely identified with an individual or a small group of persons who developed or publicized the idea. For example, cooperative learning is an instructional strategy shown by extensive research to improve students' social and academic performance, but for several years it had all the earmarks of a movement. Educators were bombarded with publications, conference sessions, and institutes on the subject. David and Roger Johnson, Edythe Johnson Holubec, and Patricia Roy helped popularize the topic with their book *Circles of Learning* (1984), which advised teachers to design their own lessons in accord with a set of general principles. Robert Slavin (1988), who had also done extensive research, took a different approach by incorporating cooperative learning into a series of published instructional programs. These programs include the currently much-respected Success for All (Slavin, 1996).

I once talked to an elementary school librarian who had volunteered, with another staff member, to teach a course in cooperative learning offered for salary credit to teachers at her school. Along with other prospective instructors, she had attended a summer training program organized by the staff development office in her large suburban school district. She had not used cooperative learning herself, because she said it did not apply to her work as a library media specialist, but she was enthusiastic and accepted by other members of the staff. Several months after the eight-week course ended, I asked if any of the teachers who had taken her class were now using cooperative learning regularly. "Not that I know of," she said.

Many similar topics have had their day in recent years—inclusion, detracking, whole language, character education. Some were backed by legislation or official policy, while others were more grassroots. It would not be at all accurate to say they came and went, because nearly all of them continue as professional challenges. But some no longer attract the attention they once did.

TEACHING THINKING

An example that is particularly instructive to SEL leaders is the crop of programs for teaching thinking that were popular in the 1980s. I use the past tense because we have heard relatively little about these programs in the last five years. I do not know how widely used they are at this point—or, for that matter, how much they ever were used. Most continue to be available, so they are clearly not obsolete, but to educators pursuing current trends, they are not the latest thing.

I refer to programs such as Instrumental Enrichment, Philosophy for Children, CORT, Tactics, (see Costa, 1991) and so on, which were refined by their developers over many years but which, as a group, caught the attention of many K–12 educators in the mid-1980s. As editor of publications for the Association for Supervision and Curriculum Development, I was intrigued by the promise of such programs and, in speeches, workshops, conferences, and numerous publications, helped promote them. I continue to believe that an important aim of education should be the cultivation of what are sometimes called higher-order thinking skills (some of which are also taught in SEL programs).

Thinking skills programs were strikingly different from one another in style, purpose, and form. Some were quite sophisticated, had elaborate support materials, and required extensive teacher training. Some were intentionally simple and flexible. Some had been thoroughly evaluated (usually by their developers because others did not have the motivation or necessary funding), while others were backed only by anecdotal evidence. In general, each program was:

- Closely identified with a forceful, charismatic developer who had devoted a great deal of time and attention to its development.
- Based on a well-articulated theory, sometimes derived from recent research (in this case, findings from cognitive science).
- Available in published form, usually with materials for students and teachers.
- Claimed to be effective only if used as intended; that is, taught by a qualified teacher on a continuous basis to attain a cumulative impact. In other words, it was to be taught separately from other curriculum content.

Administrators excited about the prospect of developing students' mental abilities could choose from among the published programs, which varied widely in their assumptions, teaching methods, and teacher preparation requirements. Or they could set out to embed direct instruction in various skills at particular points in the local curriculum (Beyer, 1997). Or they could encourage teachers, through staff development, to incorporate selected strategies in self-designed units of instruction (Marzano & Pickering, 1997). Or they could put their faith in well-designed subject-matter curriculum (Resnick, 1987), which sought to develop thinking indirectly through reasoning about academic content.

In my conversations with educators, I found that most were attracted to the idea of improving student thinking but thought it should be incorporated into regular subject-matter instruction. Though impressed with what developers had accomplished with their specialized programs, they did not like the idea of separate classes in thinking skills. They believed that setting up separate classes would be logistically difficult and hard to justify to a skeptical public. Most important, it would violate their professional conviction that all teachers should teach thinking in every class.

The current SEL movement is similar in many ways to the thinking skills movement. Some programs resemble thinking skills programs in these ways:

- Most are identified with one or more persons who devoted a great deal of time and effort to their creation and refinement.
- Each is based upon an explicit theory or set of theories derived from research (in this case from social psychology).
- They are available in published form.
- Their developers have evidence of their effectiveness if used as intended.
- They require systematic use over a period of time to achieve their effectiveness. Many are intended to be taught separately or included as part of a particular course.

Other approaches to SEL are more flexible; like some of the recommended thinking skills plans of the 1980s, they rely upon local curriculum revision or generic professional development for their implementation.

INVISIBLE INNOVATIONS

As mentioned, I have referred to thinking skills programs in the past tense because the movement is less visible now, even though most of the programs continue in use. Optimists might even contend that elements of the movement were absorbed into the system, which may be partly true; every wave of school change leaves some traces in its wake. Curriculum developers and textbook authors probably now put somewhat more emphasis on processes such as problem solving than they did in the 1970s, and some undoubtedly incorporate explicit teaching of selected thinking skills. Many teachers continue to use strategies they learned in professional development classes, some in connection with teaching special courses and some in generic programs like Dimensions of Learning (Marzano & Pickering, 1997). However, when instruction is incidental rather than deliberate, it is difficult to determine the effects on students' thinking abilities.

If my analogy is applicable, it may be appropriate to ask what can be done to keep the current generation of social and emotional programs from becoming the "been there, done that" of the next decade. Four problems help account for the shaky implementation of thinking skills programs and other well-intended innovations: lack of support, competing demands on instructional time, insufficient training, and parent and teacher opposition. Stated more positively, successful implementation requires administrative support, sound scheduling, staff development, and teacher and parent approval.

ADMINISTRATIVE SUPPORT

A critical requisite of successful implementation is official support, including both logistical support, such as making sure necessary supplies and equipment are made available, and official endorsement. Some thinking skills programs came and went because superintendents, principals, and board of education members doubted their value or had other priorities. Of special concern in many school districts in recent years has been the rapid turnover of superintendents. New superintendents, and sometimes newly elected board members, are often expected to launch their own initiatives. No matter what they choose to emphasize, the schools will almost certainly continue to teach reading and mathematics. Less well-established programs, however, such as courses in thinking, may be neglected or discontinued.

Leaders convinced of the importance of SEL must act upon their commitment by giving teachers the necessary tools and time as well as giving moral support through public encouragement and recognition. Perhaps even more essential is establishing the broad base of support that programs must have to survive changes in leadership and other challenges that will inevitably arise. A good example is the process by which the highly regarded New Haven, Connecticut, Social Development Project was developed and sustained (Weissberg, Shriver, Bose, & DeFalco, 1997).

TIME IN THE SCHEDULE

A concrete example of administrative support is making official arrangements for when a new program will be offered. As mentioned previously, many of the most effective thinking skills programs were designed to be taught as special classes, but school officials were reluctant, or unable to convince policymakers, to make such courses part of the established curriculum. Because improved thinking, like most other educational outcomes, requires cumulative development over a period of several years, a major issue for advocates was, and continues to be, finding time for thinking skills instruction. For example, Stanley Pogrow (1997), who has evidence that students become much more successful after two years in his Higher Order Thinking Skills (HOTS) program, has waged a losing battle with opponents of all "pull-out" Title I programs. Despite its apparent effectiveness, HOTS has been dropped by schools pressured to do schoolwide programming instead.

As governing agencies increase pressures on schools to achieve higher academic standards enforced through assessment programs and other accountability measures, it is increasingly difficult to make provisions for separate courses whose purpose is to contribute to academic outcomes indirectly rather than directly. Educators who believe that schools should have planned, comprehensive, sequential SEL programs must give careful thought to scheduling. Which teachers will be responsible for which aspects of the program, and when are they supposed to teach it? If SEL instruction is to be integrated with other classes, what will be done to make sure it is actually done rather than being squeezed out by competing demands?

PROFESSIONAL DEVELOPMENT

Clarifying responsibility, of course, is only the beginning; teachers must also have adequate preparation for what they are to teach—although some programs require more special preparation than others. Knowing that most teachers get very little job-specific training, creators of some thinking skills programs (notably Edward deBono, creator of Cognitive Research Trust [CORT]) designed materials for use by untrained teachers. Before teaching Matthew Lipman's Philosophy for Children, on the other hand, teachers were expected to have had at least a full year of intensive preparation. More training is undoubtedly better, especially when, as in the case of philosophy, teachers are unlikely to have had much prior experience with the subject— but staff development is costly in both money and time. Even so, if special training is needed, as it usually is, it must be provided.

No one knows how much of the inadequate implementation of thinking skills programs can be traced to ineffective or insufficient training, although it undoubtedly was a major factor (Education Commission of the States, 1997). Research is beginning to reveal the extent to which professional development must be thorough and highly focused to be effective. Researchers studying mathematics reform in California (Cohen & Hill, 1998) found that teachers' implementation and students' achievement were best when professional development was directly related to the curriculum teachers were to teach. Specifically, when teachers were taught about new mathematics materials their students were to learn from, they used the materials and related teaching practices more, and their students gained more, than when professional development dealt with slightly more generic—but subject-related—programs such as Family Math.

This suggests that leaders responsible for implementing SEL programs must not just hope that teachers will somehow pick up the knowledge and skills they need or assume that staff development must necessarily be limited to the time arbitrarily set aside for it. Instead, they must carefully analyze the situation and provide each staff member with the appropriate amount and quality of specific training, both before the program begins and throughout the implementation process.

TEACHER AND PARENT APPROVAL

Although it was probably not a major factor in implementation of thinking skills, the attitudes of teachers and parents often determine the success or failure of new programs. In the last decade, outspoken opposition from traditionalists has waylaid or damaged numerous state and local programs, especially those identified as outcome-based education or whole language. The "culture wars" between educators and religious conservatives seem somewhat less incendiary now than in the mid-1990s, but that may be only because conservatives have gained enough power to play a larger role in state politics and because educators are more respectful (or at least wary) of parents' demands. Another contributing factor may be efforts by both liberals and conservatives to more clearly define the role of religion in U.S. public life, including public schools (Haynes, 1994).

Although leaders of some traditionalist groups now openly advise Christian parents to teach their children at home (Simonds, 1998), many conservative parents will continue to send their children to public schools but will protest what they consider violations of family privacy or attempts to subvert their children's values (Burron, 1996). Because many other parents and citizens are reportedly convinced that public schools are neglecting basic skills, educators apparently need to do a better job of explaining themselves and listening to parents' concerns, as well as making sure they really are teaching well.

Results of surveys and focus groups conducted by the Education Commission of the States (1996) provide new insights on the topic of parent opinion. Asked where they got information about schools and school programs, parents listed "teachers" more than any other source, including school officials and the media. Presumably they meant teachers they knew personally as well as their children's teachers. A possible interpretation is that at least some of the opposition to school programs may be provoked by teacher criticisms. Parents may say, "I don't know what to think of these new ideas, but she should know." Despite their best intentions, school officials have not always thoroughly involved parents and teachers when considering proposed changes. If the initiative is controversial, as many things are these days, lack of public involvement may prevent its success.

Agencies working to reform public schools, including the Institute for Educational Leadership (1997), New American Schools (Bodily, 1998), and the Annenberg Institute (1998), warn that public understanding and support will continue to erode unless schools establish a much higher level of public engagement than in the past. They advise districts to hold town meetings, convene task forces, and use other means to make sure that all elements of the community have been informed and consulted. Because SEL programs deal not with conventional school subject matter but with sensitive human relationships, it is especially critical that parents and teachers be fully involved in their selection and development.

CONCLUSION

In this chapter, I have discussed four factors that are likely to affect the implementation of SEL programs, which are similar in several respects to the thinking skills programs of the 1980s. Schools will be more successful in their efforts to initiate new programs when there is strong administrative support, when the program is scheduled appropriately, and when teachers have the necessary professional development. Equally important, programs will be much stronger where parents and teachers have participated in the planning process and are convinced of their value.

REFERENCES

Annenberg Institute for School Reform. (1998). *Reasons for hope, voices for change.* Providence, RI: Author.

Beyer, B. K. (1997). *Improving student thinking: A comprehensive approach.* Boston: Allyn & Bacon.

Bodily, S. J. (with others). (1998). *Lessons from new American schools' scale-up phase* (RAND Report MR-942.0-NAS).

Burron, A. (1996). Parents' rights-_society's imperatives: A balancing act. *Educational Leadership, 53*(7), 80–82.

Cohen, D. K., & Hill, H. C. (1998). *State policy and classroom performance: Mathematics reform in California* (CPRE Policy Brief RB-23). Philadelphia: Consortium for Policy Research in Education, University of Pennsylvania.

Costa, A. L. (1991). *Developing minds: Programs for teaching thinking* (Rev. ed., Vol. 2). Alexandria, VA: Association for Supervision and Curriculum Development.

Education Commission of the States. (1996). *Listen, discuss, and act: Parents' and teachers' views on education reform.* Denver, CO: Author.

Education Commission of the States. (1997). *Investing in teacher professional development.* Denver, CO: Author.

Elias, M. J., Zins, J. E., Weissberg, R. P., Frey, K. S., Greenberg, M. T., Haynes, N. M., Kessler, R., & Schwab-Stone, M. E. (1997). *Promoting social and emotional learning.* Alexandria, VA: Association for Supervision and Curriculum Development.

Goleman, D. (1995). *Emotional intelligence.* New York: Bantam Books.

Haynes, C. (Ed.). (1994). *Finding common ground: A First Amendment guide to religion and public education.* Nashville, TN: Freedom Forum First Amendment Center at Vanderbilt University.

Institute for Educational Leadership. (1997). *Public conversations about the public's schools.* Washington, DC: Author.

Johnson, D., Johnson, R., Holubec, E. J., & Roy, P. (1984). *Circles of learning: Cooperation in the classroom.* Alexandria, VA: Association for Supervision and Curriculum Development.

Johnson, J., & Immerwahr, J. (1994). *First things first: What Americans expect from the public schools.* New York: Public Agenda.

Marzano, R. J., & Pickering, D. J. (with others). (1997). *Dimensions of learning* (2nd ed.). Alexandria, VA: Association for Supervision and Curriculum Development.

National Commission on Excellence in Education. (1983). *A nation at risk.* Washington, DC: U.S. Government Printing Office.

Pogrow, S. (1997, November 12). The tyranny and folly of ideological progressivism. *Education Week,* 34–36.

Resnick, L. (1987). *Education and learning to think*. Washington, DC: National Academy Press.

Simonds, B. (1998, April). *President's report*. Costa Mesa, CA: National Association of Christian Educators/Citizens for Excellence in Education.

Slavin, R. E. (1988). Cooperative learning and student achievement. *Educational Leadership, 46*(2), 31–33.

Slavin, R. E. (1996). Neverstreaming: Preventing learning disabilities. *Educational Leadership, 53*(5), 4–7.

Weissberg, R. P., Shriver, T. P., Bose, S., & DeFalco, K. (1997). Creating a districtwide social development project. *Educational Leadership, 54*(8), 37–39.

12

Learning about Social and Emotional Learning

Current Themes and Future Directions

Jonathan Cohen

School life *always* profoundly affects the social and emotional lives of students and educators. Teacher-student and peer relations, our pedagogic methods, and the learning process shape students' experience of themselves and others. The contributors to this volume believe that we can and must do this in thoughtful, caring, responsible ways that intentionally foster the development of social and emotional competencies. Some educators believe that the three "R's" or particular domains of intelligence (linguistic and mathematical) are most important and that school is not an appropriate forum for social and emotional learning (SEL). In any case, school and family life *are* the two major social arenas that shape and color children's social and emotional worlds.

As a learner—and a teacher—how do I feel about myself and others? What is easy and/or difficult for me to recognize in others? How do these conscious and sometimes unrecognized experiences affect motivation and social relations, as well as how and what I learn and/or teach? For example, when I am having a problem (be it mathematical or social), how do I feel and how do I (purposively and/or automatically) go about solving the problem? These are just a few of the fundamental social and emotional questions and sets of experiences that influence what we value and our ability to learn.

Social and emotional competencies provide the foundation for us to solve interpersonal and intrapsychic problems and generate creative questions. As such, these competencies represent modes of intelligence (Gardner, 1983). What we teach and how we act and learn together in school directly influence the development of these capacities, be it in facilitating, promoting, pleasurable or unpleasurable, discouraging, and/or undermining ways.

How can we learn more about SEL? Learning in schools is always influenced by our theory of who the child is and by our theories of learning and teaching; what our goals are; the modes of learning we need in order to actualize the goal(s); the process needed to convey these modes of learning; and the pedagogic methods we use to induce and sustain this process.

THEORY

Theory refers to the set of preconceived ideas or principles that we have about a topic. Our theories, for example, about learning and teaching may be recognized or not, explicit or implicit, and, upon reflection, sensible or not. In any case, they necessarily shape and even determine what we see. For instance, our theories about language learning and reading instruction determine to a greater or lesser extent when and how we seek to help a child to read. What are your theories about the nature of child development and social and emotional competencies? About the purpose of education? Theoretically, do you believe that schools should be a place where we seek to promote the acquisition of skills and knowledge related to social and emotional competencies?

The authors in this volume believe that schools can and should purposively promote social and emotional competencies in a sustained, substantive manner. Interestingly, there is little discussion here about the underlying nature of social and emotional competencies or modes of intelligence. It is important to note that in other domains (e.g., language learning), increased theoretical understanding about the underlying nature of language abilities and disabilities guides effective pedagogic and remedial methods. There is much to learn about the underlying psychobiological nature of social and emotional abilities/disabilities and the complex sets of psychosocial meanings that are attributed to them. Future learning in this area may inform educational and psychoeducational efforts.

GOALS

Educational goals vary dramatically for many reasons: political pressures; practitioners' past experiences (as learners and teachers); theories about "what really matters"; and how educators understand what our children/class need as well as our realistic appraisal of what we can provide to a given child and/or class now (see Chapter 11). Speaking very broadly, there are often two sets of educational goals that most teachers seek to balance: skill/knowledge acquisition and learning how to learn. The authors in this volume emphasize these two goals in varying ways. Some believe that the most important and effective way to promote SEL with particular populations of students is to insure that they learn sets of skills and have an opportunity to practice these skills in class (see Chapter 3). This approach emphasizes skill acquisition as an essential first step that is optimally taught in a separate K–12 class.

Others believe that self-reflection, recognizing the experience of others, and utilizing this information in a variety of helpful ways can and should be integral facets of all that we do in schools. Here learning how to learn and skills acquisition are seen as equally important pathways that can be fostered simultaneously (see Chapter 6). Although the methods vary, all of the authors in this volume share a common goal: to promote SEL in our schools. And, most implicitly or explicitly underscore the essential importance of integrating these domains into all that we do in schools linguistically, mathematically, musically, visually, and kinesthetically.

MODES OF LEARNING

Modes of learning refers to what actually happens to facilitate learning. This tends to be talked about more in universities than in teacher and parent groups. Many parents and teachers are keenly interested in the nature of learning and the dialectical, interactive, evolving process of taking in new information and integrating this with what we already know. However, most also care about what a given child knows and does not know now. What do we need to do now to promote learning within a given child and/or class?

Many different and to some extent overlapping modes of learning facilitate SEL: where students feel safe, appreciated, and respected; the creation of classrooms where students can and do engage in discovery and meaningful, creative problem solving and in the generation of new socially and emotionally informed questions; where learners are exposed to new information and the opportunity to practice new skills; and where students identify with a teacher who becomes a role model. These and additional modes of learning are probably essential ingredients that facilitate SEL. Depending on the student's endowment, home and neighborhood life, motivation, and his or her particular array of strengths and weaknesses, it is likely that different modes of learning are more or less important. I suggest that practitioners in the classrooms, professors in the university, and the students themselves potentially have much to learn from one another about these fundamental questions.

PROCESS

The process of learning refers to the actual steps that student and/or teacher and/or classroom group need to take to insure that a given topic and/or capacity is mastered. Many authors in this volume focus on what they consider to be critical elements of a successful and substantive SEL process. On a political-social level, many stress that the process must be a truly collaborative endeavor between parents and educators. Temporally, many stress that SEL in schools needs to be an extended, ongoing process to be effective. Individually, the learning process refers to what happens within the mind of each student.

The process of creating effective SEL programs optimally needs to include the "whole village": educators, school specialists, parents, and members of the community. Most new programs begin experimentally, and by definition, they are small. Ultimately, learning takes place in each child's mind, in the context of particular classroom relations and an individual classroom. But, implementing any substantive change in schools needs to include all of the significant members of the child's life. Involving more representatives of the community is important on many levels. It fosters understanding, consensus building, and the creation of common agendas and vocabularies, which have the power to transform schools (Comer, Haynes, Joyner, & Ben-Avie, 1996; also see Chapter 10). The more greatly members of the community decide to explicitly value SEL, the more a given vocabulary and way of thinking will pervasively color and shape people's developing minds. The process of a school adopting a common vocabulary is in and of itself a powerful action that occurs over time—the process necessarily affects thinking.

All of the authors in this book suggest that effective SEL needs to be an essential ongoing part of all children's education over the course of their schooling. Some practitioners (see Chapter 8) require schools to make at least a five-year commitment when a given school or district wishes to work with the Resolving Conflict Creatively Program. Others work with teachers, schools, and/or districts "one step at a time." It is common sense that substantive learning in this and any other domain is a long-term process. We can't and don't expect students to learn history or English in year or two. It is the ongoing process that provides repeated opportunities for students to discover more about themselves and others as well as to practice and further develop these competencies as they themselves develop.

On another level, process refers to what is occurring in the minds of our students. The mind is the seat of learning. On this essential level, we want to see our students involved with the process of *discovering* more about themselves and others and how this helps solve social and emotional questions and problems (see Chapter 7). This process of discovery is the heart of learning. This—I think—is why Ted Sizer (1996) and others in the Coalition for Essential Schools focus on the importance of an assessment process that is based on tracking the kinds of questions that students ask. When students are raising meaningful questions, they are by definition involved with the process of discovery.

METHODS

Most authors in this volume focus on the actual methods needed to induce and sustain the SEL process for students. Some of the authors here explicitly focus on methods that educators can use to further their own SEL (see Chapter 9). There are many methods that can be utilized, depending on the developmental stage of the person we work with, the nature of the individual's strengths and weaknesses, and the particular SEL programs and perspectives that we adopt and/or combine.

This volume—and subsequent volumes in this series—presents an array of methods that emerges from various programs and perspectives. Some of the methods presented are detailed curriculum-based methods that are quite prescriptive and structured. Specific sequences of skills are presented in ways that will be of great help to many educators wanting to experiment with and use a SEL program (see Chapter 3). Other SEL programs may be used as a curriculum-based program or integrated into whatever the educators are already doing (see Chapter 5). Other programs include a menu of options that can be integrated into any class and from which each teacher will pick and choose as he or she sees fit (see Chapter 6). Some of the methods in this volume emphasize specific sets of awareness and skills (Chapter 4); others focus on a perspective that enhances our capacity to empathize with and understand children (see Chapter 7). All of these programs and/or perspectives seek to enhance the two basic building blocks of social and emotional functioning (self-reflective capacities and the ability to recognize what the other is experiencing) so that we may become more responsible, knowledgeable, and caring with ourselves and others.

Some of our authors focus on how methods to shape classroom life: the group. For example, the work of The Responsive Classroom (see Chapter 6) underscores that teacher-student and student-student relationships are very dependent on the structures that the teacher creates in the classroom. Relationships do not just happen. The ways that we begin the day, create transitions, manage disciplinary issues, and define the process of learning become a critical part of our implicit social and emotional curriculum. Educators can—and often do—explicitly seek to promote social and emotional competencies and structure relationships throughout the day. This is a powerful communication to students, parents, and colleagues that affects the culture and life of school.

CONCLUSION

The authors in this volume share a conviction that understanding the nature of child development is the essential foundation for all that we do. Although we may have the same educational goals for kindergarten students and high school students, the nature of the process (e.g., what we can expect children to discover) and the methods we use will vary greatly depending on the ages and developmental capacities of our student(s) (see Chapter 2). Most in education theoretically agree with this basic truth. But, in practice this raises complicated questions. What does it really mean to think developmentally about a given child? How is the past affecting the present with a given child, and can this further our capacity to educate the child? How will the upcoming developmental challenges that students will encounter affect the learning process?

In recent decades, we have begun to learn much more about how particular pedagogic methods affect students' lives over time. In fact, one of the most important recent developments in SEL is that there are sustained, systematic research efforts that assess the impact that these programs and perspectives have on behavior and academic performance (Elias, Zins, Weissberg, Frey, Greenberg, Haynes, Kessler, Schwab-Stone, & Shriver, 1997). As many of the authors in this volume note, we have learned that many SEL programs have an extraordinarily positive effect on behavior. This is important news! There is preliminary evidence that some of these programs have a positive effect on academic functioning and performance. This is an area that we need to learn more about.

In conclusion, there is still much to learn about SEL. We need to learn more about the interrelationships between our theories and goals, modes of learning, the educational processes, pedagogic methods, and outcomes. We need to learn more about how these programs and perspectives affect academic performance and achievement. We also need to learn more about how we can let each other know what we are doing to further SEL. There are so many educators and school specialists who have been and continue to be involved with furthering the development of these competencies in our students today. I have been struck by how often we—inadvertently—feel alone in this work. Virtually all of the authors in this book are linked to programs that seek to further ties between practitioners committed to this task. In addition, the Collaborative for the Advancement of Social and Emotional Learning (CASEL) and the Project for Social and Emotional Learning at Teachers College, Columbia University, are also committed to furthering communication between practitioners, social scientists, school-based mental health professionals, parents, policymakers, and educational leaders. We need to learn to communicate with one another and to help one another to further the SEL that will support our children's growth and development.

REFERENCES

Comer, J. P., Haynes, N. M., Joyner, E. T., & Ben-Avie, M. (Eds.). (1996). *Rallying the whole village: The Comer process for reforming education.* New York: Teachers College Press.

Elias, M., Zins, J. E., Weissberg, R. P., Frey, K. S., Greenberg, M. T., Haynes, N. M., Kessler, R., Schwab-Stone, M. E., & Shriver, T. P. (1997). *Promoting social and emotional learning: Guidelines for educators.* Alexandria, VA: Association for Supervision and Curriculum Development.

Gardner, H. (1983). *Frames of mind: The theory of multiple intelligences.* New York: Basic Books.

Sizer, T. R. (1996). *Horace's hope: What works for the American high school.* Boston: Houghton Mifflin.

About the Contributors

Ronald S. Brandt was formerly the editor of *Educational Leadership* and other publications of the Association for Supervision and Curriculum Development (ASCD). His current professional interests include the use of knowledge from cognitive research and neuroscience to improve learning, and engagement of parents and the public in school reform. He is author or co-author of numerous publications including *The Language of Learning* (a glossary of education terminology) and *Powerful Learning,* and the editor of *Assessing Student Learning: New Rules, New Realities,* in press. In 1996 Brandt was one of the first persons inducted into the EdPress Hall of Fame for his contributions to education publishing.

Robert B. Brooks is Assistant Clinical Professor of Psychology at Harvard Medical School and has served as Director of the Department of Psychology at McLean Hospital in Belmont, Massachusetts. Dr. Brooks has lectured nationally and internationally and has written extensively about creating a positive school climate that nurtures resilience, motivation, learning, self-discipline, and self-esteem. He is the author of *The Self-Esteem Teacher* and has completed a videotape and educational guide for PBS entitled *Learning Disabilities and Self-Esteem. Look What You've Done! Stories of Hope and Resilience.*

Ruth Sidney Charney is co-founder of Northeast Foundation for Children. A classroom teacher for more than 20 years, she is the author of *Teaching Children to Care* and *Habits of Goodness.* She holds graduate degrees from Bank Street College of Education and Teachers College, Columbia University.

Linda Bruene Butler is a clinician supervisor and chief trainer for the Social Decision Making/Problem Solving Program at the University of Medicine and Dentistry of New Jersey. She was the co-director of the 1998 Teachers College Social Emotional Learning Summer Institute.

Jonathan Cohen is co-founder and Director of the Project for Social and Emotional Learning as well as Adjunct Associate Professor of Psychology and Education, Teachers College, Columbia University. He is also a faculty member and supervisor at the Institute for Child, Adolescent and Family Studies (New York, New York).

Linda Crawford is the founder and Director of Origins, a Minneapolis-based teacher education organization focusing on multi-cultural understanding through the arts. She is a former elementary school director and high school teacher. She provides Responsive Classroom professional development to schools throughout the country.

Karol DeFalco is a teacher in the Social Development Department of the New Haven Public Schools. She has been involved with teaching social and emotional learning programs to students since 1984, and is an experienced trainer and supportive coach for teachers who implement these programs. DeFalco is also a contributor to *Emotional Development and Emotional Intelligence: Educational Implications*.

Maurice J. Elias is Professor of Psychology and Coordinator of the Internship in Applied, School, and Community Psychology at Rutgers University. He is a member of the Leadership Team of the Collaborative for the Advancement of Social and Emotional Learning (CASEL). He is the author of *Emotionally Intelligent Parenting* and the award-winning *Promoting Social and Emotional Learning: Guidelines for Educators*.

Norris M. Haynes is Professor in the Counseling and School Psychology Department, and Director of the Center for School Research and Improvement, at Southern Connecticut State University. He is also Associate Clinical Professor at the Yale University Child Study Center.

Linda Lantieri is co-founder of the highly acclaimed Resolving Conflict Creatively Program (RCCP) and is currently Director of the RCCP National Center for Educators for Social Responsibility. She has been an educator—teacher, administrator, university professor, and education activist—for more than thirty years. She is co-author of *Waging Peace in Our Schools*.

Steven Marans is Harris Assistant Professor in Child Psychoanalysis and Director of the Child Development and Community Policing Program at the Yale University Child Study Center. Dr. Marans is the author of *The Police-Mental Health Partnership*.

Peggy McIntosh is Associate Director of the Wellesley College Center for Research on Women. She is founder and co-director, with Emily Style, of the National Seeking Educational Equity & Diversity (S.E.E.D.) Project on Inclusion Curriculum. McIntosh is the author of many articles on curriculum change, women's studies, and systems of unearned privilege. She is the recipient of the Klingenstein Award for Distinguished Educational Leadership from Teachers College, Columbia University.

Janet Patti is Associate Professor in the Department of Curriculum and Teaching, and Coordinator of the Educational Administration and Supervision Program, at Hunter College. She consults with Educators for Social Responsibility in the area of social emotional learning, with a focus on conflict resolution and intergroup relations. Dr. Patti is co-author of *Waging Peace in Our Schools*.

Mary E. Schwab-Stone is a child psychiatrist with training in epidemiology and is currently Harris Associate Professor of Child Psychiatry at the Yale Child Study Center. Her research has been guided by an interest in the relationship between the social environment and psychological adjustment in childhood, with a particular emphasis on children growing up in situations of social and economic disadvantage. In recent years this interest has become focused specifically on school-based programs for the prevention of psychological difficulties and the promotion of healthy development in children in urban settings. She has collaborated with the New Haven Public Schools as a program consultant, and heads the Yale-based team responsible for evaluating their social development and prevention programming. Schwab-Stone has written extensively on related issues including *Promoting Positive Social Development and Health Practices in Young Urban Adolescents* and *No Safe Haven: A Study of Violence Exposure in an Urban Community*.

Timothy P. Shriver is President and Chief Executive Officer of Special Olympics International, and Chair of the Leadership Team of the Collaborative for the Advancement of Social and Emotional Learning (CASEL). Prior to joining Special Olympics, Shriver was the Supervisor of the New Haven Public Schools' Social Development Program. In 1994, he helped launch CASEL, a national organization to promote effective school-based prevention programming, where he continues to advocate for effective primary prevention programming in schools nationwide. Shriver has written extensively on these issues and has co-authored several publications including *Promoting Positive Social Development and Health Practices in Young Urban Adolescents; Involvement in Multiple Problem Behaviors of Young Urban Adolescents; No Safe Haven: A Study of Violence Exposure in an Urban Community;* and *No New Wars*.

William J. Solodow is the consulting psychologist at the Riverdale Country School and has a private practice, working with both children and adults, in individual psychotherapy, psychological testing, and learning disabilities evaluations. He is an advanced candidate at the Columbia University Center for Psychoanalytic Training and Research.

Emily Style is an adjunct instructor for New York University and Cornell. She works regularly with K–12 educators in Philadelphia, and her essay "Curriculum as Window and Mirror" is part of the framework used by the State of Minnesota to promote a more inclusive curriculum. With Peggy McIntosh, she co-directs the National S.E.E.D. Project on Inclusive Curriculum, now in its thirteenth year.

Robert (Chip) Wood is co-founder of the Northeast Foundation for Children and author of the book *Yardsticks: Children in the Classroom, Ages 4–14*. He is an M.S.W. social worker and a former public K–8 school principal and teacher.

Index